The Death of Truth is a must-read primer on current cultural thinking and practice, a guide to the confusion of tonight's news and tomorrow's analysis of why the world stage is in chaos. Here is a compelling review that shows how completely we are embedded in postmodern philosophy, and how we as Christians can and must speak into the cultural morass of postmodernism with understanding and compassion.

Dr. Donald K. Wood
President—Christian Medical & Dental Society

Opponents of Christianity in the past charged it was a false religion. Now opponents argue that Christianity ought not to be believed because its followers *claim it is true*. This is the posture of our postmodern age—a posture traditional Christian apologists are not prepared to confront. This book is on the cutting edge and thus mandatory reading for any Christian who wants to engage this postmodern spirit. I highly recommend it.

Dr. Francis Beckwith
Author of *Politically Correct Death*

Though written for the Christian community *The Death of Truth* has great meaning for society at large. Thought-leaders in science, education, politics, and law should read this book.

Dr. William Tyler Jarvis
President—National Council Against Health Fraud

Enlightening, informative, and insightful. *The Death of Truth* explains changes happening in intellectual circles and makes an understanding of the sweeping effects of postmodernism accessible to everyone, detailing how these changes impact our lives.

Dr. Dale E. Galloway
Dean of the Beeson International Center—
Asbury Theological Seminary

The Death of Truth is a valuable survey for the layperson of postmodernism's impact on society, and the book's extensive bibliography springboards the serious student into further research. I heartily recommend it.

Dr. Hugh Ross
President—Reasons to Believe

The DEATH of TRUTH

Dennis McCallum

GENERAL EDITOR

BETHANY HOUSE PUBLISHERS
MINNEAPOLIS, MINNESOTA 55438

Published by Bethany House Publishers
A Ministry of Bethany Fellowship, Inc.
11300 Hampshire Avenue South
Minneapolis, Minnesota 55438

Printed in the United States of America.

Library of Congress Cataloging-in-Publication Data

The death of truth : what's wrong with multiculturalism, the rejection of reason, and the new postmodern diversity / Dennis McCallum, editor.
p. cm.
Includes bibliographical references.

1. Christianity and culture. 2. Christianity—20th century. 3. Postmodernism—Religious aspects—Christianity. 4. Postmodernism—Controversial literature. 5. Multiculturalism—Religious aspects—Christianity. 6. Multiculturalism—Controversial literature. 7. Evangelicalism.
I. McCallum, Dennis.
BR115.C8D34 1996
261—dc20 95-45770
ISBN 1-55661-724-0 CIP

DENNIS McCALLUM is Senior Pastor at Xenos Christian Fellowship in Columbus, Ohio, and part of the Crossroads Project, a group conducting seminars on the postmodern challenge at universities across the country. He is the author of several books, including *Christianity: The Faith That Makes Sense, The Summons, The Myth of Romance*, and *Walking in Victory.*

CONTENTS

Preface

Although this book was written by scholars, communicators, and researchers from several different fields, it isn't an academic book. *The Death of Truth* brings postmodernism and its impact on today's society within the reach of people who have never studied it before, in an attempt to move awareness of this school of thought out of academia and into popular discussion. Because our goal is to help the public at large grasp the magnitude of the postmodern shift, scholarly readers may not be happy with missing distinctions, apparent lack of subtleties, and even the complete absence of certain categories, terms, and authors in our discussion. We have ruthlessly chopped unnecessarily technical or difficult ideas and language and have grouped related concepts in an effort to make postmodernism understandable to those who most feel its effects on their world. I appreciate the way my scholarly colleagues have borne up under the profound annoyance they have at times felt as I substantially rewrote their essays for the popular audience.

A list of subjects we have eliminated along with short articles on each is available for viewing and downloading at our home page on the World Wide Web (http://www.crossrds.org). You can also call 1–800–698–7884 for a free listing of articles and other materials.

We hope academic readers will agree with us that the public should also understand, at some level, the sweeping changes going on in intellectual and professional circles and the impact of those changes on their everyday lives, and will kindly, to be colloquial, cut us some slack.

We expect that even scholars will find this volume useful in introducing postmodernism and stirring the interest of students, who can then broaden their understanding of the subject through more detailed reading. We hope to bring forth our own academic volume soon, which will expand on and clarify these chapters at a level of detail appropriate for more in-depth study.

Thank you in advance for your indulgence and help.

—Dennis McCallum

1

ARE WE READY?

DENNIS MCCALLUM, CONTRIBUTOR

Within months after Charles Darwin released his *Origin of the Species* in 1859, a revolution in thinking gripped the scientific world. Although at the time most Christians had no idea anything was happening, no one today doubts the far-reaching results of that revolution. During the decades after Darwin, the notion of a natural world with no place for God became a new, nearly unanimous understanding among intellectuals, eventually reshaping every academic discipline, as well as education, government, and even the church. Now, by the close of the twentieth century, even popular culture accepts Darwin's theory of naturalistic evolution as settled fact.

The Christian church wasn't ready for Darwin.

At the time Darwin wrote and even for decades afterward, Christian leaders thought it was important to defend the view that the world was created in exactly 4004 B.C., as commemorated in the play

---

About the Contributor:

Dennis McCallum is a writer and co-senior pastor at Xenos Christian Fellowship in Columbus, Ohio. Xenos focuses its ministry on evangelism, community development, and discipleship through home groups. Dennis is the author of numerous articles on apologetics as well as several books, including *Christianity: The Faith That Makes Sense* and *Walking in Victory*. His M.A. in biblical studies and historical theology is from Ashland Theological Seminary.

Inherit the Wind. Christian arguments against evolution reflected not only dogmatism and weak reasoning, but something much worse. Early Christian apologists in this field often showed a lack of understanding of what natural selection was, not to mention the reasons people believed in it. Christians couldn't respond in a convincing way to a doctrine they understood only dimly, and when we look back at some of the arguments Christians first advanced against the doctrine of naturalistic evolution we can only grimace in embarrassment.

Most Christians today can answer evolutionists effectively, but their ability to change any minds on this issue is minimal. Why? Too much time passed without a coherent, credible Christian voice to counteract Darwin's theory. Darwinism managed to distance God from creation and the natural world—with the effect that even people who hold a dim belief that God exists regard him as irrelevant to their daily lives. We can only wonder what would have happened if some of the current sophisticated, convincing Christian arguments were at hand when Darwin first wrote.

Unfortunately, Christian leadership wasn't ready for the intellectual challenges of the late nineteenth century, with devastating results.

The New Revolution

Now, in the late twentieth century, we are caught up in a revolution that will likely dwarf Darwinism in its impact on every aspect of thought and culture: *postmodernism*. Unlike Darwinism, postmodernism isn't a distinct set of doctrines or truth claims. It's a *mood*—a view of the world characterized by a deep distrust of reason, not to mention a disdain for the knowledge Christians believe the Bible provides. It's a *methodology*—a completely new way of analyzing ideas. For all its diverse ideas and advocates, postmodernism is also a *movement*—a fresh onslaught on truth that brings a more or less cohesive approach to literature, history, politics, education, law, sociology, linguistics, and virtually every other discipline, including science. And it is ushering in a cultural *metamorphosis*—transforming every area of everyday life as it spreads through education, movies, television, and other media.

Just as Darwinism wasn't easy to understand 150 years ago, postmodernism and its impact isn't immediately easy to grasp. But as you read this book, the who and why and what (and so what) of this shift will dawn on you. Postmodern thinking surrounds us—and sways us, even in the church. We will see how postmodernism already affects our lives, and how the effects will only intensify in the coming years.

The postmodern revolution is still happening.

We, as Christians, still have an opportunity to influence the outcome—if we don't wait too long.

The Challenge of Modernism

Until recently, the consensus in secular (non-Christian) thought has been *modernism*. Modernists view the world, including humans, as one gigantic machine, placing their faith in rationality (the ability of humans to understand their world), empiricism (the belief that knowledge can only be gained through our senses), and in the application of rationality and empiricism through science and technology. Make no mistake—the modern worldview continues to exert great influence on contemporary culture. Recent developments in the fields of animal intelligence, artificial intelligence, and the genetic basis for behavior, for example, are alarming and powerful challenges to God's Word. Each of these developments requires a response from thoughtful Christians.

> As with Darwinism, Christians again are unprepared for a major challenge to their worldview.

Modernism continues to hammer away, landing effective blows on theism, the belief in an infinite, personal God. But academicians, the thought-shapers who teach in our colleges and universities—whose opinions sooner or later influence the rest of society—are clearly discarding modernism and embracing postmodernism in growing numbers. Popularized forms of postmodern thinking are diffusing into mainstream culture with a speed never imagined in Darwin's day. If we don't energetically grapple with postmodernism and learn to communicate in its terms, we can never hope to push back the ideological tide.

The Challenge of Postmodernism: *It is the death of truth as we know it.*

Like Darwin's theory of evolution, postmodernism originated in intellectual and academic circles, which is why most Christians are unclear about what postmodernism is. Even Christian leaders and thinkers become confused as they are assaulted by the strange or even seemingly nonsensical language of postmodern analysis. But postmodernists are far from insane. They present a dangerously convincing case for their view—a view that ultimately directly undermines all possibility of knowing objective truth (that is, truth that is true whether one believes it or not).

Postmodernism, as it applies to our everyday lives, is the death of truth as we know it.

And once again, Christians aren't ready for a major challenge to the Christian worldview. Christians stand unprepared to answer postmodernism because its concepts are hard to phrase in everyday terms. Postmodern jargon is difficult for most people to decipher, and recent books on postmodernism, secular and Christian, offer little help because they are written *by* scholars *for* scholars. That wouldn't be a problem if postmodernism were just another intellectual knot for academics to busy themselves untying. Yet we see signs of postmodern analysis at every turn. We won't say whether we think the following examples are good or bad until later in the book, but you may be surprised that they share a common basis in postmodern theory:

- The "political correctness" movement, an attempt by schools and corporations to control what students and employees say.
- A ripening view around the country that courts never provide fair trials to members of racial minorities or less affluent socioeconomic groups, because courts operate only to guard the privileges of the dominant culture—wealthy white males.
- A reluctance among educational and parenting experts to correct, confront, grade, test, or group children, based on the belief that labels stuck on children stick for life—so called "labeling theory."
- Tolerance gone extreme, as in the increasingly common view that we should never criticize another culture or question an in-

dividual's moral decisions, because all views deserve equal respect.

- A declining emphasis in schools on helping students master the literature, history, values, and philosophy of Western culture, and a growing emphasis through multicultural education on students determining their own standards of literacy—accepting, for example, non-standard or "street English" as its own legitimate language.
- New calls for segregation based on race, such as Afrocentric schools.
- The increasingly widespread belief that every hurt is intentional, every accident legally actionable. Radical victimology means that victims of all kinds belong to a marginalized, repressed group with only one hope: to strip power from the dominant group—the victimizers.
- Histories that purposely leave out even major events in the past to further the agendas of oppressed special-interest groups (examples: feminist, or gay and lesbian histories).
- Fresh attacks on Christian missions, claiming that missionaries are unrelenting "destroyers of culture."
- The belief that "male" and "female" are socially created categories intended to enslave women to men. Humankind is said to comprise not two sexes but at least five genders: heterosexual women, homosexual women, heterosexual men, homosexual men, and bisexuals. These genetically rooted identities are to be affirmed by our educational system and protected by the courts.
- Hostility toward science: When, for example, the Smithsonian Institution's Museum of American History received money to add an exhibit on American science, the funders expected to see displays commemorating the achievements of science over the past century. Instead, they found mainly "a catalogue of environmental horrors, weapons of mass destruction and social injustice. Among all the displays of pesticide residue, air pollution, acid rain, ozone holes, radioactive waste, food additives, and nuclear bombs, there was no mention that the life expectancy in the United States has more than doubled in the last century, the period covered by the exhibit."[1]

The list could go on. Here is the point: Although we might not understand how all these things are connected, they are in fact all manifestations of our culture's alarming postmodern shift. In recent years Christians have been concerned about relativism and the growth of New Age religions. But these are only the tip of the postmodern iceberg.

Our Goal

In this book we seek to show where postmodernism impacts your culture. Occasionally we will refer to thinkers unfamiliar to you. Just keep going. Reading this book and finding your way through the maze of postmodernism won't be the easiest thing you've ever done, but we hope it will be one of the most rewarding. Devoting time to digest this material will give you an invaluable understanding of this powerful movement—an understanding you will need in the years to come. Parents especially can't afford to miss the material covered in this book. For interested readers we provide additional detail in notes at the end of chapters.

We'll look first at some definitions, and compare the fading secular worldview of modernism with the new worldview of postmodernism.[2]

Then we will see how postmodern thinkers analyze and interpret several areas of contemporary life and thought. Again, if you feel confused at points, keep reading. Postmodernism *is* confusing, just as Darwin's ideas were 150 years ago. But as you see how postmodernism impacts crucial areas of your life, the definitions will make more sense. Soon you will be able to spot postmodern thinking all around you—on TV, in the movies, your children's classrooms, in song lyrics, and on the news. This book brings together a group of researchers and experts who will explain in plain language how postmodernism applies to everyday concerns, such as:

- Your next visit to a doctor may drop you into the lap of occult healing techniques. Postmodern rhetoric has eased the introduction of alternative medicine into nursing and medical schools, where superstition is now taught as being no less credible than proven scientific principles.
- There's a good chance your children will be educated in student-centered classrooms—not having teachers transmit knowledge

to them, but the postmodern way—creating knowledge themselves.

- You will find out why people no longer accept the words of a written text, including the Bible, at face value, thanks to the current style in literary interpretation, postmodern "deconstruction."
- A crucial lesson for all students to grasp: History class has become a platform for radical political and social agitation. History is no longer the search for "what happened," but an opportunity for formerly excluded and silenced groups in society such as gays and lesbians to finally be heard. Postmodern analysis of history makes it possible.
- Reality is in the mind of the beholder. This central premise of postmodern psychology shouts at us in bookstores and on TV shows and in the advice our neighbors give.
- Court decisions seem increasingly absurd. Why? Postmodern legal scholars and lawyers interpret the United States Constitution to mean *what it means to them*, not what its writers intended. The real and potential changes to government and law make the "liberal vs. conservative" struggles of the past two decades seem insignificant.
- Why do our American students lag behind the rest of the developed world in the sciences? Part of the reason is that postmodernists attack science as the vanguard of Western imperialism. The front page of the *Wall Street Journal* quoted a postmodern "feminist historian of science" who said that male-dominated science has assaulted nature like a violent man exploits a helpless woman. "A passive nature had to be interrogated, unclothed, penetrated, and compelled by man to reveal her secrets."[3]
- Your neighbors think your faith is "right for you." Unlike modernism, which treated religion as superstition, postmodernists happily accept any religion—as long as it makes no claim to universal truth or authority. Religion is at the heart of the postmodern revolution. How does a Christian live and share his or her faith in a gullible, undiscerning world?
- You may even find that you have been influenced by postmodern ideas yourself!

After we see how postmodernism is impacting all these areas of life, we will work to glean some positive lessons from postmodern thought, and in the closing chapters suggest how Christians can respond to this attractive yet menacing worldview.

In Brief

- Society in the late twentieth century is facing an ominous revolution of thought that fits under the broad label of "postmodernism."
- Even though postmodernism already affects every facet of our lives, most Christians remain unaware of what it is or how to respond.

Notes

1. Robert L. Park, "The Danger of Voodoo Science," *The New York Times* (Sunday, July 9, 1995), "OP-ED."
2. The boundaries of postmodern thought aren't easy to describe, especially since postmodernists rebel against categories and labels, which they consider prisons. In addition, postmodernism has deeply influenced a number of related ideologies as they stand today, such as feminism and liberation theology. Some feminists may deplore the outcome of deconstructive postmodernism, but in fact, they depend on postmodern methods and accept basic postmodern assumptions, and are instrumental in the spread of postmodernism. Just as intellectual historians identified a romantic revolt against enlightenment modernism, which deplored the conclusions of the enlightenment while nevertheless accepting its underlying assumptions, today related groups do the same with postmodernism. For this popular study, we are lumping all such groups in with postmodernists.
3. Elizabeth Fee, *The Wall Street Journal* (Monday, July 10, 1995): p. 1.

2

OUR OLD CHALLENGE: MODERNISM

JIM LEFFEL, CONTRIBUTOR

Strange things happen these days, some so strange it seems people have lost their minds. Consider these examples:

- A large state university convenes a peer review board to assess the academic credibility of a faculty member who has been training nurses to heal by passing their hands through the *prana* energy fields said to surround sick people's bodies. The board declares the professor's theories unproven. When they recommend a ban on further teaching of this New Age-based healing technology while data is gathered to verify the healing claims, the professor pleads that the panel is championing male-dominated medicine over female-dominated nursing. The university allows her to continue offering the courses for credit.[1]
- Leading thinkers in American law, including a recent nominee to head the U.S. Civil Rights Commission, argue against majority

About the Contributor:

Jim Leffel is director of the Crossroads Project, an interdisciplinary apologetics ministry whose researchers include the authors of this book. He also serves as education director for Xenos Christian Fellowship and as adjunct professor of philosophy at Ohio Dominican College. Jim holds an M.A. in philosophy of religion from Trinity Evangelical Divinity School and a B.A. in philosophy from The Ohio State University.

rule, fighting the dangers of what they brand "majoritarian interests."

- "Outcomes" for the new Outcome-Based Education programs in many school districts focus as much on diversity training as they do on reading, writing, and arithmetic.

Modernism and *Post*modernism

All of these examples and many others like them are the direct result of a new way of viewing reality. For decades, Christians and other theists (those who believe in an infinite, personal God) have battled the anti-religious ideology called *modernism*, or what some have labeled *secular humanism*. Most Christian apologetics today target modernism, which denies the existence of God and the supernatural. But there's a new, rapidly growing view of the world that threatens to discredit modernism and theism alike: *postmodernism*. Postmodernism means *after*-modernism, in the sense that it's *beyond* modernism. Postmodernists believe they have seen through modernism.[2]

For now, we will work from an extremely brief description of postmodernism, which we will later further develop:

Postmodernists believe that truth is created, not discovered. They think things like reason, rationality, and confidence in science are cultural biases. They contend that those who trust reason—and things based on reason, like science, Western education, and governmental structures—unknowingly act out their European cultural conditioning. This conditioning seeks to keep power in the hands of the social elite.

Because postmodernists reach these conclusions in reaction to modernism, we can't understand postmodernism without first grasping the basics of modernism. In this chapter, then, we will examine four key modernist beliefs, contrasting in the next two chapters four key postmodern reactions to those beliefs. Browse the table below, which shows where we are headed. For comparison, we also include the biblical, theistic alternatives. Some definitions may be unclear now, but we will explain them as we go on:

Subject	Modernism	Postmodernism	Theism
Human Nature	Humans are purely material machines. We live in a purely physical world. Nothing exists beyond what our senses perceive.	Humans are cogs in a social machine. We are primarily social beings.	Humans are the only beings on earth created in the image of God. They are both spiritual and material.
Free Will (Autonomy)	Humans are self-governing and free to choose their own direction.	People are the product of their culture and only imagine they are self-governing.	Human free will has been drastically diminished by a moral fall from grace, but people are still responsible for the use of their remaining free will. The desire to be autonomous is sinful—we were created to depend on God.
View of Reason	People should be "rationalistic optimists" who depend only on the data of their senses and reason.	There is no such thing as objective rationality (that is, reason unaffected by bias) in the sense that modernists use the term. Objective reason is a myth.	Reason is necessary, but insufficient for understanding reality. Reason can disclose truth about reality, but faith and revelation are needed in addition.
View of Progress	Humankind is progressing by using science and reason.	"Progress" is a code-word used by modernists to justify the domination by European culture of other cultures.	Humans are not progressing toward a glorious future. Advances that relieve suffering and prolong life, however, are good.

Let's look at each of the boxes on the left in order.

Key Modernism Belief #1: Humans Are Biological Machines

Subject	Modernism	Postmodernism
Human Nature	Humans are purely material machines. We live in a purely physical world. Nothing exists beyond what our senses perceive.	Humans are cogs in a social machine. We are primarily social beings.
Free Will (Autonomy)	Humans are self-governing and free to choose their own direction.	People are the product of their culture and only imagine they are self-governing.
View of Reason	People should be "rationalistic optimists" who depend only on the data of their senses and reason.	There is no such thing as objective rationality (that is, reason unaffected by bias) in the sense that modernists use the term. Objective reason is a myth.
View of Progress	Humankind is progressing by using science and reason.	"Progress" is a code-word used by modernists to justify the domination by European culture of other cultures.

Most of us in the West have grown up under the sway of modernism, a school of thought that stretches back to the period in European history known as the Enlightenment. By the early 1700s, advances in science, most notably the findings of Galileo and Newton, had persuaded intellectuals to reject the medieval view of nature. When scientific observation directly contradicted church pronouncements, people discarded the church's dogma. They no longer accepted, for example, that the earth was the center of the universe and that the objects beyond the moon were perfect spheres revolving in orbit around the earth.[3] People became modern. They were "enlightened."

Inspired by Newton's laws of mechanics, these new modernists viewed nature as a grand machine whose processes could be understood only through the grid of natural law. People began to study nature by applying reason and increasingly standardized rules of investigation. As they searched, modern scientists discovered principles in nature that explained how the natural order worked—the same natural order that earlier thinkers had attributed to God's providence. Not surprisingly, conflict between the old way and the new way of explaining reality was often just under the surface.

Although many of the earliest scientists were Christians, in time more and more scientists came to view God as an unnecessary theory. He may have set the universe in motion, they granted, but natural laws alone now governed the universe. This belief that God started things and then disappeared, leaving them to run on their own, is termed *deism*. Deism is the stepping stone between the theistic worldview of the Middle Ages and the atheistic modernism of the present day.

Then, in 1859, Charles Darwin published *The Origin of Species*. His contemporary, Johann Gregor Mendel, made important discoveries in the field of genetics. Together, their work, now known as evolutionary theory, introduced a new era of naturalistic science.

For many, Darwin's theory of natural selection provided the overarching process and Mendel's genetics provided the mechanism by which all biological life could emerge, adapt, and develop over time without any help from God. Noted Oxford zoologist Richard Dawkins captured this sentiment recently when he said that "although atheism might have been logically tenable before Darwin, Darwin made it possible to be an intellectually fulfilled atheist."[4]

Because modernists view nature as a machine independent of God, they also directly challenge the Christian view of human nature. Modernist evolutionists, for instance, have turned the study of human behavior into a strictly biological science. Because they believe humans are merely part of the machine of nature, modernists today reach dangerous conclusions. What people once considered moral choice, they now attribute to genetic encoding or environmental conditioning. Modernist scientists confidently assert that genetics explains such things as altruism, addiction, homosexuality, infidelity, and violence.[5]

As people accept purely biological explanations for human behavior they narrow the gap between human and non-human. Similarly, qualities once thought to be uniquely human are now widely regarded as common in the animal kingdom. Anthropologists and experimental psychologists today argue that animals use language to express their thoughts and feelings.[6] Humans may differ from other animals in the size of our brains, but we otherwise are essentially the same, according to these researchers.

Artificial intelligence serves as a final example of modernism's influence on our view of human nature. Millions have been entertained by the human-like computer "Data" on *StarTrek: The Next Generation*. But what many accept as science fiction, modernism takes as real. If humans are essentially machines, they argue, then it should be possible to make a machine that does everything humans can do. As Carl Sagan put it, "Each human being is a superbly constructed, astonishingly compact, self-ambulatory computer."[7]

The point is that modernism is no friend to Christianity. Among other things, modernism is directly opposed to the biblical understanding of what it means to be human. Today, "sociobiology" denies both human freedom and uniqueness. Modernists have no room for human dignity because they think humans are essentially no different from any other species or organism. They also have no room for freedom, because they think human behavior can be explained by chemical reactions that follow impersonal laws of nature. Because modernists think we are determined by our biology and our environment, they view humans as nothing but reactive, stimulus-response machines.

To summarize:

- Modernists overthrew the medieval view of the world.
- They see nature and humans as purely physical machines.
- They trust scientific inquiry to give all the answers.

Key Modernism Belief #2: People Are *Autonomous*

Subject	Modernism	Postmodernism
Human Nature	Humans are purely material machines. We live in a purely physical world. Nothing exists beyond what our senses perceive.	Humans are cogs in a social machine. We are primarily social beings.
Free Will (Autonomy)	Humans are self-governing and free to choose their own direction.	People are the product of their culture and only imagine they are self-governing.
View of Reason	People should be "rationalistic optimists" who depend only on the data of their senses and reason.	There is no such thing as objective rationality (that is, reason unaffected by bias) in the sense that modernists use the term. Objective reason is a myth.
View of Progress	Humankind is progressing by using science and reason.	"Progress" is a code-word used by modernists to justify the domination by European culture of other cultures.

In the early days of the Enlightenment, modernist thinkers

rejected the medieval social hierarchy with its authoritarian church structure and divine right of kings, asserting instead that nature placed all humans on the same level. Political theory reflected this.

They saw humans as essentially free or "autonomous"—independent, self-contained, self-governing, a law unto themselves. They held that autonomous people need a social order that protects their "natural rights" to individual autonomy. Since reason demands that people come together for the sake of mutual protection, government "of, by and for the people" is the only way these inalienable rights can be preserved.[8] American society's highly individualistic focus is a direct result of the modernist view of human nature.[9]

The driving force behind the new social order envisioned by modernists was the "invisible hand" of capitalism. Capitalism, said moral philosopher Adam Smith, provided the moral framework for democratic society. He taught that competition for markets appeals to rational self-interest and that success in the marketplace maximizes human creativity and personal freedom. He claimed these capitalistic market forces were just as real a force in society as are physical laws in nature.

The wealth and freedom created by Western capitalistic democracies clearly is unparalleled in history. Yet democratic capitalism has produced some negative social conditions never envisioned by its Enlightenment proponents, and postmodernism is in many ways a revolt against capitalism. As we will see in Chapter 4, many postmodernists are waging ideological war against the democratic/capitalistic state.

To summarize:

- Modernists think people are free to make up their own minds and to choose between different courses of behavior.
- They revolted against the earlier medieval view that people need to be guided by the church and a king.
- They believe that freely competing market forces under democracies will lead to a healthy society.

Key Modernism Belief #3: People Can Use Unaided Reason to Find Truth

Subject	Modernism	Postmodernism
Human Nature	Humans are purely material machines. We live in a purely physical world. Nothing exists beyond what our senses perceive.	Humans are cogs in a social machine. We are primarily social beings.
Free Will (Autonomy)	Humans are self-governing and free to choose their own direction.	People are the product of their culture and only imagine they are self-governing.
View of Reason	People should be "rationalistic optimists" who depend only on the data of their senses and reason.	There is no such thing as objective rationality (that is, reason unaffected by bias) in the sense that modernists use the term. Objective reason is a myth.
View of Progress	Humankind is progressing by using science and reason.	"Progress" is a code-word used by modernists to justify the domination by European culture of other cultures.

Anselm's dictum, "I believe so that I might understand," captured the mind-set of the Middle Ages. He sought to root reason in the soil of Christian belief. Descartes' assertion, "I think, therefore I am," is the anthem of the modern period. Descartes and the modernists held that human reason by itself was sufficient to arrive at truth.

Modernists also believe people are free to think rationally and impartially. According to modernists, our minds can perceive and study reality and reach objective conclusions—that is, they believe we are able to truly understand reality as *reality*, relatively unaffected by our own bias, distortion, or previous belief systems. Our conclusions can reflect reality outside ourselves, not just thoughts within our own minds.[10]

The modernist worldview assumes naturalism—the belief that all phenomena can be explained by natural causes and laws. Naturalism is consistent with both atheism and deism, because for either worldview the things we see in the world have no spiritual cause. This assumption affects not only their view of human nature but also their understanding of human knowledge.

Modernists teach that since humans are merely biological beings, knowledge can only be based on our physical sense experience—a view of knowledge called *empiricism*, which states that "nothing is in our mind that is not first in our senses." How do we come to know something? We see it, hear it, feel it, smell it, or taste it. Put simply, "seeing is believing."

Empiricism implies limits on what we can know. If knowledge is rooted only in sense perception, we cannot know anything beyond the realm of what empiricists call "possible sense experience." They argue that since science is the objective study of sensory data, it becomes the final arbiter of truth. But there's a problem. When modernists limit knowledge to what our senses can experience, the implication is obvious: They automatically exclude the possibility of knowing spiritual or moral truths.[11] Empiricists hold that beliefs about spiritual or moral matters are rooted in non-rational faith or in personal preference, not in reason. Those who claim to know God or to recognize the rightness or wrongness of a thing make assertions beyond the nature and limits of human knowledge.

As many have pointed out, however, an empirical view of knowledge itself requires faith. Empiricism is based on what philosophers call the "correspondence theory of truth." Correspondence theory holds that a person's idea is true when it matches reality outside that person. In other words, we possess knowledge when the images inside our minds agree with the real objects outside our minds.

When modernists limit knowledge to what our senses can experience, they exclude the possibility of knowing spiritual or moral truths.

Empiricists optimistically assume that our senses can create impressions in our minds reflecting reality as it truly exists. Significant advances in science and technology have strengthened this modernist confidence in reason, and the usefulness of science is evidence of the strong correlation between reality and the ideas about reality in our minds. Postmodernists, though, doubt both the usefulness of science and the correspondence theory of knowledge, as we shall see.

Key Modernism Belief #4: Humankind Is Progressing

Subject	Modernism	Postmodernism
Human Nature	Humans are purely material machines. We live in a purely physical world. Nothing exists beyond what our senses perceive.	Humans are cogs in a social machine. We are primarily social beings.
Free Will (Autonomy)	Humans are self-governing and free to choose their own direction.	People are the product of their culture and only imagine they are self-governing.
View of Reason	People should be "rationalistic optimists" who depend only on the data of their senses and reason.	There is no such thing as objective rationality (that is, reason unaffected by bias) in the sense that modernists use the term. Objective reason is a myth.
View of Progress	Humankind is progressing by using science and reason.	"Progress" is a code-word used by modernists to justify the domination by European culture of other cultures.

Enlightenment thinkers optimistically believed that their reasoning powers and their new approaches to scientific disciplines would lead to a world free from superstition, violence, and poverty. Modernist thinkers thrive on the notion that just as the natural world had progressed through stages of evolution, human society will also evolve and progress into a bright future.

Consider the words of the Marquis De Condorcet, in his influential work, "Progress of the Human Mind":

> Such is the aim of the work that I have undertaken . . . to show by appeal to reason and fact that nature has set no term to the perfection of human faculties; that the perfectibility of man is truly infinite; and that the progress of this perfectibility from now onward is independent of any powers that might wish to halt it, has no other limit than the duration of the globe upon which nature has cast us.[12]

In these words you feel the optimism, indeed the arrogance, of the modernist mind-set. This arrogance is a large part of the motive for the postmodern revolt.

In Brief

- Modernists think people are just like the rest of the universe—purely material and, therefore, machinelike.

- They believe people are autonomous—that they have free will and should use their reasoning powers to pick the rational direction in life. They believe society should be structured to preserve freedom.
- Modernists believe it is possible to take a rational approach to life, and that this is the "enlightened" view. Superstition—the belief in the supernatural, spirits, gods—has no place in the rational approach.
- Modernists believe humanity is progressing toward a positive future based on technology and democracy.

Notes

1. We discuss this case in detail in Chapter 5.
2. Postmodernism is not a single school of thought with fixed teachings, but a rapidly evolving group of concepts. The movement may even shed the name "postmodernism" in the years to come, because leading thinkers in the movement have shown a strong inclination to devise new words and names for their positions and to shun labels and descriptions, no matter how accurate. They strongly resist being identified as a belief system in their own right, wanting only to deny other orthodoxies. We therefore need to be able to recognize postmodernism by its ideas, not by its titles. American interest in Eastern Mysticism and Native American religions, for instance, is compatible with postmodernism, not modernism or theism.
3. See the recantation of Galileo in Rome, June 22, 1633, in John Beatty and Oliver Johnson, *Heritage of Western Civilization*, Vol. 2 (Englewood Cliffs: Prentice-Hall, 1987), p. 24.
4. Cited in Alvin Plantinga, *Warrant and Proper Function* (Oxford: Oxford University Press, 1993), p. 217.
5. For an overview of the issues related to the genetics of behavior, see Charles C. Mann, "Behavioral Genetics in Transition," *Science* (264:1686–1689).
6. "Conceptual Abilities of Some Non-Primate Species, With an Emphasis on an African Gray Parrot," I. M. Pepperberg, in Susan Taylor Parker and Cathleen Rita Gibbeon, eds., *"Language" and Intelligence in Monkeys and Apes, Comparative Developmental Perspectives* (Cambridge: Cambridge University Press, 1990), p. 469.

7. Cited in Ed Miller, *Questions That Matter* (New York: McGraw-Hill, 1987), p. 162.
8. John Locke's *Second Treatise on Government* and Jean-Jacques Rousseau's *Social Contract* provided the basis for modern democracies.
9. Robert Bellah, et. al., *Habits of the Heart* (New York: Harper & Row, 1985).
10. This may seem contradictory to our earlier statement that people are stimulus-response machines without freedom under modernism. It is! In fact, this is one of the great contradictions in modernism, leading to criticism by both theists and postmodernists. See a simple explanation of theistic attacks on modernism based on this contradiction in Dennis McCallum, *Christianity: The Faith That Makes Sense* (Wheaton, Ill.: Tyndale House Publishers, 1992), pp. 46–51, or contact us via the World Wide Web at http:/www. xenos. org/presup. html. We will examine the postmodern arguments in the next chapter.
11. Though naturalists often claim they have an adequate basis for morality, they actually replace moral concepts with non-moral language such as desire, or utility. See A. J. Ayer, *Language, Truth and Logic* (New York: Dover Publications, 1952) or Charles L. Stevenson, *Ethics and Language* (New Haven, Conn.: Yale University Press, 1944).
12. Antoine-Nicolas De Condorcet, "The Progress of the Human Mind," in John L. Beatty and Oliver A. Johnson, *Heritage of Western Civilization*, Vol. 2 (Englewood Cliffs, N.Y.: Prentice-Hall, 1987), p. 90.

3

Our New Challenge: Postmodernism

Jim Leffel, Contributor

In a recent series of more than twenty interviews conducted at random at a large university, people were asked if there was such a thing as absolute truth—truth that is true across all times and cultures for all people. All but one respondent answered along these lines:

"Truth is whatever you believe."

"There is no absolute truth."

"If there *were* such a thing as absolute truth, how could we know what it is?"

"People who believe in absolute truth are dangerous."

The lone exception was an evangelical Christian, who said absolute truth was in Jesus Christ.

Truth, declares a growing collective consciousness, is *relative*: what is true, right, or beautiful for one person isn't necessarily true, right, or beautiful for another. *Relativism* says that truth isn't fixed by outside reality, but is decided by a group or individual for themselves. Truth isn't discovered, but manufactured. Truth is ever-changing not only in insignificant matters of taste or fashion, but in crucial matters of spirituality, morality, and reality itself.

This is the postmodern consensus—that truth is a slippery thing. Contemporary society's distrust of truth, though, didn't emerge from nowhere. Relativism—one facet of postmodernism—

is rooted in a distrust of the claims of modernism. Because postmodernism has risen to popularity largely as a response to modernism, we will look again at our chart contrasting these two views. In the last chapter we considered the boxes under modernism. Now let's look at the boxes under *post*modernism to understand what it is and why we see it today.

Key Postmodern Belief #1: Humans Are Cogs in a Social Machine

Subject	Modernism	Postmodernism
Human Nature	Humans are purely material machines. We live in a purely physical world. Nothing exists beyond what our senses perceive.	Humans are cogs in a social machine. We are primarily social beings.
Free Will (Autonomy)	Humans are self-governing and free to choose their own direction.	People are the product of their culture and only imagine they are self-governing.
View of Reason	People should be "rationalistic optimists" who depend only on the data of their senses and reason.	There is no such thing as objective rationality (that is, reason unaffected by bias) in the sense that modernists use the term. Objective reason is a myth.
View of Progress	Humankind is progressing by using science and reason.	"Progress" is a code-word used by modernists to justify the domination by European culture of other cultures.

Postmodernists, like modernists, believe people are no different than the rest of nature though they conceive of nature very differently. The crucial difference between modernists and postmodernists on this point is this: While modernists see people primarily as cogs in a vast *physical* machine, postmodernists see people as cogs in a *social* machine. They focus not on the effects on people of the physical processes of nature and biology, but on the effects of social processes, especially language.

Even this considerable disagreement, however, isn't the main area of conflict between the two camps. The hottest arguments are in the second, third, and fourth boxes on left and right.

Key Postmodern Belief #2: People Are Never Really Autonomous

Subject	Modernism	Postmodernism
Human Nature	Humans are purely material machines. We live in a purely physical world. Nothing exists beyond what our senses perceive.	Humans are cogs in a social machine. We are primarily social beings.
Free Will (Autonomy)	Humans are self-governing and free to choose their own direction.	People are the product of their culture and only imagine they are self-governing.
View of Reason	People should be "rationalistic optimists" who depend only on the data of their senses and reason.	There is no such thing as objective rationality (that is, reason unaffected by bias) in the sense that modernists use the term. Objective reason is a myth.
View of Progress	Humankind is progressing by using science and reason.	"Progress" is a code-word used by modernists to justify the domination by European culture of other cultures.

Modernism's focus on the individual birthed Western democracy. Humans, modernists declare, begin as autonomous, self-governed individuals in a sea of other individuals, each self-interested and consequently each a threat to the other. Modernist political theorists argue that from this primal "state of nature" people come together—for reasons of individual self-interest. They agree to voluntarily limit freedom for the sake of protection. They assume that a person is first an individual, and becomes a social being by choice. Society exists as the creation of individuals, and its ongoing existence is dependent on the consent of rationally self-interested individuals. Society is constructed by individuals, not vice versa.

Liberal democracy holds water only if humans are free to select between alternative actions. Postmodern theorists, however, reject the idea that people freely reason and choose. Human thought, in their view, can't exist independent of our social environment.[1] Postmodernists draw their conception of human rationality largely from Marx, who said that rational thought is the product of people's interaction with their socioeconomic environment.[2] He claimed our thought is derived from social forces imposed upon us. Consequently, postmodernists say that all thoughts are "social constructs."

Have you ever noticed the common attitude that society *ines-*

capably molds people's thinking? Our society readily accepts the postmodern proposition that people are entirely the product of their cultural conditioning. People can hardly be expected to think or act in any way other than how their culture shapes them. An inner-city boy, for instance, lands in jail because his culture made him a certain way. We increasingly view the differences between people not as the result of life decisions or directions chosen by the individual, but as the result of different cultural backgrounds or social forces.

These truths are undeniable to an extent, yet the postmodern conclusions are, we believe, grossly exaggerated. How do some individuals—for better or for worse—end up behaving in ways totally different from the culture in which they were raised? We will evaluate this and other postmodern positions later, but for now must limit ourselves to understanding them.[3]

Marx developed his claim that people are the product of culture through studying economic history and philosophy. Later, based on Marx's theory, sociologist Karl Mannheim developed what he called the "sociology of knowledge," which sought to identify the social factors giving rise to people's ideas and their identities.[4] His approach is expressed by Peter Berger, one of today's best-known sociologists:

> A thought of any kind is grounded in society. . . . The individual, then, derives his worldview socially in very much the same way that he derives his roles and his identity. In other words, his emotions and his self-interpretation like his actions are predefined for him by society, and so is his cognitive approach to the universe that surrounds him.[5]

Since this "sociology of knowledge" is almost universally accepted among postmodernists, we will briefly explain its meaning and implications. The sociology of knowledge makes two important claims:

1. Human beings are what their cultural environments make them. In answer to the question, "Who am I?" the postmodern sociologist answers, "You—your thoughts, your attitudes, your very existence—are a 'social construction,' " a creation of society and cultural conditioning. In the postmodern view, the institutions, language, and symbolic forms that make up a culture also define the individual:

Society shapes our aspirations, expectations, sense of self-worth, and purpose for being. While postmodernists would not use the term "determinism" (because they see it as an unacceptable rationalistic idea), their view of humans implies that people are largely determined by their culture.[6]

Postmodernists have a problem with individual identity. They use language that implies the existence of the personal self, but their outlook points to the disintegration of self. The notion of distinct personhood, according to postmodernists, is an illusion. From their view, individuals are actually "nodes" or particular expressions of wider social reality. Postmodern anthropologists and literary theorists often view the purpose of their work not as bettering the self, but as eliminating it.[7]

2. *All our thinking is a social construct.* Postmodernists also assert that our pattern of thought, our "cognitive approach" to the universe, is also a social construction. This means that the beginning truths or "axioms" we bring to the reasoning process are beliefs we have been conditioned to accept by our society, just as others have been conditioned to accept a completely different set of beliefs. Postmodernists assert that all such beginning beliefs are arbitrary.

For instance, we in the West have been taught that truth cannot be self-contradictory. But in Asian religion and culture, truths can often be contradictory. Although we in the West may think we are being rational and objective, we aren't. Postmodernists point out that we already have a cultural and social beginning point that makes objectivity impossible. We trust our assumptions about the validity of "reason," they argue, because our culture is that of Enlightenment Europe. Other cultures may trust their shaman or their guru for the same reason.[8]

In the absence of objective truth, there is no final bar of appeal to determine truth and reality when cultures view the world in different or mutually exclusive ways. We are left with cultural relativism, or what the postmodernists term "local knowledges" or "paradigms." Within each paradigm people think differently and have their own truth, which is real to them alone.

Key Postmodern Belief #3: People Are Never Objective or Rational

Subject	Modernism	Postmodernism
Human Nature	Humans are purely material machines. We live in a purely physical world. Nothing exists beyond what our senses perceive.	Humans are cogs in a social machine. We are primarily social beings.
Free Will (Autonomy)	Humans are self-governing and free to choose their own direction.	People are the product of their culture and only imagine they are self-governing.
View of Reason	People should be "rationalistic optimists" who depend only on the data of their senses and reason.	There is no such thing as objective rationality (that is, reason unaffected by bias) in the sense that modernists use the term. Objective reason is a myth.
View of Progress	Humankind is progressing by using science and reason.	"Progress" is a code-word used by modernists to justify the domination by European culture of other cultures.

Modernists say that when we observe something, our senses show us the same thing again and again, which suggests that what we see reflects what is really there—that is, modernists, being empiricists, assume that the images our senses bring to our minds correctly reflect reality outside our minds. John Locke used the image of waves carving out the contour of a beach as an analogy for how our senses imprint with increasing clarity the data of the external world on our conscious minds. In the same way, he argued, our sense experiences that create impressions in our minds correspond to the contour of reality outside our minds—the correspondence theory of knowledge.[9]

But how can we know if the images our senses bring to our minds genuinely match reality outside our minds? Ultimately, the only way to be sure would be to stand outside ourselves and compare our mental images with the real world. But since we can't stand outside ourselves, we have no way to know whether the correspondence is accurate. We are left with skepticism.

This is one reason postmodernists contend that empirical "objectivity" doesn't exist. They raise the problem of *representation*—how we perceive reality, and whether our perceptions accurately reflect the external world. Postmodernists say they don't. They point out that different people see the same things differently. Recall the accounts of the Los Angeles riots of 1993—the varying descriptions from white observers and black observers. Often, the white observers described a group of lawless hoodlums wrecking a neighborhood. But black observers often described a group of frustrated people seeking justice the only way they knew. Some leaders, both black and white, repeatedly stressed that further riots of the same kind are *inevitable* unless the economic and judicial conditions leading to the riots are changed. Apparently, people's cultures condition them to perceive the same events differently.

For exactly this reason, police at the site of a car accident know well the need to correlate the testimony of witnesses. Each source sees events from its own point of view. One group of observers sees their point of view as reality. But to a different group, reality looks different.

People's inherent subjectivity—their tendency to see things from their own point of view, and to conclude that their view of reality is real and correct—leads postmodern analysts to question the objectivity of people's every perception. "How can we ever trust objectivity," they ask, "when there is no way to objectively check on the validity of our perceptions?"[10]

How Language Makes Objectivity Impossible

Postmodernists talk at length about language and its effects on our thinking. They believe studies of language provide evidence for their critique of modernist views of reason and freedom. Several of the more complex postmodern assumptions come from the sometimes cryptic field of linguistics, the analysis of language.

We saw earlier that postmodernists deny we have a "self" that exists independent of our social reality. Culture and society *create* individuals as well as their thoughts and attitudes. One of the main ways society shapes individuals is through language.

Postmodernists point out that individuals always interact with reality through the medium of language. All mental activities, they say, are based in language—that is, we *think* in words and *communicate* with words. People are connected to reality through the labels they assign to their perceptions and ideas. These labels—words—are arbitrary, assigned by society. The more abstract—and often the more important—our ideas are, the more dependent we are on words alone to provide meaning. But if language is the way people relate to reality, then we must understand the nature of language.

Two components in the study of language stand out in importance for postmodernists: *semantics* (the *meaning* of words and language forms such as phrases and clauses) and *syntax* (the arrangement or *structure* of those words and forms). If we understand the postmodern perspective on these two areas, we will also understand much of the postmodern analysis of language, truth, and reason.

The Prison of Semantics

In the early 1930s Polish mathematician Alfred Korzybski raised some intriguing issues about words and their meanings.[11] He pointed out a problem with the use of the word "is." When we use "is," he claimed, we collapse into a naive realism. We confuse perceptions with reality. If we say, for example, "the room is hot," we unconsciously substitute perception for reality, subjectivity for objectivity. We should say, "the room *appears* to be hot," or "I *perceive* it to be hot." Instead, by stating perceptions as though they are reality, our words actually insulate us from reality. We confuse the symbol—words—with reality. We think we understand something because we have formed a word for it. As cultures accept definitions for words, they solidify the confusion between the symbolic and the real.

Ironically, postmodernists have no shortage of new vocabulary for conveying these concepts. They call the symbol or word the "signifier," and the reality it supposedly describes the "signified." Words, to postmodernists, are "maps" while the reality they supposedly describe is the "territory."

Words	**Reality**
Signifiers	Signified
Maps	Territory

We might say the field of semantics deals with the relationship between words and reality, and this is just where postmodernists have a problem. They argue that we have no access to the territory (reality) without the map (words). But since we can't check the territory against the map, we have no way of knowing how reliable the map is. We are caught up in a circle of words, with no way out. Just as empiricists can never stand outside themselves to compare sense perceptions with external reality, so language-users can never depart from the world of words to consider their own ideas.

Take, for example, the Eskimo language. They have dozens of words for "snow." We have only a few. What difference would it make to grow up in a culture using a language with different words than ours? Some cultures have no word that corresponds to a certain word from another culture. How, then, can they think the same thoughts? How can their reality be considered the same as that of the other culture? Postmodernists argue that we are locked out of their world, and they out of ours. Language is like a "prison house."[12] We cannot go outside our language in either thought or experience.

The Prison of Syntax

If semantics, the meaning of words, subverts our *impressions* of reality, then syntax does the same for our *reasoning* about reality. Syntax is the structure of a language, the rules for using language. Postmodernists claim that syntax, by governing the way we relate words to each other, establishes a logic within language. Yet they go on to argue that the logic of language effectively overthrows the laws of objective reason itself.

Linguist Benjamin Whorf, for example, argues that we categorize perceptions and thoughts based on the language we use. And since the logic (or syntax) of one language cannot be applied to the logic (syntax) of another, we are confronted with separate, culturally isolated systems for thinking.[13] This difference between systems goes beyond the fact that cultures say different things. They actually *think* in different *ways* because their languages arrange and interpret ideas differently, according to postmodernists.

These observations carry a certain amount of weight. Careful Bible students, for instance, know that Hebrew thinking is different than modern Western thinking, which in turn is different than Greco-Roman thinking. These differences are evident in the structure of these languages themselves, even when discussing the same subject. Of course, the differences are usually subtle: different expressions, different emphases, ideas little known in one culture compared to another. The differences sometimes include elements of culturally accepted but fundamentally false worldviews, such as belief in a flat earth.

Most of us would observe these latter differences without conceding that, for them, the world *was* flat. Postmodernists, though, take these observations to an extreme. They say that once we admit different language systems lead to different ways of thinking, we lose the ability to judge the ideas of other cultures. To do so, they argue, would be to impose our own language and thought patterns on their way of thinking. Since we cannot say one language is superior to another, we cannot evaluate or criticize the ideas, facts, or truths a language conveys. So, for instance, some postmodern theorists regard standard English to be inappropriate for teaching African-American or Latino children. (See Chapter 7.)

Imprisoned in Our Own Language

For the postmodernist, problems exist not just between cultures, but within a single culture. Have you ever driven down a freeway and looked up to gauge how fast the clouds are moving? Very quickly you realize it's impossible. Your own car is moving, so you have no objective way to know how much of the cloud movement is the result of your movement, and how much is the result of the clouds' movement. If you want to be sure of the direction or the speed of the clouds, you will have to stop your car.

> To postmodernists, confidence in Western rationality is a failure to understand the difference between our culture and others.

In the same way, we understand nature through the grid of our language. We cannot think about nature without using language. If language has a logic of its own based on its syntax, we have no way of knowing how our language affects our perceptions. Our language is the moving car from which we view the world.

We could ask if the sky is really blue, but if everyone is wearing rose-colored glasses, we could never be sure of our answer. We could assign terms such as "cause" and "effect" to the things we behold in nature. But how do we know the things we see are actually "causes" or "effects," or whether we have arbitrarily assigned these terms to something that *could* be viewed altogether differently? So, postmodernists argue, there is no way to know if the laws of language and the laws governing reality are the same. Postmodernism leaves us in an all-pervasive skepticism, locked up in what they call the prison house of language. Reality is defined or constructed by culture and language, not discovered by reason and observation.

This leads to some alarming conclusions. Recently, for example, a panel of nineteen experts appointed by the National Institutes of Health recommended that federal funding be used for producing and harvesting—and destroying—fetuses for laboratory experimentation. The panel's reasoning is that "personhood" is a "social construct." Human beings, in other words, aren't born, but defined.[14] According to them, cultural consensus (not always popular, but that of the experts) defines reality.

What happens, however, when culture decides a certain race or gender is non-human, and those non-humans are targeted for extinction? If reality is culture-bound, it would be an act of imperialism for another culture to intervene. Without an absolute standard, there is no basis for judging a Nazi or a misogynist any more than there is for defining a human life.

Postmodernists and Progress

Subject	Modernism	Postmodernism
Human Nature	Humans are purely material machines. We live in a purely physical world. Nothing exists beyond what our senses perceive.	Humans are cogs in a social machine. We are primarily social beings.
Free Will (Autonomy)	Humans are self-governing and free to choose their own direction.	People are the product of their culture and only imagine they are self-governing.
View of Reason	People should be "rationalistic optimists" who depend only on the data of their senses and reason.	There is no such thing as objective rationality (that is, reason unaffected by bias) in the sense that modernists use the term. Objective reason is a myth.
View of Progress	Humankind is progressing by using science and reason.	"Progress" is a code-word used by modernists to justify the domination by European culture of other cultures.

Postmodernists reject the notion that humanity is progressing through the use of reason and technology. Their response is so important that we have devoted the next chapter to it. Before moving on to examine the impact of postmodernism on our society, we will also briefly critique the postmodern beliefs examined in these chapters.

In Brief

- Postmodernism views human beings as cogs in a giant social machine, or more precisely, as "nodes," extensions of their culture.
- Postmodernists reject the modernist idea that people can ever be rationally objective. We can never take the self or culture out of reason, and therefore reason can't be trusted any more than intuition or feeling.
- Postmodernists argue that people believe they are free to think what they want, but their thoughts in fact inescapably reflect their social environment. We think in the language of our culture and through the personal identity our culture has bestowed on us; for both these reasons, personal freedom—in the Enlightenment sense of autonomy—is an illusion.

Notes

1. People sometimes wonder whether postmodern thinkers are merely denying the *amount* of autonomy and freedom that modernists claim, or denying the very *possibility* of all freedom and autonomy. Careful reading usually shows the latter. For example, note John McGowan's comments in his survey of postmodernism: "Autonomy is a [central] plank of humanism, with its insistence that humans can produce their lives and their social world on their own. For this reason, much postmodern work, with its antihumanist slant, has been at pains both to deny the possibility of achieving autonomy and to indicate autonomy's pernicious consequences." John McGowan, *Postmodernism and Its Critics* (Ithaca, N.Y.: Cornell University Press, 1991), p. 4. He continues: "Willful modernist self-exclusion, the claim to stand outside, is only a delusion; the postmodernist insists that everything is included [within social reality], that nothing can achieve the autonomy or distance in which the mod-

ernists found their last defense against all-encompassing capitalism," p. 13.

2. See Arthur Mendel, *The Essential Works of Marxism* (New York: Bantam Books, 1961), p. 5ff. See also "Socialism: Utopian and Scientific," Karl Marx and Fredrich Engels, in *The Essential Works of Marxism* (New York: Bantam Books, 1961), pp. 45ff.
3. See Chapter 14 for a summarized critical assessment of postmodernism in light of Christianity.
4. Defined in Karl Mannheim, *Ideology and Utopia* (New York: Harcourt, Brace, 1936).
5. Peter Berger, *Invitation to Sociology* (Garden City: Doubleday & Co., Inc., 1963), p. 117.
6. Carravetta states that the self is "only a mask, a role, a victim, at worst an ideological construct, at best a nostalgic effigy." Peter Carravetta, "On Gianni Vittamo's Postmodern Hermeneutics," *Theory, Culture and Society*, 5 (February 3), pp. 395–99.
7. Ironically, postmodernism and modernism hold this essentially impersonal view of humans in common. Modernism sees people as impersonal because they are machines. Postmodernism sees them as nodes or extensions of their culture. See Terry Eagleton, *Literary Theory* (Minneapolis: University of Minnesota Press, 1983), p. 104ff.
8. In the view of postmodernists, Western culture uses reason mainly as a weapon for division. As John McGowan explains it, "Western reason's fundamental attachment to the law of noncontradiction can thus be seen as based on the instrumental utility of that principle in the attempt to assert control. The repression of contradiction both within the self and within the social body favors integrity and unanimity over difference and multiplicity." John McGowan, *Postmodernism and Its Critics*, p. 19.
9. See John Locke, *Essay Concerning Human Understanding* (London: Oxford University Press, 1924).
10. See discussions on this problem in Richard Rorty, *Philosophy and the Mirror of Nature* (Princeton: Princeton University Press, 1979), and Madan Sarup, *An Introductory Guide to Post-Structuralism and Postmodernism* (Athens: University of Georgia Press, 1989).
11. Cited in Walter Truett Anderson, *Reality Isn't What It Used to Be* (San Francisco: Harper & Row, 1990), p. 40. We can trace the postmodern view of semantics to the *general semantics* movement Korzybski initiated with his 1933 publication of *Science and Sanity*.
12. Fredrick Jameson, *The Prison House of Language* (Princeton, N.J.: Princeton University Press, 1972) is one of the defining works of postmodern literary theory.
13. See Benjamin Whorf, *Language, Thought and Reality* (New York: Wiley, 1956). The Sapir-Whorf hypothesis has had a significant influence in developing a postmodern theory of language. "The forms of a person's thought are controlled by inexorable laws of pattern of which he is unconscious. These patterns are the unperceived intricate systematizations of his own language . . . every language is a vast pattern-system, different from others, in which are culturally ordained forms and categories by which the personality not only

communicates, but also analyzes nature, notices or neglects types of relationships and phenomena, channels his reasoning, and builds the house of his consciousness."

14. R. Neuhaus, *Redefining Humanity: Crossing the Threshold of Embryo Experimentation* (New York: *The Wall Street Journal*: Dow Jones, 1994).

4

Postmodernism and "The Myth of Progress": Two Visions

Jim Leffel, Contributor

Postmodernism leaves its adherents awash in an ocean of divergent "truths." Without ultimate truth and meaning to cling to, what keeps postmodernists afloat? Surprisingly, many turn to analyzing and applying power. When truth dies, power fills the vacuum. Postmodernists concern themselves with the rhetorical significance of ideas, not their truth or rationality.

The racial struggles raging in public education mirror the rest of our culture. Notice how two prominent scholars describe the heart of these struggles less as fights over truth—curriculum, content, knowledge bases—and more as the maneuverings of power blocks:

> (American) schools were used to "adjust" the African-American child to white middle-class norms and to educate an African-American elite to aspire to what whites had in a society that denied African Americans dominant group privileges. Northern, urban blacks who rejected segregation based on the experience of the South found that integration meant direct domination and degradation in white schools.
>
> While the debate about multiculturalism in education is concerned with minority groups determining what counts as knowledge, what knowledge should be submitted, and who controls access to education, *the core of the debates is the greater*

> *or lesser degree of political power any one group holds in relation to others.* [Emphasis added][1]

Postmodernists agree that various groups' attempts to wield power is what drives society, yet their reactions to these struggles split them into two camps. *Skeptical postmodernists* regard power negatively, as an overwhelming force of repression. They view the cultural relativity of truth as an occasion for a cynical posture toward all commitments to truth. *Affirmative postmodernists* see power positively, as a tool. They see the rise of subjective, culturally based truth and reality as an opportunity to create new realities and, by extension, new kinds of individuals. Since both skeptics and affirmatives are readily recognizable in our culture, we will discuss each in turn.

Skeptical Postmodernism

Skeptical postmodernists devote themselves to uncovering what they regard as the underlying motivations for others' truth claims. In their cynicism, they unmask what they consider to be the hidden agendas that drive social life.

According to postmodernists, people who claim to know truth or absolutes have an ugly history. Their wide-ranging truth claims are embedded in language, and as we have seen, postmodernists believe language is by nature metaphorical and relative, not objective. In other words, language is a big step removed from reality. Those making truth claims forget the symbolic nature of language, and as time passes, they begin to mistake culturally fashioned myth for "natural law" or the "will of God."

Nineteenth-century Americans, for example, believed in so-called "Manifest Destiny," a view that said it was somehow "obvious" or "manifest" that God wanted the United States to own all the land between the eastern seaboard and the Pacific Ocean. The Mexicans and Native Americans who possessed the land at the time, of course, found that concept less obvious. Manifest Destiny eventually became a justification for subjugating native tribes in the American West as well as for an unjust war with Mexico.

The inferiority of Blacks alleged throughout American history is another example of a dominant group using what they think they know to demean and disempower others, what postmodernists call "epistemological tyranny."[2] According to postmodernists, human history is marked by the tragedy of so-called rational, objective "truth" being inflicted on the weak in society. This has been especially true of the twentieth century, as seen in the mythologies surrounding Jews in Nazi Europe, or the "dictatorship of the proletariat" in Marxism.[3] Skeptical postmodernists refuse to carry on what they see as the fiction of truth. They use the tools of their trade to assume the posture of a critic.

What, then, is the skeptics' posture toward society? Clearly, skeptics can't be optimistic about the course of history. Postmodernists of this sort therefore often suggest withdrawal or "ironic detachment" from culture. In the face of the individual's powerlessness to change reality, the skeptics often despair. One analyst of postmodernism explains:

> The skeptics represent a current of desperation and defeatism. By opting out of politics they leave power relations and formal authority untouched. This engenders a cynical, nihilist, and pessimistic political tone. . . . Their attraction with death and suicide evokes much the same message, however: whatever political scenarios emerge, none is different enough from the status quo to matter to them.[4]

Such postmodern cynicism is reflected in art, including popular cinema and music. Cynical and polemical movies, for instance, portraying Christian missions or Western culture in general as guilty of cultural imperialism speak eloquently of postmodern cynicism. Examples of this genre would be *The Mission, At Play in the Fields of the Lord, The Black Robe, Do the Right Thing,* and *Dances With Wolves*. *Jurassic Park*, written by New Age faithful Michael Crichton, is a powerful polemic against the arrogance of human technology, pretended truth claims, and so-called "progress" at the expense of nature.

Current musical lyrics contain unqualified cynicism toward government, education, business, law and, in a word, all of society. The lyrics of Offspring, Nine Inch Nails, Green Day, Bash, Nirvana, Hole, Live, Pearl Jam, Soundgarden, or any of a host of popular bands reflect skeptical postmodernism in the vast majority of their songs. The skeptics' view contains great pain and anguish, but they argue that we need to muster courage to face the emptiness of a world without absolutes.

Affirmative Postmodernism

Affirmative postmodernists are more difficult to describe because they are active in so many diverse causes. Indeed, eclecticism (borrowing from a variety of worldviews) and an ability to maintain even contradictory positions simultaneously are common among affirmative postmodernists. They argue that self-contradiction isn't a problem once we remove the modernist burden of rational consistency. While affirmative postmodernists also believe our confidence in enlightenment reason is a cultural bias, they attach a significance to this insight different from the skeptics. For them, the annihilation of objective truth (that is, truth that's true for everyone) opens the door to cultural change.

Affirmative postmodernists are sometimes referred to as "constructivists." They are constructivists because, not believing in any objective foundation for reality, or knowledge claims about reality, these postmodernists feel free to *create*, or *construct*, "knowledges" and "realities." Many American postmodernists work to create "socially constructed reality" through political and social activism. They argue that if reality is rooted in culture, then we can actually construct new realities through social change.

The people leading the way today in the so-called politics of race, gender, sexuality, ecology, poverty, and religion are mostly affirmative postmodernists, even though some would be unaware that their views fit this description. Some analysts lump postmodern social activism together under the term "the politics of difference" and "the politics of inclusion." We will cover some of these issues when we talk about law, history, education, psychology, and spirituality.

A clear example of constructivism is the political-correctness movement thriving on college campuses. Behind this movement is the supposition that the way we speak of others perpetuates a cultural climate of race and gender bias mythologies. The key to doing away with these mythologies isn't challenging attitudes, but talking differently. Words don't *describe* reality; they *create* reality. We will never form a society free from such prejudice, they believe, unless we control the words and language upon which that prejudice is based. The political-correctness movement isn't just an attempt to keep from hurting people's feelings, but an attempt to create different kinds of people by changing the cultural environment.

We may wonder how affirmative postmodernists make their jump from being openly critical of ideology to being ideologically active. What twist of logic enables those who deny the knowability of truth to aggressively advance certain viewpoints? Affirmative postmodernists substitute power for truth.

Many constructivists declare openly that since truth cannot tell us how to order society, our only recourse is to assert whatever power is necessary to carry out our agenda. No justification need be given—though it usually is—because no justification is ever possible. Constructivists argue that the dominant culture has asserted its power in the past, and this is how we came to have certain cultural "truths." In fact, they argue that the main reason society's "received truth" exists is to promote the cause of the privileged at the expense of the oppressed. Consequently, postmodern activists advocate the cause of the oppressed by offering new versions of "truth." Michel Foucault, one of the most prominent postmodern intellectuals, argues that "We are subjected to the reproduction of truth through power, and we cannot exercise power except through the production of truth."[5]

> A clear example of constructivism on the college campus is the political-correctness movement.

Politicizing truth, a practice once called "propagandizing," is now central in the theater of postmodern political action. Once we accept that we cannot objectively distinguish between right and wrong views, "truth" becomes the tool of interest groups who promote their agenda using political and cultural power. Rhetoric replaces rational pleas. Power becomes the only arbiter of which version of reality—past or future—will prevail. So, for example, we no longer have "history"; we now have "feminist history" or "gay and lesbian history." We no longer have politicians who strive to represent all constituents fairly based on some understanding of right and wrong; instead we have officials who pander to the power of special interests groups of the right and left.

When postmodernists agree with Plato's adversaries that "justice is the interest of the stronger," the result is a menacing vision of future public life. In the remainder of this book, we will examine this vision of public life under the growing postmodern consensus.

Living in a Postmodern Culture

Lest we think that postmodernists are academics or activists "out there" somewhere, we need to note that today we are fast becoming a *postmodern culture*. Our culture widely accepts the basic tenets of postmodernism:

- Reality is in the mind of the beholder. Reality is what's real to me, and I construct my own reality in my mind.
- People are not able to think independently because they are defined—"scripted," molded—by their culture.
- We cannot judge things in another culture or in another person's life, because our reality may be different from theirs. There is no possibility of "transcultural objectivity."
- We are not moving in the direction of progress, but are arrogantly dominating nature and threatening our future.
- Nothing is ever proven, either by science, history, or any other discipline.

People accept these propositions without necessarily understanding their origin. When that happens, a society has become postmodern, based on postmodern assumptions. Although individual members of a culture may not understand postmodern literary theory or the philosophical roots of the movement, for example, they nevertheless stand in the postmodern flow of thought.

A perfect example of this is the New Age movement. Having evolved rapidly along with the rest of culture, the movement has now moved almost completely into the sphere of the postmodern. Today, New Age consciousness and postmodernism share an overlapping philosophical base. This isn't evidence of a conspiracy, but a shift in thinking permeating all of society. It's similar to earlier decades, when many stood in the Judeo-Christian flow of thought even though they never understood Christianity, Judaism, or the Bible.

As we will see in later chapters, some do understand the connection between contemporary cultural shifts and postmodernism, but most people on the street aren't sure how they got their ideas. They are, nevertheless, thinking within a broad postmodern framework if they:

- think intuition and feelings might tell us more about reality than does reason;
- believe people do what they do because their culture made them who they are;
- think pessimistically or cynically about the future;
- view technology, government, and the legal system with cynicism;
- are interested in "spirituality," but reject biblical Christianity.

Are Postmodernists Correct?

We will be examining some of the postmodernists' positive contributions throughout the rest of this book. However, before going further, we have some objections to raise regarding their core views.

Of all the questions raised by postmodern thought, the most fundamental is its critique of reason. Postmodernists offer important challenges to the overly optimistic modernist reliance on unaided human reason. The modernist belief that science will unravel all of the mysteries of the universe *is* arrogant, as postmodernists have argued. Yet if postmodern skeptics are right, there can be no basis for knowledge of *any* kind. In a postmodern culture, truth as we know it is dead. We feel the effects of the postmodern rejection of reason in every field of knowledge today, from natural science, to law, education, medicine, and many other vital areas of social life.

The postmodern shift could leave us despairing and hopeless. What difference can any of us make if our thoughts do not apply beyond ourselves? Christians must feel particularly disturbed by this shift. How can we convince anyone that Jesus and his Word have the answers not just for his day but for any day?

But if postmodernists are wrong, we have a mission before us. We believe they *are* largely wrong. We also believe we can understand *why* they are wrong and demonstrate this to those trapped in the postmodern web of confusion. Before we turn in the following chapters to examine postmodernism's impact on distinct areas of our culture and then to a biblical critique of postmodernism, let's look briefly at a few obvious gaps in postmodern thought.

Can We Trust Our Impressions?

Postmodernists hold that since we can't stand outside of ourselves to compare mental image with external reality, we are forced to reject the idea that we can know reality in an objective way. We would answer, to the contrary, that our judgments about the world, while not infallibly accurate, are open to revision by further investigation. Just because we lack absolute *certainty* about the external world doesn't mean we can't know *anything* about what exists apart from us. We don't have to wallow in postmodern skepticism.

The success of scientific technology is a strong argument that our perceptions of the world are relatively accurate. Countless achievements attest to the reliability of human knowledge. We can engineer enormously sophisticated rockets to propel men to the moon, and provide health care that has more than doubled human life expectancy. We couldn't do these things without an essentially reliable correspondence between our ideas of reality and reality itself. Moreover, if scientific knowledge is a figment of culture as postmodernists claim, why can scientists from different cultures replicate experiments that yield exactly the same results?

Science provides limited but genuine insight into many parts of the world's one, shared, and *only* reality. Science isn't just a Western paradigm, as postmodernists claim.

Postmodernists who hold that scientific knowledge based on the correspondence view of truth is merely a "Western cultural paradigm" err seriously. They jettison the possibility of knowledge, mistaking it for modernism's overconfidence in unaided human reason. But even the most primal cultures display powerful evidence of "scientific reasoning." The Amazonian Indian who knows nothing of Western technology has a technology of his own. It isn't accidental, for example, that he hunts with a blow-

If we look even to the most primal culture, we find powerful evidence of "scientific reasoning."

gun of, say, eight feet as opposed to two. His choice of a poison to kill his prey certainly isn't arbitrary. Just as we refine our knowledge of the world by learning from experience, hypothesizing, and repeating successful results, others around the world have used similar processes throughout history.

Postmodern cynics betray the inconsistency of their skepticism every time they drive a car, ride on a airplane, dial a telephone, or write on a computer. They depend on the very science they claim cannot know reality. Our knowledge of the world is limited, and we have used technology in oppressive ways. But we still possess a vast amount of objective knowledge of the world.

Postmodernism Is Self-Defeating

When postmodernists call all knowledge "arbitrary social constructions," they again overplay an important observation. Culture certainly significantly affects identity, beliefs, and values. Personal identity is, in part, based in our social identity. But postmodernists go beyond observing the influence of culture to declaring that all beliefs and knowledge claims are "arbitrary social constructs," fabrications of culture. This claim, however, is self-defeating on two counts:

1. From the postmodern point of view, postmodernism itself can only be seen as another "arbitrary social construction" like all other ideologies. As such, we have no compelling reason to accept the theory. We can simply dismiss it as the creative work of extremely cynical people.
2. If postmodernism can be shown to be true, a worldview with objective merit, then postmodernism's main thesis (rejection of objective truth) is wrong. It ends up teaching that there is at least some objective truth—namely, that postmodernism is right!

In either case, postmodernism's rejection of rational objectivity is self-defeating. It either denies the plausibility of its own position, or it presumes the reliability of reason and the objectivity of truth.

Is Language a Prison House?

Postmodern linguistic theory poses a real threat to the possibility of rational thought and meaningful communication. But are we obliged to accept the postmodern assessment of language?

Postmodernists, remember, begin by asserting that all human thought is rooted in language. Consequently, they say, no reasoning is possible without the ability to understand and use words. But here we find helpful insight from developmental psychology. In surveying key research in infant psychology, Donald McIntosh states that infants recognize a world of objects and events.[6] He shows how research indicates infants can think even at a *prelinguistic* stage of development, that is, before they can speak. Research indicates that children want to acquire language because of an *already existing* framework of thought.[7]

How different these findings are from postmodern speculations! Instead of our thoughts being shaped by the words we learn, research actually shows that what we learn motivates us to acquire language.

Finally, researchers discover that, before children can talk, they demonstrate a certain uniformity in thought.[8] In other words, the human approach to the world is pretty much the same prior to the acquisition of language. Our language may be arbitrary, but we do know something objectively for which these words serve as labels.

Is Truth Always Culture-Bound?

Postmodernists miss another important point in their view of language. According to their view, because each language has its own logic (syntax) and meaning (semantics) it should be impossible to communicate meaningfully or to translate accurately from one language to another. To do so would subjugate the unique, culturally contained meaning of one language to another.

But multilingual speakers know that despite differences, sometimes significant ones, between languages, concepts can almost always be meaningfully expressed. Reality isn't divided along language lines in the way many postmodernists have claimed.

Cultures do often approach reality differently. Historians from different cultures sometimes write wildly different accounts of the same event. And pantheists and animists view nature in a radically different way than do naturalistic scientists. But that's not the same as being unable to grasp what the other means. Postmodernists focus on the fringe of the language question—the five percent of language that is hard to translate—and ignore the ninety-five percent that is perfectly clear.

While communicating truth or views of reality across cultures can be difficult, we have no reason to believe it's impossible. The very fact that we are aware of differences proves we can detect and understand our differences if we are careful. Because of our ability to communicate, we can begin to understand one another and think about why we often view things differently. And that communication opens the door to genuine exchange and evaluation of ideas, even concerning abstract concepts such as spirituality and morality. As we will see in the following chapters, without the ability to genuinely understand one another we can only anticipate an increasingly fragmented and dangerous world.

For the sake of fairness, this brief critique of postmodernism has been based only on secular—non-biblical—evidence. If we turn to the Bible, we discover a whole new list of criticisms. We will study these in Chapter 14.

Postmodern Impact

Without understanding the principles of postmodernism we explored in these beginning chapters, we can't interact intelligently with postmodernists. We can fully expect that postmodern labels and slogans will change in the future, but these undergirding ideas will be the same. We have to learn to recognize postmodern assumptions and patterns of thought no matter what they are called.

The next chapters look at the impact of postmodernism in several key areas of culture. For the most part, we see affirmative postmodernists in action, aiming to empower the weak and exploited sub-groupings in society while unmasking the hidden agendas of the ruling classes. We will continue to trace the ideas behind our culture's contemporary attitudes in order to understand how our culture has arrived at its postmodern attitudes and values. When we come to the end of that study, we will use that insight to map out a plan for engaging our culture.

In Brief

- Postmodern thinkers reject theories that human society is advancing toward a glorious future. Such views are considered artificial constructs—the mythology of Western culture.

- Skeptical postmodernists take the position of cynical critics of other worldviews. They advance no particular alternative.
- Affirmative postmodernists set out to apply the postmodern view of socially constructed reality as a blueprint for activism. They agitate on behalf of groups they consider oppressed, arguing that existing social systems don't make room for such groups.
- For several important reasons, we have argued that the major premises of postmodernism are mistaken. The valid parts of the postmodern position are exaggerated to the point that they become false.

Notes

1. Thomas J. La Belle and Christopher R. Ward, *Multiculturalism and Education: Diversity and Its Impact on Schools and Society* (Albany, N.Y.: State University of New York Press, 1994), pp. 12, 34–35.
2. Epistemology is the study of how we know things. Epistemological tyranny means the tyranny of what we think we know, using our belief systems to justify repression of others.
3. It may seem contradictory that postmodernists derive much of their analysis from Marxism on one hand, and criticize Marxist governments as tyrannical on the other. But postmodernists derive only their *epistemology*—or method of approaching truth—from Marxism. They generally have rejected Marxism itself, especially as it has been embodied by various cultures. They see the outworking of Marxism as a social construct buttressed by nationalistic mythology.
4. Pauline Rosenau, *Postmodernism and the Social Sciences* (Princeton: Princeton University Press, 1992), p. 143.
5. Michel Foucault, *Power/Knowledge* (New York: Pantheon Books, 1980), p. 132.
6. He says that "The world of the infant is a world of coherent, sharply delineated objects and events, to which she relates powerfully, though in an undifferentiated way, in the modes of perception, cognition, and emotion." Donald McIntosh, "Language, Self, and Lifeworld in Habermas's Theory of

Communicative Action," *Theory and Society* 23:1994, p. 22.

7. McIntosh writes, "At the one-word level, the words learned most readily are those that refer to objects and events already well-established in prelinguistic intentionality. The word becomes attached as additional property, a kind of 'handle' to the already existing prototype in terms of which the object . . . has been *conceptualized.* The fact that these words refer to things *already known* explains the startling rapidity of the growth of the child's vocabulary." Donald McIntosh, "Language, Self, and Lifeworld," p. 23. See also Carolyn B. Mervis, "On the Existence of Prelinguistic Categories: A Case Study," *Infant Behavior and Development* 8:1985.
8. Donald McIntosh, "Language, Self, and Lifeworld," p. 27. McIntosh concludes, "Beneath the welter of lifeworld (worldview) perspectives and the differences among individuals who share the same perspective, there is a level of thought and interaction on which people everywhere have pretty much the same outlook. Here is where the relativism of the lifeworlds comes to an end. . . ." See also Carolyn B. Mervis, "On the Existence of Prelinguistic Categories," p. 39, #21.

5

Postmodern Impact: Health Care

Dónal P. O'Mathúna, Contributor

Postmodernism is both a philosophy and a cultural movement. While few people understand the philosophy, all of us experience the cultural movement—the impact made when the ideological changes are put into practice. The changing face of health care stands as a prime example of how the new thinking affects us. Although health care seems like an unquestionable accomplishment of Western culture, postmodern tampering could turn all that around, as this true story illustrates.

A woman in her thirties awakens one morning with severe abdominal pain. The intensity of the pain makes it difficult for her to get out of bed. She takes some pain-killers and tries to sleep, but the pain remains. Finally, she calls her doctor. A nurse answers and courteously inquires about the symptoms and her recent activities.

The nurse tells the woman there is nothing seriously wrong with

About the Contributor:

Dónal P. O'Mathúna is an Irish scholar now living in the United States. His B.S. is in pharmacy from Trinity College, Dublin, Ireland, and his Ph.D. is from The Ohio State University in medicinal chemistry. He has also earned an M.A. in Biblical Studies from Ashland Theological Seminary. He is Associate Professor at Mt. Carmel College of Nursing, the author of several articles and a contributor to *Bioethics and the Future of Medicine*. This chapter expresses his views, not those of Mt. Carmel College of Nursing.

her. She doesn't need to see the doctor, nor take any medication. Instead, this is an opportunity to explore her body and the meaning of her pain. The real source of her problem is her stress and anxiety about the pain. She needs to get in touch with her inner self and be enlightened by what her body can tell her. She should take two or three days to relax and focus on herself, and all will be well. In fact, she could be at a turning point in her life if she learns more about herself and how to listen to her body.

Not impressed by what the nurse tells her, the woman insists on talking to someone else. She eventually gets an appointment with the doctor. He discovers a huge growth on her ovary and recommends immediate surgery. The growth is very fragile, bursting immediately upon removal. If it had burst while inside her, the consequences could have been much worse—serious infection, at least, and possibly death. After surgery, the pain disappeared and has not recurred.[1]

This surreal account is, strangely enough, the direct result of postmodern thinking. The nurse had accepted some of the new alternative approaches to health and healing being widely taught for academic credit today. Today, more than 80 nursing schools are teaching one type of alternative medicine. The number teaching other types is unknown. If you live in a major city, you may have had a seminar at work focusing on alternative medical techniques. The nurse in this story, like thousands of others graduating from our postmodern-influenced health care training institutions, no longer believes that clinically sound medicine is any more effective than practices seen as superstition only a short time ago.

The number of popular books promoting alternative healing is exploding. These therapies are known variously as "alternative medicine," "fringe medicine," "New Age healing," or "nonlocal medicine." For the purpose of clarity, we will use the term "alternative medicine" in this chapter. This is a good term because the National Institutes of Health recently formed the Office of Alternative Medicine to investigate these therapies, thus lending them governmental credibility.[2]

To further illustrate what we mean by "alternative medicine," we will look at two popular practices: *Ayurvedic* Medicine, and a related alternative nursing technique called Therapeutic Touch. Both draw their views from the same two sources: Eastern mystical religion and postmodernism.

Ayurvedic Medicine

The woman in our illustration was probably being encouraged to use Ayurvedic Medicine. *Ayurveda*, the traditional medicine of India, literally means "science of life," but the basis for the practice is actually more deeply spiritual.[3] Best-selling author Deepak Chopra, M.D., is the best-known proponent of Ayurvedic Medicine in the United States. His books *Quantum Healing, Perfect Health* and *Ageless Body, Timeless Mind* have been translated into twenty-five languages, and he also appears in his own PBS special. Chopra practiced modern Western medicine until returning to India to learn Ayurveda from Maharishi Mehesh Yogi, (the same guru who introduced Transcendental Meditation to the West with the help of the Beatles). Maharishi has bestowed Chopra with the title "Dhanvantari (Lord of Immortality), the keeper of perfect health for the world."[4]

Chopra teaches that the basic substance of our bodies isn't matter, but energy and information.[5] This life energy, or *Prana*, is nonphysical and flows through everyone, animating and sustaining us. The energy of each person is a localization of infinite fields of energy which pervade the universe. This energy enters the human body through channels known as *chakras*. True health results from a balanced flow of this energy through the body. Imbalances in the flow lead to physical symptoms which we recognize as illness, aging, and death.[6]

A balanced flow of *Prana* is said to be maintained by such things as a balanced diet, moderate exercise, stable relationships, and appropriate handling of stress, though Ayurvedic practitioners use a variety of other products and practices to improve this balance. These include *rasayanas* (herbal supplements), gemstones, meditation, *panchakarmas* (purification procedures), diagnosis of disease by pulse monitoring, personality typing, and *yagyas* (religious ceremonies to solicit the aid of Hindu deities).[7]

Therapeutic Touch

While Ayurveda gains popularity in the general population, Therapeutic Touch is popular in the nursing profession.[8] It is currently taught in more than 80 colleges and universities in the United States, and in more than 70 other countries, especially in schools of nursing.[9] The National League for Nursing, which accredits nursing colleges in the United States, promotes Therapeutic Touch.[10]

This recent popularity began in the 1960s with Dora Kunz, a clairvoyant, while she was president of The Theosophical Society in America. Kunz observed the healing practices of a Hungarian "faith healer" which seemed to require only the intention to heal.[11] She joined forces with Dolores Krieger, R.N., Ph.D., to study and promote this practice. Krieger's teaching and writing while she was on the faculty at New York University's School of Nursing did much to popularize the practice. Therapeutic Touch is also strongly promoted by the Center for Human Caring at the University of Colorado.[12]

According to Krieger, "Therapeutic Touch is a healing practice based on the conscious use of the hands to direct or modulate, for therapeutic purposes, selected nonphysical human energies that activate the physical body."[13]

In practice, a healer must become "centered" before attempting Therapeutic Touch. Centering is "an act of self-searching, a going within to explore the deeper levels of yourself."[14]

When centered, a person is aware of the flow of human energy and any imbalances in it. This is assessed by passing the hands over the other person, but *without* making contact. For this reason, Therapeutic *Touch* is actually a misnomer. Contact isn't needed because *Prana*, the vital energy, extends a few inches beyond one's skin.

Practitioners detect imbalances in the energy field through a variety of cues: "vague hunches, passing impressions, flights of fancy, or, in precious moments, true insights or intuitions." Or, "very frequently" the healer finds "the cues constellate into a clear visualization within your mind of an ongoing process or some aspect of it."[15] These imbalances are then corrected in a variety of ways. Through " 'effortless effort' that is guided by conscious, mindful action" the healer redirects any imbalanced energy and restores health by simply intending to do so.[16] Most importantly, compassionate concern must motivate the healer.

Therapeutic Touch has a strong religious dimension, though some practitioners deny this. "Therapeutic Touch is an interior experience, a seeking within. As you make these techniques your own, there will be an upwelling of the further reaches of your own consciousness."[17] In the foreword to Krieger's latest book, Stanley Krippner, a psychology professor and author in this field, notes that to attain the goals of Therapeutic Touch, "spiritual orientation may be a key element."[18] One training manual describes centering as a way to connect more deeply with "a Higher Power."[19]

Therapeutic Touch is based on many of the same principles as Ayurvedic Medicine, as can be seen from Therapeutic Touch's four assumptions.

As with Ayurveda, energy is the fundamental nature of reality, with human energy again called *Prana*.

Health is a balance in the flow of this energy.

Healing involves a variety of techniques for restoring balance.

The body should be altered through awareness and mental disciplines.

For these, and other reasons, the president of the National Council Against Health Fraud, William T. Jarvis, Ph.D., described Therapeutic Touch as "a spin-off of Ayurvedic Medicine."[20]

From this short description, it should be clear that both Ayurvedic Medicine and Therapeutic Touch draw most of their ideas from Eastern religions, not from postmodernism. Yet without the advent of postmodern thinking, neither would have a place in modern health care. They are perfect examples of how widely differing ideologies have actively used postmodern analysis to propagate their views.

Alternative Medicine and Postmodernism

Postmodernism isn't the source for alternative medical ideas, but it's the Trojan Horse that has brought dubious practices such as alternative medicine to prominence and acceptability on campuses today.[21] Modern scientists have known the views behind alternative medicine for a long time. But these views have been rejected for some solid scientific reasons. Most important, as we shall see, proponents of alternative medicine cannot demonstrate that it works. However, in the postmodern environment of countless academic institutions, theories like those used in alternative medicine cannot be freely critiqued.

Postmodernism rejects many of the ways by which a worldview—or a medical therapy—can be assessed and judged. Bad research, therefore, carries as much weight as properly structured and controlled studies. Likewise, with the lack of certainty about our ability to discover or know truth, arguments against these therapies may carry no more weight than the cries of one religion against another. Almost anything can gain credibility, *once scientific methodology is declared nothing more than a cultural bias*—namely, that of Western Europe.

The consequences of this shift may be serious, including dangerous long-term effects on people's health.

Postmodern Reality: A New Dark Age

Postmodernism calls for a radical restructuring of the way we think. Postmodernists argue that reality isn't as rigid as we once thought. They claim that the idea of objective reality is a metaphor to help us communicate. Such a view of reality is compatible with alternative medicine in a way modernism never was. Proponents of alternative medicine acknowledge postmodernism's impact in their favor. Dolores Krieger, for example, admits that the postmodern view of reality has benefited Therapeutic Touch and led to widespread interest in it.[22] Moreover, having come from traditions of the East, these theories bear the hallowed title of "oppressed" and "non-Western." Both mean the same thing to postmodernists: Any attack on alternative medicine is an effort to extend the control of dominant culture over weaker subcultures.

Postmodernism rejects many of the ways by which a medical therapy can be judged.

Again, although the *content* of alternative medical teaching isn't explicitly postmodern, it is much more compatible with postmodernism than with modernism. Also, even more importantly, alternative medicine apologists use the postmodern method to establish the acceptability of their view. To be specific, they use three postmodern arguments:

1. They cast doubt on the findings of biochemical medicine, arguing that it is merely an outgrowth of a Western (modernist) men-

tality, which is materialistic, male-dominated, and cold.

2. They argue that alternative medicine is the product of the "marginalized" or oppressed minority culture in the West. They claim that criticisms of alternative medicine are nothing but power posturing by the medical establishment, which endeavors to preserve its control over medicine.

3. They seek to replace objective, rational, experimental data as the basis for accepting the value of a therapy with a new basis: personal experience.

We now turn to examine each of these claims.

Rejection of the Medical Model

Earlier chapters described postmodernism's rejection of modernism. Proponents of alternative medicine critique and either reject or downplay the value of the biochemical model of medicine, the majority view in America and a direct outgrowth of modernist science.

Modernists view humans basically as bags of chemicals. The more we know about the chemical reactions of the body, the better we can understand health and illness. To diagnose illnesses, doctors either test body fluids or tissues or do hi-tech scans. They believe they can restore good health by correcting abnormal body chemistry, and treatments focus mainly on things like drugs, radiation, and surgery. They assume that illness and health are physical phenomena, and view medicine as an applied physical science.

Proponents of alternative medicines vigorously attack this modernist view. In her talk on Postmodern Nursing, Jean Watson identified modern medicine with technology, money, and products.[23] She wants her holistic metaphor of the body to replace the medical metaphor of the body as a machine. Another proponent suggests that Therapeutic Touch can move us from "a world of technology," "mechanistic reductionistic language," and "the machinery of curing" back to the "art of caring."[24] According to a third proponent, the physical aspects of healing and treatment are the least important. Rather, he argues, healing is "a quantum event first, a mental one second, and physical only in its last stages."[25]

Of course, postmodernists aren't the only critics of modern medicine. Anyone who has experienced cold, inhumane treatment from the modern health care system can sympathize with their observations.[26] People grow angry at modern medicine when their high expectations aren't met, and such frustrations make them more willing to listen to extravagant claims. Our postmodern culture has an antiestablishment ethos which makes alternative medicine more acceptable to those frustrated with established medicine.

Postmodernism also promotes a "back to the good old days" mentality. Apologists for alternative medicine claim—truly enough—that they derive insight from ancient traditional medicines. In their attempts to reject modern medicine, many proponents of alternative medicine claim that human life was healthier when it was more natural and less civilized.[27] The postmodern reshaping of history supports this claim even though it goes against well-substantiated historical facts to the contrary (see Chapter 8 on the postmodern distortion of history).

Chopra, for instance, uses postmodern analysis to his advantage by making use of both sides of the argument on this point. He claims that people in the past lived less fulfilling lives and died younger because of the severity of their living conditions.[28] But elsewhere he claims that people in the past lived to great old ages because they worked hard and had less stressful lives.[29]

Alternative medicine's critique of modern medicine, then, pictures modern medicine as an enterprise characterized by uncaring chrome, concrete, and stainless steel. Alternative medicines are postured as the soothing, wise hand of the ancients. These postmodern critics of the medical model make some good points. Many in mainstream medicine would agree, for instance, that the medical community has lost some of its humanitarian and spiritual roots. People are wise to approach science and modern medicine with a degree of skepticism, rather than the almost sacred confidence of earlier decades. Modern medical fixes can condone or promote a lack of personal responsibility in our behavior. Increased interest in euthanasia, for example, is another reaction to the lack of dignified care for the dying.

These criticisms, however, aren't enough to justify a wholesale rejection of modern medicine. While science *can* lead to dehumanization, materialism, and immoral pragmatism, many of the first modern scientists were devoted Christians who saw their work as a way to glorify God and serve others. In addition, the application of science to medicine has brought many benefits. The increase in longevity and health in much of Western society attests to this. But problems arise when humans are seen as purely physical. Humans are emotional, intellectual, and spiritual persons who also have physical bodies. All of these dimensions should be taken into consideration by health care, but often they are not. To this extent, Christians can agree with some of the criticisms of modern medicine. But this shouldn't lead to a total conversion in our worldview.

An Appraisal From the Laboratory

Apologists for alternative medicine reject the use of science, which fathered the medical model, yet they attempt to retain science as a way to validate their own therapies and gain wider credibility. They do this in spite of the fact that science is a method of investigating the *physical* universe, while these therapies are based on *nonphysical* entities.[30] According to Larry Dossey, another proponent of alternative medicine, these newer therapies "seem to have no possibility, even in principle, of being explained in the local, physicalistic, reductionistic framework" of modern medicine.[31]

Even though practitioners of alternative medicines seek to heal using nonphysical energies, they persist in claiming scientific validation for their arts. Sharma and others claim that over 500 studies support Transcendental Meditation's claim to reduce health care use and increase longevity.[32] They go on to claim that "with rigorous scientific investigation, Maharishi Ayur-Veda may provide useful new insights and approaches to the prevention and treatment of disease."[33]

Janet Quinn, a leading promoter of Therapeutic Touch, admitted recently that "we don't have empirical data to demonstrate the existence of a personal energy field." But she felt this lack of data hardly removes alternative medicine from the realm of science. "It's a working hypothesis," she explains. "In science, you're allowed to do that."[34] She offered no comment on the fact that scientific hypotheses must be tested by experiments.

So how well do these therapies perform in scientific studies? Poorly! Larry Dossey admits that "although there is plenty of anecdotal evidence that many such therapies improve the quality of life . . . [there is] little scientific evidence that such methods extend life beyond what could be achieved with conventional treatments."[35]

Analysis of the 500 meditation studies cited by Sharma has failed to reveal the types of benefits claimed by Ayurvedic practitioners.[36]

Alternative medical experiments and studies have been poorly structured, rendering their results invalid. When studying the health effects of meditation, for instance, the meditating subjects should be compared to a control group of other subjects who simply rest or lie quietly for a period every day. Otherwise, how do we know whether any improvement is the result of daily rest or of ancient meditation techniques?

Alternative medical researchers have usually missed this obvious question. A recent review of meditation research by the National Research Council found that resting-only controls were rarely used in research on meditation. "When resting-only controls are present, there is virtually no evidence that reductions in somatic arousal (heart rate, respiration rate, skin conductance fluctuations, blood pressure) are any less than those found in experienced meditators who are meditating."[37]

Adherents claim to have broad research to back up the effectiveness of the herbal supplements and remedies used in Ayurvedic medicine. There is disagreement, though, regarding the quality of this research. Two papers were presented on Ayurvedic preparations at the Twenty-eighth Annual Meeting of the Society for Economic Botany at the University of Illinois at Chicago in June 1987. While the Ayurvedic community cites these as scientific research papers, others have called them "a publicity stunt." According to some, the presenters offered no hard results.[38]

Similarly, Therapeutic Touch claims to have twenty years of "basic, formal, and clinical research" to back it up.[39]

However, independent examination of this research has found it seriously deficient. In 1975, a letter signed by twelve nursing professors pointed out serious flaws in the design of Krieger's early research.[40] Ten years later, a survey of the research supporting Therapeutic Touch again found poor research design and defective statistical methods.[41]

A very recent survey of all the research up to 1994 concluded, "One thing leaps out in surveying these papers. The more rigorous the research design, the more detailed the statistical analysis, the less evidence there is that there is any observed—or observable—phenomenon here."[42]

As expected, alternative medicine rejects these charges of inconsistencies and contradictions in their own research. They claim the charges are the result of flaws and biases in modern science. However, they continue to insist that their practices are scientific. The burden of proof is on them, as it should be with any new therapy. They must show that their therapy is effective. So far, they have failed to do so.

When the evidence goes against alternative medicine, its proponents turn quickly to one of postmodernism's other rhetorical tactics to authenticate their practices.

The Voice of the Marginalized

Postmodernists often claim to speak on behalf of a "marginalized," or oppressed, group. When talking on Postmodern Nursing, Jean Watson emphasized how the medical model had marginalized nursing with its "caring model." Also marginalized are the poor, those with AIDS, and the homeless. She called on nurses to speak up for these groups by emphasizing human consciousness and "centering." She argued that Western society has not used this knowledge because it has been "systematically excluded from human consciousness" by biases of the modern era.[43] Thus, the view that life consists of energy fields has been rejected not because it lacks scientific validation, but because modern researchers have marginalized it.[44] Similarly, Sharma points out that Ayurvedic medicine has been suppressed due to "centuries of foreign rule in India."[45]

A recent investigation into the teaching of Therapeutic Touch at the University of Colorado provides a good example of postmodern debating tactics.

A group of citizens in Colorado questioned the teaching of Therapeutic Touch at the University of Colorado's *Center of Human Caring*. They complained that tax money shouldn't be spent teaching a technique which was based, not in science, but in New Age religion.[46] The University convened a panel of faculty from both that university and elsewhere to examine the scientific evidence for Therapeutic Touch. The peer review panel concluded that "there is not a sufficient body of data, both in quality and quantity, to establish TT as a unique and efficacious healing modality."[47] They found it unacceptable that the practice might continue to be taught without better evidence to validate it.

The response to this report was pure postmodernism. According to one of the critics of Therapeutic Touch, the University of Colorado's Nursing School viewed the finding "as male-dominated medical imperialism against female-dominated nursing."[48] In their view, the evidence wasn't as important as the ones interpreting it. One critic of the report claimed, "We would like to imagine our whole lives are rational and science-based, but only fifteen percent of medical interventions are supported by solid scientific evidence."[49] In the end, the University allowed the teaching of Therapeutic Touch to continue on the basis of academic freedom.

Of course, if it were true that 85 percent of medicine is unsupported by scientific evidence, it would suggest we reevaluate all medical procedures. It would not mean we should dismiss the scientific method. Postmodernists often use this tactic of diverting attention from the actual data to the views of the interpreters of the data. These are *ad hominem* (against the man) arguments which seek to disqualify the critic, rather than to answer criticisms. They carry little rational weight, but in today's postmodern climate, they often get more results than well-reasoned arguments.

A similar example of spurious *ad hominem* support for alternative medicine is the body of research on Ayurvedic herbal remedies allegedly done by Tony Nader, Ph.D. He claims that when he was a graduate student at both Harvard and MIT he was told to stop research on these products. Chopra commented on this: "This in no way reflects on the quality of the research. If anything, it reflects the prejudice and bigotry of so-called objective scientists."[50] He offers no evaluation of the research itself. The institutions and Nader's former advisors claim the research was never performed.

This type of response distracts attention from an evaluation of the evidence. Instead, people grow sympathetic to the underdog, and more inclined to reject the conclusions of the "establishment." Postmodern ideology thus outweighs physical evidence. The most recent edition of a mainstream nursing textbook recommends accepting Therapeutic Touch as a way to "celebrate the diversity among us. . . . Therapeutic Touch is rooted in Eastern philosophy. Because of our Western culture orientation, we search for research to explain its effects. To the Eastern mind, if it works, one doesn't need research to prove how it works. The Eastern mind doesn't care how it works, only that it does."[51]

This new way of thinking about science and medicine menaces public health. Chopra revels in this state of affairs when he says that once a person has accepted the Ayurvedic way of thinking, "you will no longer be bound by society's notions of what you should be doing, saying, thinking, or feeling."[52] Students of frontier American history will remember snake oil and diet pills made from the eggs of tapeworms. When medicine is unaccountable the results can be terrifying.

Reliance on Experience

Chopra places a higher priority on experience than reason itself. He argues, "You sometimes see *Prana* defined as 'life force' or 'life energy,' but what is more important than a definition is to get experiential knowledge of it."[53] In his instructions about doing some of his exercises he states: "In the three related procedures given here, you will experience the effortless way that intentions can get fulfilled, bypassing the ego and the rational mind."[54]

Postmodern alternative medical apologists actually dare to argue that therapies should not be evaluated on the basis of objective evidence or quantitative results. Rather, they say, individual experience should be the judge. Krieger encourages her readers: "Therapeutic Touch works. . . . You can do it; everyone who is willing to undertake the discipline to learn Therapeutic Touch can do it. You need only try in order to determine the truth of this statement for yourself. So, I invite you: TRY."[55]

Although Krieger claims that experiential knowledge is the key to assessing this therapy, educated people are aware that every quack healing method ever devised has those who claim it worked for them![56] Scientists call this *anecdotal evidence*. People can, and do, tell anecdotes about how they can levitate while meditating or how a shaman was able to heal cancer. But strangely, when these events are brought into the laboratory, scientists are unable to duplicate the results. Reliance on anecdotal evidence falls short of the standards of modern science and medicine, but postmodern apologists answer that such objections are nothing but prejudice.

A practical example of the problems with anecdotal evidence can be seen in the benefits cited by Chopra for meditation. These include lowering of blood pressure, improved vision and hearing, and better overall quality of life.[57] However, these very same benefits have been reported for people who attend church regularly and hold their relationship with God to be important.[58] One study found that this wasn't just due to social support, but to some "uniquely religious factor."[59] These studies suggest health benefits resulting from taking the spiritual dimension of our lives seriously, but they cannot prove a given therapy is effective.

Postmodernists interpret this to mean that the content of our beliefs isn't important. Any belief works! But this is a separate issue. The truthfulness of a scientific theory must be shown by more than just experiential, anecdotal claims. This is the underlying premise of scientific research. If personal experience were the only way to know if a medical theory worked, we would end up trying out untested, harmful therapies on ourselves, or at the least, wasting time and money on ineffective therapies. We need some prior evaluation of potential therapies so that we experiment with only the relatively safe and effective ones.

The task of evaluating medical therapies and products falls to a number of government agencies and professional organizations. While the larger marketplace is governed by the premise "let the buyer beware," the health marketplace is governed by the more cautious premise, "let the seller beware."[60] This is why we have consumer protection laws. Few would argue that medicine should not be regulated when the dangers of bogus therapies are so great. Like the woman at the beginning of this chapter who had a cyst, our lives could be threatened by well-meaning but mistaken medical practitioners unless we regulate medicine.

However, accepting regulation of medicine involves giving over a certain amount of personal authority to the state. We decide not to experience everything for ourselves, but to let someone else test things and then we take their advice. Postmodern rejection of all forms of authority and their suspicion of government and law leads alternative medicine proponents to reject accountability for their own therapies.

Today's abundance of self-help books promotes the postmodern idea of everyone deciding for him or herself. But with so many things to know and understand about health care, how can a person decide what is reliable? By law, advertisements may not be false or misleading, but popular literature isn't regulated. Jarvis points out that, "The public is at a major disadvantage when faced with false and unproven remedies in books, magazines, and newspaper articles, lectures, audio and video cassettes, talk show appearances, etc. The financial interests of the promoters are often disguised in such communications."[61]

The evidence suggests that people frequently fall prey to health care quackery and fraud. One survey in 1987 found that 26.6 percent of the American public had used a questionable health care treatment.[62] These are high costs paid for the postmodern right to "determine our own reality." As a result of this broad rejection of authority, billions of dollars is being wasted, harm is being done, and people are being diverted from proven, helpful therapies.

Impacting the Health Care System

We have noted that there are skeptical and affirmative forms of postmodernism. Alternative medicine receives most of its support from the affirmative postmodernists. Jean Watson claims that health care is about to move into a transcendent, caring framework, once her ideas are accepted and promoted by nurses.[63] Dossey is hopeful about the future once we realize that "the world, at heart, is more glorious, benevolent, and friendlier than we have recently supposed."[64]

This optimism is based in part on a positive view of human nature. Chopra claims that at our core, we are love, truth, compassion, beauty, awareness, and spirit.[65] To put it more bluntly, "I am perfect as I am!"[66] Our problems all stem from the fact that we do not believe this. Like other New Age schools, Ayurvedic Medicine involves coming to see our inherently perfect nature, and then living according to that nature.[67]

This positive view of human nature leads to some dangerous conclusions in alternative medicine. Since there is no objective reality with which to compare therapists' evaluations, much depends on their inherently good nature. Krieger explains, "In Therapeutic Touch, you, as the healer, are the sole determiner of what will happen during the therapeutic process. . . . It [is] imperative that you feel quite sure of your judgments, which are largely subjective in nature."[68]

Not only do people have a good nature, the universal energy field of life (*Prana*) is also inherently good. *Prana* is the source of life and health in both Ayurvedic Medicine and Therapeutic Touch.[69] Dossey claims there is "an intrinsic order in the world" that will express itself in "what's best for the organism" if we attune to it correctly.[70] He adds that the best attitude is one that "honors the rightness of whatever happens, even cancer."[71] But if cancer is right, why try to overcome it?

Chopra agrees. He claims that "every moment is as it should be."[72] Under such fatalistic theories, we lose one of the greatest motivations for changing people's conditions in this world: the belief that things aren't as they should be (Romans 8:18–25).

Effect on Medical Ethics

What is the right way to change things—to ease pain, to bring healing, to provide for death with dignity? Medical ethics seeks to give direction in the midst of dilemmas. However, alternative medicines support a view that makes all ethics redundant. They support the idea that whatever happens is right. Dossey says we should not try to waste time figuring out the "right" thing. He recommends allowing our unconscious to direct our actions, even if it violates "the values we hold dearest in our aware, conscious life, such as our moral and ethical codes."[73] Our responsibility is to "allow events to unfold around [us] and react to them spontaneously, without suppression."[74]

Chopra adopts the postmodern idea that we do not have the truth; we only have an interpretation. For good health, he advocates "acknowledging that two opposing viewpoints can both be valid."[75] Yet in spite of their relativism and irrationality, they all have one rule: The right way to act is when we are filled with love and compassion.[76] This love isn't an emotion or an action. It's "a state of being" when you are "in contact with Being."[77]

Because of this, there are no moral guidelines for our actions. When we act while at one with the universal energy field (centered), our actions will be right since our nature is perfect and loving, and the universal energy field moves in our best interests. Because of this,

Dossey naively rejects the idea of informed consent (telling the patient what the doctor proposes to do and why) when using mental therapies, so long as the practitioner has only loving intentions.[78]

When we view the universe as inherently good we cannot see it as the source of suffering or illness. Instead, the root cause of all illness is in sick people themselves. Krieger notes with approval that "several views of reality do not perceive illness as bad; rather, they see illness as an individual's reaction to circumstances."[79] This is good, she argues, because it means healing is completely within one's own control. Chopra admits that his views are just human inventions, "but they allow us much more freedom and power. They give us the ability to rewrite the program of aging."[80] In both writers we see a belief that individuals have power over their own lives, including the ability to heal themselves.

However, this emphasis on personal power can have detrimental effects on how we respond to illness in ourselves and others. Many users of alternative therapies blame themselves when they get ill.[81] They put great pressure on themselves to think correctly, and often avoid seeking other forms of proven treatment. To seek mainstream help is seen as an admission of failure or weakness of mind. Thus, these therapies can indirectly harm people if they fail to get effective help.[82]

Placing sole responsibility for illness on the sick person easily leads away from compassionate concern for the suffering. This implication has been lived out in Eastern cultures where the caste system has historically allowed many of the wealthy to ignore the suffering of the poor. According to the Hindu idea of *karma*, people bring on their own suffering by their actions in a former life. To relieve such suffering would be a violation of *karmic law*.[83] Similarly, if people are the root causes of their illnesses, and have complete healing power within themselves, there is little reason for others to get involved.

The narcissistic lifestyle advocated by teachers of alternative medicine makes ignoring others' suffering even more likely. Chopra notes that "successful aging . . . involves a lifelong commitment to oneself every day."[84] He claims that we all have a "fundamental need for comfort and well-being that [we] must fulfill."[85] We can imagine this self-centeredness being coupled with their beliefs about suffering described above. Could not such a worldview create a health care system that has little concern for the ill and underprivileged? The president of the National Council Against Health Fraud envisions such a situation:

> Ineffective, albeit emotionally appealing, pseudo-medicine could lower health care costs by substituting cheap dietary supplements for expensive prescription medication, and/or by shortening patient survival times. Such a scenario would produce a better bottom line financially, and be more attractive than the blatant rationing of expensive health care, but would not pass muster ethically.[86]

The Spiritual Cost of Alternative Medicine

Not only do alternative medical apologists call on people to experiment with herbs and physical practices, they also encourage them to dabble in the spiritual realm. The appeals are not only spiritually mistaken, they are dishonest. These therapists introduce people to spiritual disciplines without disclosing their religious nature. People looking for a book on healthy living instead find themselves experimenting with the occult. What these therapists promote as medicine is in fact a religion.[87]

> Apologists for alternative medicine don't just ask people to experiment with herbs. They encourage them to dabble in the spiritual realm.

Christianity and alternative medicines both make some similar claims. Both claim that people are much more than physical beings, but are also spiritual (Genesis 1:26). Both claim that good health may be dependent on more than just physical factors (2 Samuel 13:2; 1 Corinthians 11:29–30). Both claim that spiritual factors can bring about cures (James 5:14–16). Both claim that great power becomes available upon accepting their worldview (Ephesians 1:19). Both claim that believers see the world through different eyes compared to non-believers (1 Corinthians 2:14).

But the Bible teaches that spiritual healing comes through faith and conversion in Jesus Christ (John 5:24; Romans 10:9–11). The need for religious conversion is never explicitly stated in Ayurvedic Medicine or Therapeutic Touch. However, ultimately this is what occurs. (Postmodernism as well calls for a paradigm shift, which is a type of conversion experience.) But rather than being explicit about the need for conversion, these therapies call for a gradual increase in involvement and a building up of experiential verification. Frequently, alternative medicine leads people unknowingly into a conversion to spiritism and the occult.[88]

The problem is that all spiritual beliefs are not what postmodernists claim: different ways of describing the same thing. Dossey claims that "Goddess, God, Allah, Krishna, Brahman, the Tao, the Universal Mind, the Almighty, Alpha and Omega, the One" are just different names for the same absolute consciousness.[89] They see different religions and spiritual practices as different ways of reaching the same goal. Hence, as with other postmodernists, they have no reason or ability to evaluate or pass judgment upon anyone else's beliefs.

We can see the strong religious overtones involved in alternative medicine when we consider the line between the development of Therapeutic Touch and theosophy. Theosophy is a school of nature mysticism and spiritism heavily involved in the occult. Two of the top apologists for Therapeutic Touch, Dora Kunz and Dolores Krieger collaborated on a book published by The Theosophical Society in America. This series of books had the goal of making "well-known occult works . . . available in popular editions."[90]

When people are called to just "Try it!" they may be getting much more than they bargained for. "Apart from the occult, Therapeutic Touch would not exist," declares Sharon Fish.[91] A popular witchcraft book describes a practice called "Pranic Healing." This is identical to Therapeutic Touch except that the Wiccan version is performed within a circle, with both healer and patient naked.[92]

Ayurvedic Medicine is much more candid about its spiritual agenda. Chopra claims that true healing will occur when we finally realize that each one of us literally is God. "I know myself as the immeasurable potential of all that was, is, and will be. . . . There is no other I in the entire universe. I am being and I am nowhere and everywhere at the same time. I am omnipresent, omniscient; I am the eternal spirit that animates everything in existence."[93]

While postmodernism would not critique this position, Christians must. This is self-worship in its most blatant form. In Genesis, Adam and Eve usurped God's authority to be like him. The Bible teaches that the root of all our problems is our desire to be gods. Here is a worldview that claims the solution to our problems will come when we truly believe that we are gods.

Explaining Reported Benefits

Some will counter that these therapies really do seem to help and to heal. In spite of the lack of qualified scientific evidence, anecdotal evidence suggests they may work in some cases. Why?

Some positive experiences may result from a general relaxation due to the presence of a caring person. Others may be a placebo effect.[94] Others may be due to the fact that some illnesses just naturally go away.

Another possibility, however, is that authentic healing occurs in some cases through occult spiritual power. Occult healers may, at times, be able to heal through the power of occult, evil spirits. The Bible declares that the powers of the evil one are great, and that he will perform miracles to draw people away from God (2 Thessalonians 2:9; Matthew 7:22–23).[95]

In alternative medicine, people seeking health care advice are receiving religious instruction. This would be less of a problem if practitioners openly declared their religious agenda and received informed consent. We aren't arguing against freedom of speech. But it is unethical for these religious practices to promote themselves as medicine. These therapies are spiritually based and ought to be presented as such. Even more disturbing, these therapies are propagated at taxpayer expense through public universities, where students are not only taught these practices but also required to *practice* them. This is promotion of religion and should be declared as such.

Postmodern Barricades

Postmodernism erects barricades against criticism of alternative medicines. Part of postmodernism is a rejection of objective (universal) truth, to which Christianity holds fast. Therapists will argue that Christian prejudices and narrowmindedness prevent us from seeing the value in these therapies. They will argue that fundamentalists, once again, are excluding and marginalizing others. They will point to Christian criticisms as disrespect for other cultures. They will note that rejection of traditional Christianity has helped to promote acceptance of these therapies.[96]

Christians need to understand both alternative medicine and the postmodern underpinnings their practitioners use in their defense. Only then will we mount an effective opposition to the spread of these dangerous therapies.

In Brief

- Alternative medicines such as Ayurvedic Medicine and Therapeutic Touch are advancing in the health care community at a startling rate, especially in nursing schools.
- Although these techniques draw their content from Eastern mysticism rather than from postmodernism, they are related to postmodernism in that they use postmodern analysis to establish and defend their place in secular universities.
- Alternative medical apologists justify or excuse their lack of credible scientific support by resorting to postmodern arguments against the possibility of scientific objectivity. By discrediting the idea of unbiased, repeatable, and controlled scientific findings, they successfully resist pressure to demonstrate their own effectiveness and safety.
- Alternative medical apologists also use postmodern concepts of inclusion to justify teaching for undergraduate and graduate credit material that is religious and not proven to heal.

Notes

1. This account, shared with me by the victim, may not be considered fair, because it involves not only alternative medical theory, but malpractice as well. We aren't suggesting that anyone who adopts alternative medicine will engage in malpractice. But the incident does illustrate how people trained to view illness as illusion or as a merely spiritual problem may reasonably conclude that physical remedies are unnecessary.
2. C. Maswick, "Alternative Medicine Office Urged to Act Rapidly," *Journal of the American Medical Association*, Vol. 270 (September 1993): p. 1400.
3. Deepak Chopra, *Ageless Body, Timeless Mind: The Quantum Alternative to Growing Old* (New York: Harmony Books, 1993), p. 269.
4. Andrew A. Skolnick, "Maharishi Ayur-Veda: Guru's Marketing Scheme Promises the World Eternal 'Perfect Health,'" *Journal of the American Medical Association*, 266 (October 2, 1991): p. 1742.
5. Deepak Chopra, *Ageless Body, Timeless Mind*, pp. 5–6, 16.
6. Ibid., p. 270.
7. Hari M. Sharma, Brihaspati Dev Triguna, Deepak Chopra, "Maharishi Ayur-Veda: Modern Insights Into Ancient Medicine," *Journal of the American Medical Association*, 265 (May 1991): pp. 2633–2635; Andrew A. Skolnick, "Maharishi Ayur-Veda: Guru's Marketing Scheme Promises the World Eternal 'Perfect Health,'" pp. 1741–1750.
8. "Acceptance of therapeutic touch by the nursing community has become widespread." Lyda Hill and Nancy Oliver, "Therapeutic Touch and Theory-Based Mental Health Nursing," *Journal of Psychosocial Nursing*, 31 (1993): p. 19.
9. Dolores Krieger, *Accepting Your Power to Heal: The Personal Practice of Therapeutic Touch* (Santa Fe, N.M.: Bear & Company, 1993), pp. xv, 5.
10. Brian Booth, "Therapeutic Touch," *Nursing Times*, 89 (1993): pp. 48–50.
11. Linda A. Rosa, "Therapeutic Touch: Skeptics in Hand to Hand Combat Over the Latest New Age Health Fad," *Skeptic*, 3 (Fall, 1994): p. 41.
12. Its main proponents there are Janet Quinn, R.N., who obtained her Ph.D. under Krieger, and its director, Jean Watson, R.N., Ph.D., who is also President of the National League for Nursing for 1995–1997.
13. Dolores Krieger, *Accepting Your Power to Heal*, pp. 3–4, 11–13. Therapeutic Touch is based on four assumptions. First, humans are fundamentally open energy fields. All humans are connected to one another and the environment through a universal energy field. Second, humans are bilaterally symmetrical. This is the basis for assuming that the energy fields around humans are also symmetrical. Third, illness is an imbalance in an individual's energy field. Fourth, human beings have natural abilities to transform and transcend their conditions of living.

14. Dolores Krieger, *Accepting Your Power to Heal*, p. 17.
15. Ibid., p. 29.
16. Ibid., p. 12.
17. Ibid., p. 15.
18. Stanley Krippner, foreword to Dolores Krieger, *Accepting Your Power to Heal*, p. xvi.
19. Janet Mentgen and Mary Jo Trapp-Bulbrook, *Healing Touch, Level 1 Notebook* (Lakewood, Colo.: Healing Touch, 1994), p. 51. Centering, as a form of meditation, is a religious practice, very different from relaxation techniques. According to the National Research Council: "Although there is overlap with some meditation techniques, relaxation training is readily distinguishable insofar as it does not try to teach a person to gain philosophical-religious insights or to get close to a supreme being." Daniel Druckman and Robert A. Bjork, eds., *In the Mind's Eye: Enhancing Human Performance*, Committee on Techniques for the Enhancement of Human Performance, Commission on Behavioral and Social Sciences and Education, National Research Council (Washington, D.C.: National Academy Press, 1991), p. 124. Chopra is candid on this point. He states, "meditation is a spiritual practice." Deepak Chopra, *Ageless Body, Timeless Mind*, p. 167.
20. William T. Jarvis, "Quackery: A National Scandal," *Clinical Chemistry*, 38 (1992): p. 1579.
21. We do not find fault with some recent developments in health care which some label "alternative," such as the recognition of the role in health care of nutrition, exercise, stress reduction, and so on.
22. Dolores Krieger, *Accepting Your Power to Heal*, pp. 6–7. Jean Watson, in a lecture entitled "Postmodern Nursing," called for a "radical rethinking" about health and healing which would "turn our ideas upside down." Jean Watson, "Postmodern Nursing," lecture at Mt. Carmel College of Nursing, Columbus, Ohio, October 24, 1994. Chopra gives ten assumptions of the Western worldview and calls for "a completely new worldview" which will give us "the makings of a new reality." He goes on to say this change in worldview falls in line with the "paradigmatic retransformation" and "coming revolution" of the New Age movement. Deepak Chopra, *Ageless Body, Timeless Mind*, pp. 5, 7.
23. Jean Watson, lecture, "Postmodern Nursing."
24. Charlotte A. Wytias, "Therapeutic Touch in Primary Care," *Nurse Practitioner Forum*, 5 (June 1994): p. 91.
25. John W. Zamarra, "Quantum Healing: Exploring the Frontiers of Mind/Body Medicine," *New England Journal of Medicine*, 321 (December 1989): p. 1688.
26. William T. Jarvis, "Allergy-Related Quackery," *New York State Journal of Medicine*, 93 (February 1993): p. 101.
27. Thurstan B. Brewin claims this view is "disturbingly on the increase in the health field." "Logic and Magic in Mainstream and Fringe Medicine," *Journal of the Royal Society of Medicine*, 86 (December 1993): p. 721.
28. Deepak Chopra, *Ageless Body, Timeless Mind*, p. 61.
29. Ibid., pp. 54, 82–83.
30. Krieger defines Therapeutic Touch as a therapy using "nonphysical human energies." Dolores Krieger, *Accepting Your Power to Heal*, p. 4.

31. Larry Dossey, *Healing Words: The Power of Prayer and the Practice of Medicine* (New York: HarperSanFrancisco, 1993), p. 44.
32. Hari M. Sharma, Brihaspati Dev Triguna, Deepak Chopra, "Maharishi Ayur-Veda: Modern Insights Into Ancient Medicine," p. 2634.
33. Ibid., p. 2637.
34. L. Jasoff, "A No-Touch Therapy," *Time* (November 21, 1994): p. 89.
35. Larry Dossey, *Healing Words: The Power of Prayer and the Practice of Medicine*, p. 35.
36. Numerous articles were cited in response to Sharma's article: "Letters," *Journal of the American Medical Association*, 266 (October 2, 1991): pp. 1770–1774; and 267 (March 11, 1992): pp. 1337–1340.
37. Daniel Druckman and Robert A. Bjork, eds., *In the Mind's Eye: Enhancing Human Performance*, p. 122.
38. One of the organizers of the meeting commented: "While the submitted abstracts seemed reasonable, what they presented had little to do with their abstracts. In one presentation, they couldn't even provide the scientific names of the medicinal plants they claimed to have tested. The other presentation was a pitch for the Maharishi's meditation techniques—hardly appropriate for a botany meeting." Charlotte Gyllenhaal, Ph.D., cited in Andrew A. Skolnick, "Maharishi Ayur-Veda: Guru's Marketing Scheme Promises the World Eternal 'Perfect Health,' " p. 1745.
39. Dolores Krieger, *Accepting Your Power to Heal*, p. 8.
40. Barbara C. Walike, *et al*, "Attempts to Embellish a Totally Unscientific Process With the Aura of Science," *American Journal of Nursing*, Vol. 75 (August 1975): pp. 1275, 1278, 1282.
41. The critical authors concluded: "The current research base supporting continued nursing practice of Therapeutic Touch is, at best, weak. Well-designed, double-blind studies have thus far shown transient results, no significant results, or are in need of independent replication." Philip E. Clarke and Mary Jo Clarke, "Therapeutic Touch: Is There a Scientific Basis for the Practice?" *Nursing Research*, 33 (1984): p. 40.
42. Linda Rosa, *Survey of "Research" on Therapeutic Touch: A Report to the Therapeutic Touch Review Committee, Health Sciences Center, University of Colorado* (Loveland, Colo.: Front Range Skeptics, 1994), p. 9.
43. Jean Watson, lecture, "Postmodern Nursing."
44. Edward W. Russell, "The Fields of Life," in John White and Stanley Krippner, eds., *Future Science: Life Energies and the Physics of Paranormal Phenomena* (Garden City, N.Y.: Anchor Books, 1977), pp. 59–64.
45. Hari M. Sharma, Brihaspati Dev Triguna, Deepak Chopra, "Maharishi Ayur-Veda: Modern Insights Into Ancient Medicine," p. 2633.
46. Linda Rosa, "Therapeutic Touch," p. 47.
47. H. N. Claman, *Report of the Chancellor's Committee on Therapeutic Touch* (Denver: University of Colorado Health Sciences Center, 1994), p. 6.
48. Rosa., p. 48.
49. Clair Martin, then dean of the University of Colorado's Nursing School; quoted in D. Casper, "Healing Touch Wins Bout," *Boulder Daily Camera*, 25 (August 1994): pp. 1B, 3B.

50. Deepak Chopra; quoted in Andrew A. Skolnick, "Maharishi Ayur-Veda: Guru's Marketing Scheme Promises the World Eternal 'Perfect Health,'" p. 1744.
51. Lynda Juall Carpenito, *Nursing Diagnosis: Application to Clinical Practice*, 6th Edition (Philadelphia: J. B. Lippincott, 1995), p. 356.
52. Deepak Chopra, *Perfect Health: The Complete Mind/Body Guide* (New York: Harmony Books, 1990), p. 24.
53. Deepak Chopra, *Ageless Body, Timeless Mind*, p. 261.
54. Ibid., p. 99. We will comment further on the connection between the similar rejection of reason found in Eastern religion and in postmodernism in Chapter 12.
55. Dolores Krieger, *Accepting Your Power to Heal*, p. 8.
56. "Nearly every major erroneous theory of health and disease of the past can cite practices that appeared to work according to their theories." William T. Jarvis, "Quackery, a National Scandal," p. 1580. Also, we should note that even when people get better, this could be for reasons other than those they think. Experience can attest to an improvement in health, but this does not necessarily validate the underlying theory. "Evidence for effectiveness and evidence to support the relevance of some suggested explanatory theory are two different things." Thurstan B. Brewin, "Logic and Magic," p. 721.
57. Deepak Chopra, *Ageless Body, Timeless Mind*, pp. 162–167.
58. David B. Larson and Susan S. Larson, *The Forgotten Factor in Physical and Mental Health: What Does the Research Show?* (Rockville, Md.: National Institute for Healthcare Research, 1994), pp. 107–124.
59. Ibid., p. 122.
60. William T. Jarvis, "Quackery, a National Scandal," p. 1576.
61. Ibid., p. 1574.
62. Louis Harris and Associates, *Health, Information and the Use of Questionable Treatments; a Study of the American Public* (Washington, D.C.: U.S. Department of Health and Human Services, 1987); cited in William T. Jarvis, "Quackery, a National Scandal," p. 1574.
63. Jean Watson, lecture, "Postmodern Medicine."
64. Larry Dossey, *Healing Words: The Power of Prayer and the Practice of Medicine*, p. 207.
65. Deepak Chopra, *Ageless Body, Timeless Mind*, pp. 182–185.
66. Ibid., p. 183.
67. Ibid., p. 173.
68. Dolores Krieger, *Accepting Your Power to Heal*, p. 17.
69. Deepak Chopra, *Ageless Body, Timeless Mind*, pp. 261–267; Dolores Krieger, *Accepting Your Power to Heal*, pp. 112–117.
70. Larry Dossey, *Healing Words: The Power of Prayer and the Practice of Medicine*, pp. 98–99, 104.
71. Ibid., p. 24.
72. Deepak Chopra, *Ageless Body, Timeless Mind*, p. 170.
73. Larry Dossey, *Healing Words: The Power of Prayer and the Practice of Medicine*, p. 61.
74. Deepak Chopra, *Ageless Body, Timeless Mind*, p. 173.
75. Ibid., p. 179.

76. Larry Dossey, *Healing Words: The Power of Prayer and the Practice of Medicine*, p. 80; Dolores Krieger, *Accepting Your Power to Heal*, p. 7; Deepak Chopra, *Ageless Body, Timeless Mind*, p. 185.
77. Deepak Chopra, *Ageless Body, Timeless Mind*, p. 329.
78. Larry Dossey, *Healing Words: The Power of Prayer and the Practice of Medicine*, pp. 79–80.
79. Dolores Krieger, *Accepting Your Power to Heal*, p. 6.
80. Deepak Chopra, *Ageless Body, Timeless Mind*, p. 5.
81. Larry Dossey, *Healing Words: The Power of Prayer and the Practice of Medicine*, pp. 57–59.
82. For example, two physicians were charged in 1991 by the British General Medical Council with "serious professional misconduct" for endangering the health of patients by promoting Ayurvedic remedies in place of approved therapies. Andrew A. Skolnick, "Maharishi Ayur-Veda: Guru's Marketing Scheme Promises the World Eternal 'Perfect Health,' " p. 1750.
83. V. S. Naipul, a Hindu author, describes in *India: A Wounded Civilization* (New York: Vintage Books, 1978) how "popular Hinduism so easily decays into barbarism," p. 7. He comments on a quote from an Indian newspaper about how upper-caste Indians make slaves of "the Untouchables." "The practice of slavery had attained [such] a sophistication that the victims themselves were made to feel a moral obligation to remain in slavery. *Karma!*" p. 44 (emphasis his). He summarizes: "Hinduism hasn't been good enough for the millions [in India]. . . . It has given men no idea of a contract with other men, no idea of the state. It has enslaved one quarter of the population and always left the whole fragmented and vulnerable," p. 50.
84. Deepak Chopra, *Ageless Body, Timeless Mind*, pp. 249–250.
85. Ibid., p. 99.
86. William T. Jarvis, personal communication, August 8, 1995.
87. This is the position taken by the Equal Employment Opportunity Commission (EEOC): EEOC *Notice* N–915.022 (September 1988). See also, Thomas D. Brierton, "Employers' New Age Training Programs Fail to Alter the Consciousness of the EEOC," *Labor Law Journal* (July 1992): pp. 411–420.
88. Sharon Fish, "Therapeutic Touch: Healing Science or Psychic Midwife?" *Christian Research Journal* (Summer 1995): pp. 28–38.
89. Larry Dossey, *Healing Words: The Power of Prayer and the Practice of Medicine*, p. xiv.
90. Dora Kunz, ed. *Spiritual Aspects of the Healing Arts* (Wheaton, Ill.: Theosophical Publishing House, 1982), inside cover.
91. Sharon Fish, "Therapeutic Touch," p. 38.
92. Raymond Buckland, *Buckland's Complete Book of Witchcraft* (St. Paul, Minn.: Llewellyn Publications, 1987), pp. 194–195.
93. Deepak Chopra, *Escaping the Prison of the Mind: A Journey From Here to Here* (San Rafael, Calif.: New World Library, 1992), audiocassette.
94. The placebo effect is the measurable improvement in some clients' health when they are given a sugar pill, but are told it is a powerful new medicine. Somehow, the human body is able to mobilize its own healing powers when

the person believes he or she is taking medicine, even though the pill is made of plain sugar.

95. Notice also that Satan was able to cause boils on Job, implying that if he can cause illness to occur, he probably can cause it to go away as well. (See Job 1–3.)
96. Jeffrey S. Levin and Jeannine Coreil, " 'New Age' Healing in the U.S.," *Social Science and Medicine*, Vol. 23 (1986): p. 890.

6

Postmodern Impact: Literature

Jim Leffel, Contributor

As communication technologies grow ever more sophisticated, we find our ears and eyes endlessly assaulted by sounds and pictures—images that try to sell, persuade, and entertain. Educators tell us that given this environment, today's students process information from non-written sources far better than their parents. Serious readers ponder whether the printed word is dead.

Nevertheless, our society relies largely on the written word—from books, journals, and magazines, to dictionaries, encyclopedias, reports, records, and contracts—to define and communicate truth. We have always known that we can't believe everything we read. Postmodernism, advancing a completely new approach to the written word, tells us we can't *understand* what we read, at least not by attempting to discern what an author meant to communicate. In postmodern literary analysis, texts no longer have a particular meaning. They become nothing but the images projected by an author and mean whatever we create them to say.

Imagine how tremendous the impact of such a difference in approach to written texts would be:

- The United States Constitution is a text. So are laws, regulations, and ordinances. How will society be affected when courts interpret our legal standards using postmodern techniques? We will look closely at this question in Chapter 10.
- What about the Bible? To postmodern thinkers, the Bible doesn't

record an objective message to humankind from its human authors—much less the words of God to his world. It is a religious text which each reader should "deconstruct" and assess in light of postmodern principles of interpretation. We will touch on this issue both here and in the latter chapters of the book.

- History is based largely on written accounts. We shouldn't be surprised to find history literally being rewritten by postmodern thinkers, as we will explore in Chapter 8.

When postmodern literary analysis says that the words on a page no longer mean what an author intended them to mean, we see the potential dismantling of every area of scholarship and daily life.

Unlocking Postmodernism

Postmodernism isn't a collection of beliefs or dogmas as much as a *way of viewing* other schools of thought, artistic expression, and behavior. Postmodernists have developed what philosophers say is a new epistemology—a new way of knowing what we know. Unless we understand this way of approaching reality in principle, postmodern statements seem like nonsense. But once we grasp the postmodern method, everything postmodernists say comes into focus.

So even if we don't consider ourselves lovers of great literature, stepping back to look briefly at the postmodern approach to literature is important for three reasons: First, the ideas we call postmodernism were first formalized in the field of literary analysis. Second, the postmodern approach to the written text is reaching beyond university literature classes to affect how we and our children will read and interpret the most significant and the most mundane documents of our society. Third, postmodernists view all areas of knowledge as "texts" subject to their methods of literary analysis. Therefore, once we understand postmodern literary theory, other areas will be much easier to understand.

Postmodernists view the written word in a way totally different from what we are accustomed to. In this chapter we will look first at the older *grammatical-historical* approach to literature, then the new *postmodern* approach.

The Grammatical-Historical View of Literature

In all literature we encounter three things: an author, a text, and of course ourselves, the readers. How have these elements been viewed by thinkers prior to the advent of postmodernism, and how are they viewed by postmodernists?

Literary Element	Grammatical-Historical Method	Postmodern Method
Author	The author intended to convey a message through the text. That intent is the true meaning of the text. The author, therefore, is the authority over the text.	The author is irrelevant to meaning or unaware of the meaning of the text. The author doesn't stand over the text as an authority.
Text	The text is to be interpreted in light of the rules of grammar at the time it was written, the historical worldview of the intended readers, and the thought development throughout the text.	Texts are to be "deconstructed" and freed from "logocentrism." Behind the text lies the "metanarrative" and internal contradictions that discerning readers detect and expose. The text is an artifact of a particular cultural reality.
Reader	The reader is to use the tools of interpretation to discover the original intention of the author for the original audience. The reader's goal is to let the text speak while avoiding, as much as possible, introducing reader bias.	No reader can eliminate reader bias. Whatever the author intended, we will never know exactly. The reader, therefore, becomes the center of meaning. Authority over the text shifts from the author to the reader.

Let's look at these boxes from top to bottom.

Author: According to the grammatical-historical method, the author is a text's authority, the source of a text's meaning. When you write a letter, you are the one who decides what the letter says, and you know what it means. Likewise, a piece of literature is the expression of the author's reasoning, observations, inner life, and so on. For these reasons, we see the author standing "above" both the text and the reader because he or she is the source and arbiter of meaning.

Text: In the grammatical-historical model, a literary text, whether fiction or nonfiction, is a medium of communication. The grammatical-historical method views the words of the text as a medium where the author and the reader meet. The words in the text correspond to some reality either within the author's world of ideas, or in the physical world. It assumes that author and reader both live in the same world, are both humans, and can therefore communicate in words. Since words and sentences mean something, the text has an objective, stable meaning.

Readers: According to the grammatical-historical approach, we, the readers, should approach a text as learners to find that objective meaning. We should try to discover what the author meant to say in the text. To do this, we might need to study the text's literary form, its original vocabulary, and the background of its author. When we grasp the author's original intent, we have done our job as readers, and learned what the author wanted to communicate. Since the grammatical-historical method views literature as communication, it strives to know as much as possible about the author so the communication will be received accurately.

We can see from this description that the grammatical-historical method is the way most evangelical Christians read the Bible. When we approach Scripture, we believe God has inspired the author to give a certain message, and that message is the meaning of the text. We can deepen our understanding of the text as we investigate the languages used, the cultural setting of the human author, and the historical framework of the original audience. The reason such information enriches our understanding of Scripture is because it helps us to understand more clearly the message God and the human author intended.[1]

The Postmodern View of Literature

Postmodernism assigns completely different roles to the author, the text, and the readers.

Author: Consider the author. Who is he or she? Unlike modernists, who view the author as an autonomous center of reason, free choice, and creativity, postmodernists view the author as the expression of a particular cultural outlook, whether or not he or she ever realized it. This is different from the grammatical-historical approach, which acknowledges that culture may influence the author but holds that the author is able to transcend cultural influences, at least to the extent that he can communicate his individual message. Postmodernists deny that any author can transcend cultural influences in *any* way. Therefore, while the grammatical-historical method asserts that the author is capable of expressing objective and rational meaning, the postmodern method says he can't.

Postmodernists reject the grammatical-historical view of human nature and authors. Authors, they claim, are social constructs—virtually impersonal, socially constructed "nodes." According to postmodernists, authors can't create unique or original works that express their thoughts and feelings as individuals. They can only restate what is "already present" in their social reality. This means there is little value in viewing the author as the one who gives a text its meaning, as though he or she occupies some privileged place in the communication process.

Most postmodern scholars, in viewing the author as a social construct, assert that he is unaware of the meaning of his own work. The inner motivations driving the author are deeply imbedded and not consciously understood. The author is viewed as merely an extension of the underlying social forces that constitute his identity. Postmodern literary critics often interpret authors' underlying motivations through the framework of psychoanalysis (Freud), feminism, or Marxism.

> We have always known we can't believe everything we read. Postmodernism tells us we can't *understand* what an author meant to say.

Text: Postmodernists also advance a different view of the text. In their view, *everything* is a "text." All communication is a text. Social reality is a text—the story of particular social settings, which differ for various participants. Individual texts are part of the larger social text. Individuals are a "text" because their lives are narratives. We "live in story," declares one postmodern commentator. Because texts are essentially an expression of social reality, postmodernists refer to the interplay between a literary piece and social reality as "intertextuality." Since everything is a text, postmodern literary analysis extends to all branches of knowledge, as the chart in Appendix A explains.

This is where a text quickly becomes less than a communication of objective truth. Postmodernists charge that texts lack any objective meaning, because they are rooted in language, and language, as we have seen, contains its own arbitrary logic. As such, a work of literature isn't capable of possessing a stable meaning. Instead, an infinite number of interpretations are possible. A text means different things to different cultures, and no interpretation is "better" than any other.[2] All texts provide social interpretations, which change with the ebb and flow of social reality and "social consciousness."

Under postmodern analysis, any claim to truth in a text is self-contradictory propaganda. The claims are propaganda, because all communication has social or political implications. In the postmodern view, so-called "truth," because it is socially constructed, is always political.

Reader: The postmodern approach calls on readers to provide new meaning for the text by using an analytical technique called "deconstruction." The reader must first understand that language is inherently ambiguous and self-contradictory. As we noted earlier in this book, postmodernists refer to words as "signifiers." These signifiers are linked to human ideas, or "signifieds." But the connection between signifier and signified is arbitrary. The link between signifiers and signifieds exists *only in the mind* of the speaker. In other words, there is no *inherent* or *objective* (outside the mind) linkage between words and ideas or things. No word has a meaning in and of itself. It only means what a given group *assigns* it to mean. One could just as easily call a "door" a "rood" or something else. After all, other languages and cultures have completely different words for everything.

On one level, everyone agrees with these points, but in the conventional view of language, it doesn't matter, because we agree with each other on meanings. Postmodernists, on the other hand, draw radical conclusions from the arbitrary nature of vocabulary, largely because they see language as our *only* connection to reality. The meaning of any given signifier, understood in the postmodern way, turns out to be circular. This is easily illustrated by an experience every student has had—looking up a word in a dictionary that happens to be defined by other words he or she understands no better. Postmodernists say this confusion is the case with *every* word. If we looked up "signifier" in the dictionary, for example, it is defined by other signifiers which can in turn be looked up and so on forever. One arbitrary signifier is defined by other arbitrary signifiers. Here's the point: No meaning can be given to the text itself—only meanings we assign to the text based on our arbitrarily defined set of signifiers.

Postmodern critics commonly attempt to demonstrate the incoherence of language through the technique of "deconstruction." Deconstruction is a tool used to identify arbitrary hierarchies, presuppositions, exclusions, and contradictions in a text. Jacques Derrida, father of literary deconstruction, argues that when a text asserts a *thesis*, it implicitly gives validity to its *antithesis*.[3] When we talk about "good," we must accept the meaningfulness of "bad," because good can only be understood when set in opposition to bad. When an author discusses "culture," he tacitly affirms "nature," (meaning the absence of culture) and so on for any assertion.

Derrida argues that all literature is based on these oppositions. But he also argues that authors set one opposition "above" the other. In this way, authors construct arbitrary hierarchies. For example, Western writers have tended to see culture over, or superior to, nature. When authors choose to picture one side of such an opposition as superior to the other, they become, according to Derrida, "logocentric" ("word-" or "reason-" centered). To postmodernists, being logocentric is a great sin. Logocentrists are the ideologues, the cultural imperialists who attempt to subjugate others to their version of the truth.

Inventing Meaning

The mission of literary deconstruction is to identify these implicit antitheses and to unveil the slanted intent of the author—to show that his work undermines itself. The resulting analysis concludes that nothing rationally meaningful is being asserted through the words of a text. Instead, authors are merely pushing the arbitrary hierarchies of meaning defined by their culture. Deconstructionists are just as interested in what is *not emphasized* or is *not included* in a text as with what is central to that text. This is one good way to reveal hidden arbitrary hierarchies. Postmodern literary critics sometimes call this process of revealing the unstated hierarchies in a text the "subversive reading" of the text.

Let's do a subversive reading on a popular children's film. The movie *Beauty and the Beast* seems harmless to us—charming, vintage Disney, a story about the transforming power of love. But under postmodern analysis, the underlying oppositions create an entirely different picture. The heroine is defined by her physical appearance, "Belle." Therefore, women are important primarily in terms of their looks, and, consequently, how they can please men. The film explains that Belle is responsible for her fumbling father. In other words, like all patriarchy, the father has the authority, but his wards are responsible to make things come out right.

In love, the movie pictures a woman as giving herself wholly for the reform of the "Beast," or man whom she loves. Indeed, his good is accomplished *only* through her love and sacrifice. Deep inside a man, as beastly as he might appear on the outside, is a gentle, loving prince. The responsibility to manifest this good side falls, not to the man, but to his servile lover. The story is made to appear to be a law of nature; as the theme song proclaims, "tale as old as time, song as old as rhyme. . . ." In reality, according to the subversive reading of the script, a postmodern critic might see this film as a prescription for neurosis, abuse, and patriarchy.

To postmodern thinkers, readers—or moviegoers—aren't learners standing under the authority of the author and text. They are no longer on a quest to discover what the author and the words of the text mean. Instead, readers are elevated to the status of authority *over* the text. As the text is divested of hierarchy and logocentrism, the intent of the author becomes irrelevant. The reader is free from any norms of interpretation. The text is opened up to explore an endless array of possible meanings.

According to postmodern critics, deconstruction empowers readers and liberates them from the oppressive authority of the text and author. At the same time, though, even the reader isn't an authority in any objective or final sense. All readings are equally valid, and all readers are their own authorities. Edgar McKnight explains how this applies to the Bible. Readers don't search for the communication of God through his prophets. Rather, the reader inserts his own meaning. "The biblical writings," McKnight says, "are designed for readers who will find and create meanings that involve them, that match their needs and capacity. . . ."[4]

Of course readers never develop meaning in a cultural vacuum. Individual readers are strands in the fabric of a larger "cultural text," or "interpretative community." That community orients readers to the text, and consequently shapes their interpretation. Examples of interpretive community include the feminist community, lesbians, gays, a racial minority, or a religious group.

As we continue to cover different areas of contemporary society, we will see these postmodern literary principles in use in one area after another. Postmodern thinkers have extrapolated their literary theories into a general philosophy of life, where everyone is a text and every part of society is a text. Literary theory is the backbone of postmodern ideology where truth is narrative, or story, and interpretation is substituted for reason.

In Brief

- Postmodernists reject the grammatical-historical understanding of author, audience, and text in favor of a new view of each.
- Authors are no longer authorities over their texts in the sense that readers must look to understand what that author meant to say. Now the authority resides in the postmodern reader to interject his own meaning into the text.
- Postmodern readers "deconstruct" texts, unveiling their cultural constructions. Readers are empowered and liberated from the cultural constructs of the powerful—liberated from the text—and freed to give texts their own meanings.

Notes

1. For an extensive presentation of the grammatical-historical method of interpretation, see E. D. Hirsch, *Validity in Interpretation* (New Haven: Yale University Press, 1967).
2. Naturally, this includes the Bible. Postmodern biblical scholar Edgar McKnight explains, "The biblical text is like the artistic text in general, which is so filled with meaning that it transmits different information to different readers in proportion to each one's comprehension." Edgar V. McKnight, *Postmodern Use of the Bible: The Emergence of Reader-Oriented Criticism* (Nashville: Abingdon Press, 1988), p. 168, citing Jurij Lotman, *The Structure of the Artistic Text*.
3. Readability is a serious problem when trying to digest Derrida's theories. A more accessible source than most, but certainly not readable in the usual sense, is Jacques Derrida, *Points* . . . Interviews 1974–1994, Elisabeth Weber, ed. (Stanford: Stanford University Press, 1995).
4. Edgar V. McKnight, *Postmodern Use of the Bible*, p. 170. Again, "A sensitive reader may, in fact, be 'creating' a new world in the process of reading. . . . Experience with the text is an experience that alters needs and possibilities. The reader is then creating a world effectively in experience with the text." p. 176.

7

POSTMODERN IMPACT: EDUCATION

GARY DELASHMUTT AND ROGER BRAUND, CONTRIBUTORS

If you have children, they likely attend public schools—or you have found reasons to make a conscious choice to send them to a private school or to school them at home. Will the arrival of postmodernism affect our children's education? The answer is an unqualified yes. Consider this statement recently generated by the state of New York's educational task force:

> African Americans, Asian Americans, Puerto Ricans/Latinos, and Native Americans have all been the victims of an intellectual and educational oppression that has characterized the culture and institutions of the United States and the European world for centuries.

Our point isn't to condone the racism this quote implies. Our

About the Contributors:

Gary DeLashmutt is co-senior pastor at Xenos Christian Fellowship. He is author of *Loving God's Way* and coauthor of *The Myth of Romance*. He is also a member of the Board of Education for Calumet Christian School, where he has worked often on curriculum issues.

Roger Braund is an educator who first studied postmodernism while getting his degree in architecture. Later, he became a teacher and received his master's degree in science education.

goal is to trace the source of these ideas, this framing of the educational crisis. What we quickly discover is that this statement expresses the convictions of postmodern educators working to further what they term "multiculturalism." Raising awareness of "Eurocentric oppression" and its effects is but one facet of their agenda, which will increasingly dominate schools in the near future. They go on to say that

> [This] systematic bias toward Europe and its derivatives . . . [has had] a terribly damaging effect on the psyche of young people of African, Asian, Latino, and Native American descent. . . . [This] European-American monocultural perspective . . . [explains why] large numbers of children of non-European descent are not doing as well as expected.[1]

No area of society has been more influenced by postmodern thought than education. Yet the terminology educators use is rarely specifically or exclusively postmodern, and the concepts they discuss are confusing unless we understand their source.

Gauging the Postmodern Shift

Underlying postmodern educational proposals are important assumptions about knowledge, culture, values, and human nature, all of which are touched on in the task force's statements above.

As we discuss postmodernism's impact on education, we will compare each aspect of postmodern ideology to modernist educational ideology. This will help us to see both the ideas that have controlled education until recently and the reforms postmodernists are already implementing. Postmodern educators tend to be eclectic (borrowing from different views) and pragmatic (doing whatever works). They therefore accept practices and ideas they deem effective, including a number of modernist practices. It would be thus incorrect and misleading to think of postmodern education as an organized movement. We believe it is possible, however, to identify the key assumptions of postmodernism in various theories of education. When these assumptions predominate within a theory it can rightly be called postmodern, even when some modernist points are included.

The following chart summarizes our discussion.

	Modernist Theory[2]	Postmodern Theory
Knowledge	Educators should be authoritative transmitters of unbiased knowledge.	Educators are biased facilitators and co-"constructors" of knowledge.
Culture	Culture is both an object of study and a barrier to learning. Students from diverse cultures must be trained in a shared language before teachers can transmit knowledge to them.	The modernist goal of unifying society results in domination and exploitation, because unity is always based on dominant culture. All cultures are not only of equal value, but also constitute equally important *realities*. Minority students must be empowered to fight against Eurocentric enculturation.
Values	Traditional modernists believe that educators are legitimate authorities on values, and therefore *they should train students in universal values*. More liberal modernists argue that *education should be "values-neutral."* Teachers help students with "values clarification"—deciding what values each individual student will hold. Values can and should be separated from facts. The most important values are *rationality, freedom, and progress*.	Education should help *students construct diverse and personally useful values in the context of their cultures*. Values are considered *useful for a given culture*, not *true* or *right* in any universal sense. Since teachers cannot avoid teaching their own values, it is okay for teachers to openly promote their values and social agendas in the classroom as long as these are not "fundamentalist" or totalistic." Important values to teach include diversity, tolerance, freedom, creativity, emotional expressiveness, and use of intuition.
Human Nature	Modernists generally *believe in a stable, inherent self that can be objectively known*. Since humans are thought to have a stable essential nature, IQ tests, and other similar "objective tests," can be used to discover students' innate intelligence. By giving students mastery over subject matter, teachers enhance students' self-esteem. Education helps individuals discover their identities. Individuals and society progress by learning and applying objective knowledge.	Students have no "true self" or innate essence. Rather, selves are social constructs. Postmodern educators believe *self-esteem is a precondition for learning*. They view education as a type of therapy. Education helps individuals appreciate their identities rather than discover them. Individuals and society progress when people are empowered to attain their own chosen goals.

Just what is Postmodern Education? Postmodern educators, as do postmodernists in general, reject the two pillars of modernism: rationalism and progress. Instead, they praise conceptions of human thought that are subjective (intuitive and emotive), pragmatic, pluralistic, and relativistic. Postmodern educators also tend to be "affirmative" postmodernists, that is, they seek to create new realities through education to change society for the better.[3]

A New Way to View Knowledge

Knowledge According to Modernists

Modern education has tended to have characteristics similar to those found in other modern disciplines; in particular, the "two pillars" of modernism: rationalism and progress.[3] Modernists think educators ideally should be authoritative transmitters of unbiased knowledge. Even if teachers fail to be completely rational and objective educators all the time, they are still more rational and more objective than students. Teachers, therefore, have legitimate authority over students in deciding what is valid knowledge and what is not.

The source of teachers' authority is first and foremost a base of accepted knowledge derived from university research in the natural and social sciences, which shows them how and what to teach. Modernists don't claim to have found the final truth regarding the best teaching methods, though they believe they are well on their way.

These empirical studies also provide modernist teachers with much of their teaching content, curricula such as textbooks and workbooks. This is most readily apparent in science and social studies classes, where textbook content flows from the most up-to-date scientific findings. In the modernist view, sciences and school curricula progress together, replacing mythology, speculation, and mere opinion with objective knowledge.

Since modernists see teachers as authoritative communicators of knowledge, it follows that students are receivers of knowledge. The students could be considered passive, in that their main job is to acquire knowledge from the teacher, the expert. Even when students are assigned an active role in attempting to discover knowledge, as in formulating a scientific hypothesis, their ideas are still subject to correction by the teacher.

Modernist educators strive for a unified curriculum (content) and pedagogy (teaching method) based on the ideal of "one truth" as discovered by scientific study, seeking to transmit *the* correct set of concepts and/or facts for any given topic. Modernists furthermore want to test students with "objective" tools—multiple-choice and fill-in-the-blank tests, for example—where mastery of material can be quantified and analyzed statistically.

Knowledge According to Postmodernists

Constructivism is the main learning theory underlying postmodern education. According to constructivists, knowledge isn't *discovered* as modernists claim; all knowledge is invented or "constructed" in the minds of learners. It can't be any other way, postmodernists say, because the ideas teachers teach and students learn don't correspond to any objective reality. They are mere human constructions. Knowledge, ideas, and language are created by people not because they are "true," but rather because they are useful.[4]

According to postmodernism, educators are biased facilitators and co-constructors of knowledge. If all reality exists not "out there" but only in the minds of those who perceive it, then no one can claim authority. All versions of truth are merely human creations. Educators—whether classroom teachers, researchers, or textbook authors—are *not* objective, legitimate authorities. Instead, they view educational activities from their own constructed, biased perspective, and therefore have no "privileged relationship to the truth." Ruth Zuzovsky points out the startling implication of this radical constructivist viewpoint: the knowledge constructed by learners, teachers, or scientists *are all of equal worth*.[5]

For postmodernists, all knowledge is of "equal worth," at least in the traditional sense of its truth value. As we will see below, the postmodernists still have ways of evaluating knowledge claims that do not involve absolute, or objective truth. Knowledge claims, since they have no truth value, no verifiable relationship to ultimate reality, are nevertheless considered tools that people may or may not find useful.[6]

If teachers and textbook writers are dethroned, and the knowledge of any one person or group is no more true than the next, what happens at school can't help but change radically. What knowledge should be taught, for example, isn't a matter of objective evidence or arguments, but a matter of *power*. Those who have the power can make sure that their views dominate the curriculum, while other opposing viewpoints are at least partially suppressed, ignored, or "marginalized." As educational theorist Michael Apple says regarding textbooks used in the schools, "Texts aren't simply 'delivery systems' of 'facts.' They are at once the results of political, economic, and cultural activities, battles, and compromises."[7] Postmodernists claim that the knowledge incorporated in school curriculum isn't the result of what society as a whole views as legitimate knowledge. It is, in fact, a knowledge base created by specific groups of people who, because of their power, have been able to decide what is or should be "official knowledge."[8]

Those who hold the reins of power make sure their version of truth dominates the curriculum.

Researchers, postmodernists assert, are constructors of knowledge caught up in power relations just like the subjects of their studies. Postmodernists believe it is *impossible* to be unbiased and objective (and many think it is not *preferable* either) and therefore many purposefully use their research to further their own social and political agendas. As Patti Lather of Ohio State University says of qualitative research, "Such work argues that overtly value-based, advocacy research openly opposed to the maldistribution of power is neither more nor less ideological than is mainstream research. . . . No method can completely filter out widespread social biases that are deeply inscribed in a culture."[9] This concern with "curricular dominance" by those in power is clear in the statement at the beginning of this chapter that various minority groups "have all been victims of an intellectual and educational oppression."

Postmodern educators shun the reform proposals of people like E. D. Hirsch, Allan Bloom, and William Bennett, which call for teaching a "common culture," a common knowledge base. They pursue instead a variety of topics claimed to be more interesting and useful to marginalized groups.

Besides arguing that objective knowledge doesn't exist, postmodernists also argue that we are unable to *communicate* knowledge objectively. Christine Sleeter says that under the old, modernist model, "Knowledge as information is passed on from the teacher to the student as if it were a basket of eggs. Effective teaching and learning are achieved if the 'eggs' are conveyed safely, intact, and without damage."[10] Postmodern educators claim this modernist model seeks something it can never attain—the objective transmission of truth. Teachers should instead strive to say and do things that might potentially stimulate the students to construct knowledge in their own minds, which may or may not resemble knowledge in the teacher's mind (not a concern, of course—since teachers can't enter the minds of their students, they can never know if students' constructs match their own).

Sleeter explains how two schools of thought involve the student:

> Critical [postmodern] pedagogy emphasizes the collective analysis of oppression, and feminist pedagogy focuses more on personal feelings and experiences, but *both place the student at the center of teaching and learning. Neither imposes the teacher's view of reality on the students.* (emphasis added)[11]

It is important to remember that when Sleeter suggests students should be free from the oppression of teachers imposing their views of reality, she isn't referring to the teacher's religion or artistic tastes. The context of this statement is teachers imposing their rules for *English grammar* on kids from the inner city, who have their own rules of grammar!

Postmodernists see the construction of knowledge as a *social activity* and not only as something that takes place in the privacy of an individual student's mind. One practical result of this social focus is an emphasis on cooperative learning, where students, and in some situations the teacher, construct knowledge together.[12]

When postmodern education shifts the focus of learning to the students' construction of knowledge, classrooms move from a teacher-centered environment where lectures or recitation are prevalent to a more *student-centered* environment. A teacher's job isn't to pour a set of skills and knowledge into children's heads, but to provide the creative conditions where knowledge can be constructed.[13] A student-centered classroom in this context is likely to have minimal structure. It usually involves opportunities for social interaction, independent investigations and study, and the expression of creativity, as well as provision for different learning styles.[14] There, "students create knowledge, and are no longer forced to bow to the subjugation of traditional objective 'knowledge.' " As Everhard explains, "School knowledge disables to the extent that it silences students, usurps their minds or at least demands acquiescence. . . . [such knowledge] usually places boundaries between emotion and knowledge; students do not control knowledge, but rather must unite their student roles and scenarios in conformity to the teacher's master script."[15]

The debates raging over teaching inner-city children to speak "proper" classroom English illustrate how postmodern theorists view knowledge constructed by students apart from a repressive educational setting. Here is how Judith Renyi envisions the difference between traditional and postmodern modes of instruction in language arts:

> The gloomy classroom full of strictures about correctness and the lively classroom full of emergent poets define two opposing attitudes toward the children of the poor and their language competence. The first says that children must set aside what they know and how they use language to fulfill language tasks that exist nowhere in the world but in such classrooms. The second says that children already know a lot about both language and the world it can describe; it encourages using language to construct new visions and meanings. The first seeks to constrain language by grammatical minutiae. The second seeks to constrain language in poetic forms constructed by the children themselves.[16]

The postmodern view of literacy may virtually do away with grammar as a category of teaching in the years to come.

We shouldn't jump to the conclusion that postmodernists have no standards by which to judge between conflicting knowledge constructs. To the contrary, postmodern educators are often promoters of "critical thinking" in the classroom; that is, they often do encourage the evaluation of claims. But their concept of critical thinking is completely different from that of traditional education. Instead of critical approaches based on rational criteria, such as internal and external consistency, or whether a position makes sense, postmodern theory introduces new criteria for criticism:

1. *What is right for the community of which an individual or group is a part?* In other words, postmodernists apply a *culturally relative standard*. In particular, a radical constructionist asks if a piece of knowledge "resonates" with others of the community of which the individual is a part, or desires to be a part.[17] If a student wants to become an artist, for example, he will need to conform his ways of thinking and talking about art to those of the arts community.

2. *Does it help the individual or group attain their chosen goals?* This amounts to a *pragmatic standard*. If a graduate student in genetics wants to do research to help people with genetic defects, then she will accept and work with the theories and laboratory techniques that the genetics community currently considers to be essential.

In evaluating knowledge claims, teachers may to some extent guide students' conclusions, based on their greater amount of experience of what "resonates" with a given community and what is useful for attaining various ends. But in situations where students and teacher disagree over what is best, the teacher should not merely *tolerate* the choice of the "other construct" but *affirm* it. Teachers should affirm student effort expended formulating solutions to problems, because this is important for their self-esteem; von Glasersfeld explains:

> No longer would it be possible to cling to the notion that a given task has one solution and only one way of arriving at it. The teacher would come to realize that what he or she presents as a "problem" may be seen differently by the student. Consequently, the student may produce a sensible solution that makes no sense to the teacher. To be then told that it is *wrong* is unhelpful and inhibiting . . . because it disregards the effort the student has made.[18]

Consider one education professor's advice on how teachers can nonjudgmentally acknowledge students' responses:

> The list included "Um-hmmm," "That's a thought," "That's one possibility," "That's one idea," "That's another way to look at it," "I hear you," and eleven other ways not to tell a student the answer was . . . wrong.[19]

While nonjudgmental statements may be mainly a teaching strategy rather than an affirmation of error, in practice it amounts to relativism at work in a menacing fashion: Critics argue that children aren't taught right from wrong, even in areas like science and social studies. Will their employers be so tolerant?

Knowledge in the Bible

Good teachers have always realized that students are more than passive receptacles of knowledge, and have found ways to motivate their students to take an active role in the learning process. Group study projects, interactive learning, critical thinking, and attention to the learning environment can be used effectively to motivate active learning.

But postmodernism denies the correspondence between what humans perceive and the "real reality" of our world. Taken to its logical conclusion, this view undermines the whole basis for education. Why teach at all if we have no true knowledge to communicate? The biblical worldview affirms that humans cannot know exhaustively, but it insists that we can know some things truly. Because we are made in God's image as rational beings, there is substantial correspondence between what we think and external reality. The fact that we can sinfully use our brain's abilities to distort the truth (Romans 1:18ff) doesn't prove that there is no truth or that we are unable to know the truth.

Educators must always be aware of the limitations of their knowledge. Modernist educators are often guilty of unfounded dogmatism, especially about their presuppositions. Their denial of the supernatural is a statement of faith, not a proven fact. In the same way, modernist confidence in human goodness and progress fly in the face of overwhelming historical evidence. Nor have modernists ever demonstrated that more knowledge improves moral or social conditions in human society. Neither modernists nor postmodernists come to grips with human sin and its effects on thought and perception.

We also cannot accept the way radical constructivism rejects teacher/student roles and transmission of knowledge. Scripture repeatedly urges young and old alike to accept instruction and reproof (Proverbs 22:15).

Does an approach that refuses to call any answer "wrong" deserve to be called education? In the biblical worldview, answers that correspond to reality are true or correct, while answers that do not are false or wrong.

A student at a major secular university recently exposed the inconsistency of this educational approach. During the first class, the instructor showed the students a painting and asked them for their interpretations of it. After one student offered his interpretation, another disagreed. The instructor then criticized that student for being arrogant enough to think he could know what the artist really meant. Our interpretations are merely social constructs and are therefore all equally valid. The student then held up the instructor's class syllabus and declared that he interpreted it to mean that all students would receive an "A" for the course whether or not they completed any assignments!

The extreme reluctance of postmodern educators to judge, test, and evaluate seems destined to produce occupationally inept people who can't handle being told they are wrong. America may become the first country in the world afraid to tell its children that they got the wrong answer on a math problem!

Does an approach that refuses to call any answer "wrong" deserve to be called education?

Finally, parents and teachers should be clear that the educational theories underlying these bizarre practices haven't been proven. On the contrary, the new *qualitative* research used to back up many postmodern conclusions is mostly speculation. It proves nothing. Indeed, the vast majority of the material in this field makes no claim to any kind of substantiation, its authors holding that such proof is impossible anyway. Instead, we see freeform speculation regarding why, for example, many minority children are failing at school. Many critics warn that minority children who are educated using these methods will be less able to succeed in mainstream American culture. Ironically, no one is more menaced by postmodern educational theory than the minorities it purports to help.

Multicultural Education

Modernism and Culture

Modernist educators see culture, on one hand, as something students should learn about. But it is also, on the other hand, a *barrier* to learning. People from diverse cultures have differences in language that must be bridged before classroom communication can occur. Before teachers can transmit the body of knowledge available, they must train students in a shared language, or medium of communication. In America it makes sense, they argue, for the minority groups to learn English, rather than for the majority to learn minority languages or dialects.

In fairness, modernists have been willing to advance bilingual education, beginning with the mother tongue of immigrants. But the goal is always the same: to teach them "American" culture and language. After all, for them to compete in the majority culture for jobs those tools are essential.

Postmodernism and Culture

As an outgrowth of their emphasis on socially constructed knowledge, postmodern educators have hijacked the movement known as *multicultural education*. Multicultural education started as a worthwhile project concerned with familiarizing students with important cultural differences in our society. Originally, the movement embodied a liberal concern for understanding one another. However, today multicultural education has been radicalized until it has become virtually synonymous with postmodern education.

Multiculturalism asserts that social realities are, and should be, diverse. But while even modernists admit culture is diverse, they do not generally see this as an ideal or a goal. They favor the "melting pot" theory—that each cultural group contributes something at the same time they are assimilated.

Multiculturalists consider the modernist goal of unifying society to be domineering and exploitive. If society is to become one, on whose terms will it unify? The dominant culture is almost always the standard. Though lesser, oppressed cultures may contribute a thing or two, they must essentially conform to the majority standard. Multiculturalists see the dominant culture imposing its own way on minorities, perhaps without conscious planning and intent, yet with devastating consistency. When conformity proves impossible, the dominant culture seeks to "marginalize" the nonconforming—that is, to relegate those who are different to the margins of society where they can be safely ignored.

No one can deny that to some extent this proposition is true. Multicultural education, however, goes far beyond decrying excessive pressure to conform. It advances a relativistic conception of diversity where all cultures are not only of equal value but also constitute equally true and important *realities*.[20]

Multiculturalism also leads to the "politicization of education," because equalizing the power relations between opposing cultures is crucial for having a multicultural society.[21]

Postmodern multiculturalists aim to produce a humility in students concerning their own culture, believing this leads to tolerance of conflicting views. The increase in humility, however, is directed at whites, Europeans, heterosexuals, and males, more so than at their counterparts. These students represent the dominant culture, whose views (often labeled "Eurocentric") have controlled Western education for centuries.

For people of color, non-Europeans, gays, lesbians, the disabled, and women, the goal is different. Because these groups have been on the margins of the educational system for centuries, they need their self-esteem *raised* by affirming their views. Kids from minority cultures, most importantly, should never be asked to conform in any way to school or societal standards different from the standards of their own communities.

Multiculturalists also believe that no one from one culture can fully understand another culture. This leads radical multiculturalists to conclude that only a native of a given culture can accurately teach about that culture. We see this perspective most clearly in the movement known as "Afrocentric" education. For example, John Hendrik Clarke, writing for the Portland Public Schools, says that "African scholars are the final authority on Africa."[22] In order to have an accurate and positive portrayal of African-American culture, curriculum writers and instructors must be of African descent.

Afrocentric educators see a need to correct existing Eurocentric views. Johnella Butler states,

> In Black Studies we have set many tasks for ourselves: to correct distortions, to revise the history and other studies of people of African ancestry, and to critique the educational process itself by identifying how the colonization of minds is characteristic of American education.[23]

The phrase "colonization of minds" is revealing. It means that when the dominant culture calls on minorities to speak classroom English, or to do math, history, and science the white man's way, they have again acted out their old colonial role. Earlier, they argue, Europeans believed it was their responsibility to colonize non-white cultures and lands, imposing European standards, dress, religion, and language on those cultures (the so-called "white man's burden"). Now, in public education this process continues through conquering children's minds.

This radical form of multiculturalism leads some postmodern educators to reject desegregation and integration of schools, goals popular just a couple of decades ago. Instead, they promote the idea of subcultures having their own separate but equal schools, such as Afrocentric schools with Afrocentric curricula.

Again, behind this extreme view of cultural diversity is the idea that different cultures have different ways of thinking. Lynn Cheney, in her important book, *Telling the Truth: A Report on the State of Humanities in Higher Education*, describes the experience of a school system in Massachusetts:

> Like many schools reforming their curricula, the Brookline system hired consultants, two of whom advanced the idea that women and minorities think differently, learn differently, and require different standards. While explaining to Brookline teachers that white male logic involves such dichotomies as "right-wrong" and "kill-or-be-killed," one of the advisers observed that this way of thinking has made "young white males dangerous to themselves and the rest of us, especially in a nuclear age."[24]

This view may seem extreme, but it is consistent with what many postmodern scholars have said. For many, such conclusions follow logically from the postmodern understanding of the horrors, such as world wars, that have occurred while white males have been dominant in Western society. Many non-postmodernists wonder whether this ideology heralds a new wave of racism.

Culture in the Bible

God has created a world of tremendous diversity, and culture is one example of that diversity. Multicultural education, when approached within the absolutes of Scripture, is an important endeavor. Understanding other cultures can only further the communication and understanding needed for social harmony in today's global village.

However, God has given us moral and doctrinal absolutes that judge all cultures, *including our own*. Some aspects of culture—clothing styles, food, art forms, and so on—are mere matters of taste or preference. We can and should be flexible in these areas of legitimate cultural diversity, being willing even to change from our own to another pattern for the sake of better communication, according to 1 Corinthians 9:19–23. But biblical Christians believe in the existence of universal right and wrong—a measure based on the character of God and standing above all cultures.

Christians certainly should agree with postmodernists who advocate teaching about other cultures as a way of resisting the fallen human tendency to persecute the culturally different. The Bible also commands a certain kind of tolerance toward those who differ from us. Specifically, we are called to love those unlike us (Matthew 6:43–47). It would be naive to think public education will teach Christian love as its ethic, and it would be pointless if they did. Christianity without Christ doesn't work.

Because postmodern education has rejected the possibility of absolutes, it has *no basis for moral critique or limits on diversity*. The well-known controversy over accepting the gay and lesbian communities as normal manifestations of diversity is a case in point. Without authoritative moral norms based on the Bible and natural law, anything is possible.

Many Outcome-Based Education (OBE) programs emphasize not just academic performance but specific values as "outcomes" to be demonstrated before graduating to the next schooling level. Tolerance for diversity is one of the key "values outcomes" advanced in OBE programs. But when we look at what tolerance means in the postmodern world—a refusal to critique anything as either false or wrong—we recoil in horror. Our children aren't learning a valid social value under the code-word "tolerance." They are instead learning that no value is normative, and no truth is objective.

A New View of Right and Wrong

Modernism and Values

Modernists generally believe that at least some values—judgments of what is worthwhile, good, and valuable—are universal and can be objectively and rationally known. The sciences have never had much success in providing undeniable evidence for specific values, however. Still, many modernists do at least hope they will be found eventually. This has led to a division in modernist theory of education.

Traditional modernists believe that educators are legitimate authorities on values, and therefore they should train students in universal values or at least impart objective methods for arriving at values.[25] A more liberal modernist approach is that education should be "values-neutral." Some modernist educators even argued for an intermediate position between modernism and postmodernism, where the teacher is to encourage *values clarification*—helping students decide what their personal values will be. Students are viewed as free-thinking individuals selecting values based on the tools of modernism—rational thought and individual choice.

Modernists make a strong distinction between values and facts. Values can be separated from facts, they believe, so that factual knowledge can be discovered without interference from the values of the researcher. They also believe the teacher and the textbook can then without bias communicate facts to the students.

Some values are evident throughout modernist education, such as the importance of rationality and progress. This stress isn't always overt. But in the answers teachers accept and give as well as in the content of what students study, these values are always strongly implied. In addition, modernists also see education itself as a foundational value because it is the primary means for bringing about social and individual progress. People who are rational, scientifically literate, and advocates of democracy are those who can foster progress.

Postmodernism and Values

The postmodern view of values is similar to their view of knowledge: Both are social constructions. As with knowledge, education should therefore help students construct diverse and personally useful values in the context of their cultures. Since, again, no individual or group is more authoritative than any other, classes should study and affirm the diverse values held by students. Values are considered useful for a given culture, not true or right in any universal sense.

Unlike modernists, postmodernists do not accept the fact/value distinction. Rather, they see values and knowledge as interrelated. They think it is impossible for teachers to teach "just the facts," because no teacher can present his subject matter without bias, that is, without being influenced by his own values. Some postmodern educators openly promote their values and social agendas in the classroom, claiming it is impossible to do otherwise. Cheney notes: "Since power and politics are part of every quest for knowledge—so it is argued—professors are perfectly justified in using the classroom to advance political agendas. . . ."[26] At the least, most postmodernists argue that openly advancing one's values is preferable to hiding them. It's more honest—and, they feel, more appropriate, since changing society is the main goal of postmodern education.

Postmodern educators specifically promote striving for:

- *Diversity*—Diversity means guarding, unchanged, the existing values, tastes, and way of life of each subculture in our society. Charles Tesconi describes the multicultural viewpoint that "any human society is best served by maximizing (or at least maintaining) the distinctiveness of different tastes and values in just about every conceivable realm of human experience—political, religious, social, linguistic."[27] He explains that inculcating these values in students will lead to "self-understanding, self-esteem, inter-group understanding and harmony, and equal opportunity."
- *Equality*—In postmodern ideology, equality means equality *in power relationships*. Postmodernists' concerns for oppressed

groups might mean empowering minorities and women by giving their views a significant place in the curriculum. They also try to provide them with opportunities to escape the debilitating circumstances in which they have grown up by providing special scholarships or lower entrance requirements for college.

- *Tolerance and freedom*—Tolerance has a new meaning: roughly, never negating or criticizing oppressed groups. Freedom is allowing cultures and communities to express themselves. Ironically, this freedom is only extended in certain directions, as we will see in Chapters 14 and 15.
- *Creativity*—Creativity is clearly an ally of the postmodern emphases on the construction of knowledge and diversity. Stimulating and affirming creativity in students is important if diverse viewpoints are to be encouraged in constructing knowledge and values.
- *Emotions*—Affirmation of emotions follows from the importance postmodern educators place on self-esteem. They believe that any time children's emotions are challenged—even hate or selfish jealousy—the child is being disabled by having the teacher's reality imposed on her. Teachers are to empower children by affirming and "validating" any and all emotions they feel.
- *Intuition*—Intuition rises in importance because rational thought has lost its authority as a means for dealing with ideas. Modernists tend to suppress intuition and feelings, according to postmodernists, even though they are just as legitimate and perhaps even more important than rational, conceptual (or "linear") thought.

Values From the Biblical Worldview

Though there may be superficial similarities, at a deeper level, we find virtually no overlap between the postmodern view of values and the biblical view. Neither do we have much in common with modernist theories. Because we draw our values from an authority source which stands outside culture as absolute—God, as revealed in his Word—we cannot agree completely with either of our antagonists, even when we hold a particular moral view in common.

For instance, we believe in including all people in society, but not for the postmodernists' reasons. We include the weak and minorities because they are created in the image of God, not because we believe in a culture or class struggle. We share a number of the values inherent in democratic thinking—such as the belief in human freedom—but not because we are modernists. We receive our insight into human freedom—diminished though it is, by sin—from Scripture's teaching about human responsibility.

So how can Christians respond to the precipitous decline of values in our schools? Christian ethicists argue that Christians should engage the broader public, starting with appeals to "natural law"—the attributes of God, human nature, and God's ways that the Bible says are written on the hearts of all people.[28] Apart from such an objective base, prejudice and persecution are no longer necessarily wrong, nor is anything else. How pointless it is for postmodernists to beat the drum for tolerance apart from any moral basis for tolerance! A strong stand for natural moral laws based on the fact that people are created in the image of God is the only hope for equality for minority groups. And if Christians can win points in this way, we will retard further disintegration of society's concept of right and wrong.

Apart from objective, absolute truth, prejudice and persecution are no longer wrong. Nor is anything else.

God has seen fit in this age to allow sinful ideas and lifestyles to co-exist with his church in the same world.[29] Because of this, Christians should be careful not to impose biblical standards in ways that ignore this God-given freedom.[30] We need discernment for parents and their children, not censorship. (Again, ironically, postmodernists themselves are engaging in cultural censorship, as seen in the "United States History Standards," proposed as a basis for high school history education. These standards omit Thomas Edison and the Wright brothers altogether, while mentioning the 1848 Seneca Falls Convention on Women's Rights nine times.)[31]

Christians should also avoid mythical portrayals of America's past as though our country has been sinless. Our country may have been more free than most for more people than most, but it too must be judged based on the Word of God. Distorting history and denying truth are not paths to freedom in society. Unless culture stands under the judgment of God's absolutes, it becomes, as postmodernists claim, an absolute itself.

Finally, no amount of political wrangling will ever return the days when Christian values were the norm in public schools, because hundreds of thousands of teachers no longer agree with the Judeo-Christian values base. Even laws requiring proper values teaching would not be effective if the teachers don't personally embrace those values. Sadly, our best hope may be either school choice, where parents receive vouchers to use either in public or private schools, or failing that, a continuation of modernist values-neutral education. At least under the modernists the focus was on academic performance instead of racist and sexist social revolution.

The Nature of People

Modernism and Human Nature

Modernists generally believe in a stable, inherent self that can be objectively known. Though modernists view people as merely biological organisms, many still see people as rational and freely choosing individuals. This is one of the great contradictions in modernism. Other modernists, like behaviorists, see humans as essentially biologically or environmentally determined machines.[32]

In general, however, most modernist educators are optimistic humanists who think that we as individuals have inherent value and rights, such as the right to an education. They believe we are capable of bettering ourselves and our society. In addition, since humans are thought to have a stable, essential nature, teachers can employ IQ tests and other similar "objective tests" to discover the innate intelligence of a student. The modernists' belief in a stable self also leads them to conclude that students won't change beyond reasonable limits. It poses no difficulty for them to put students into educational "tracks" to help them fulfill their individual potentials within those limits.

For the modernist educator, students' self-esteem results from learning. Compared to postmodernism, though, self-esteem or self-concept isn't a primary concern, as we shall see. Rather, modernists focus on students acquiring knowledge and self-discipline. How a student feels about himself or herself is secondary. For most modernists, the first concern is whether students are acquiring mastery and competence. Students will feel good about themselves when they realize they have mastered their studies.

Since people have a "true" self, according to modernists, education helps individuals discover their identities. Through rational investigation and insight from helpers such as teachers, who are more knowledgeable about human nature (as known especially through psychology), students can find an objective understanding of who they are.

Finally, for the modernist, individuals and society progress by learning and applying objective knowledge. They think that, as they teach scientifically derived knowledge in the schools, people and society will improve because newfound knowledge makes us better able to act in accordance with what is true. Modernists believe education, more than anything else, is crucial to the progress of humanity.

Postmodernism and Human Nature

Postmodern educators believe a student's identity isn't determined by a "true self" or innate essence. It is, rather, a construct. Postmodernists generally assert that a person's self-concept is significantly impacted—if not determined—by the social group of which he or she is a part. Identity is a social construction. Also, since people live in a diverse society, the individual's socially constructed self is often thought to be fragmented.

For postmodern educators, an individual student's self-concept *is* that student's self. Since our reality is constructed in our minds, self-esteem isn't the *result* of reality but the *basis* of reality. Also, since educators have no basis for saying one construct is right and another wrong, they think it "unhelpful and inhibiting" to reject rather than to value a student's ideas. Particularly, educators should applaud the effort students expend in formulating these ideas. Failing to build up the student's self-esteem will result in negative consequences for the student and for society: "Hatred and prejudice are tools of the subconscious that ease the feeling of insecurity," David Aronson explains. This insecurity results from low self-esteem.[33] Aronson goes on to approvingly quote Schwallie-Giddis: "Those persons with high self-esteem have fewer inhibitions and can relate to and accept others far more easily than those who do not. By contrast, vengeful, intolerant behavior reflects poor self-esteem."[34] In this view, education becomes a type of therapy designed to alleviate the hate and conflict in society and bring about social harmony by increasing students' self-esteem.[35]

Because most of our social interactions involve language and because postmodernists believe language provides the basis for human thinking, language is of primary importance in constructing the self. In the context of multicultural education, one author shows the connection between the importance of language and self-esteem:

> To take the position that these [minority] children speak a substandard brand of English is a blatant imposition of school English as the only standard brand of English capable of use for learning, which is an untenable, ethnocentric position unsupported by linguistic research. The natural language research of Labov, Baratz, Garcia, has affirmed that all dialects and languages are capable of abstract reasoning, mathematical reasoning, and human communications. . . . Students have a right to their particular dialects, and teachers have a responsibility to use that language as a means to expand the students' perceptual, cognitive, and emotional development. The students' language, after all, is as intimate as their mother's love, and any educational practice that seeks to strip away this language is morally and humanly reprehensible. Yet all students have the right to expect the school to teach them mainstream English literacy.[36]

Others go further, openly declaring that the failure to use African-American language in schools as the primary teaching language is motivated by the desire to dominate and marginalize minorities:

> There is a real fear on the part of many European-Americans that, with these growing numbers of non-English-speaking peoples, the utility of English in American education will sharply decrease. Along with this decrease in utility will come a decrease in the political economic and social advantage of European-Americans over African-Americans, Hispanic-Americans and Asian-Americans.[37]

These aren't fringe views. They are views that may control education in the near future. In Columbus, Ohio, the public school system ran into terrible financial trouble in 1994. With an anticipated deficit of over $30 million for the year, the board engaged in real estate liquidations and a hiring freeze. Yet when the bare bones budget proposal came out, it included more than $3 million in new spending to launch an Afrocentric High School. In one metropolitan city after another, multicultural education is the battle cry for the wholesale introduction of postmodern ideology into public education.

Postmodern educators believe self-esteem is a *prerequisite* to learning. As mentioned above, they view education as therapy. "A Curriculum of Inclusion," once again, states that "educational oppression" has had a "terribly damaging effect on the psyche" of minority students and that this is the reason for any disappointing performance in school. This is a key issue in much Afrocentric education: If African-American students are taught in an environment that emphasizes and gives a positive portrayal of their African heritage, this will, postmodernists believe, increase their self-esteem and enable them to succeed academically. Unfortunately, their theory has never been proven. Some suspect that racism, not better performance, will result. Both reverse discrimination and resulting backlash against minorities are predictable.

Postmodern educators view self-esteem not as a by-product of learning, but a prerequisite. They view education as therapy.

As education helps individuals construct their identities, teachers must be careful not to impose their views and preferences on their students. Instead, they should respect and affirm the diversity of those identities groups choose for themselves. Postmodernists stress that educators should be aware of and work to minimize their own racism, sexism, classism, homophobia—problems which they believe all members of majority society have, and which can never be completely eradicated. Sociologist Becky Thompson, in a manual for race, class, and gender education distributed by the American Sociological Association, states:

> I begin the course with the basic feminist principle that in a racist, classist, and sexist society we all have swallowed oppressive ways of being, whether intentionally or not. Specifically, this means that it is not open to debate whether a white student is racist or a male student is sexist. He/she simply is.[38]

Educators should strive to avoid infecting their students with these harmful attitudes. Strangely, postmodern literature contains few warnings against racism and prejudice within minority groups, no doubt because these problems are seen as predominantly resident in dominant culture.

Some teaching materials are explicitly designed to assist teachers in affirming marginal lifestyles. The controversial Rainbow Curriculum was written for elementary school classrooms to affirm the gay and lesbian lifestyles. Although this curriculum was voted out in New York, the books involved, such as *Two Moms, Zark and Me*, and *Daddy's Roommate*, are commonly found in school libraries all over the country. We are not suggesting such books should be banned, although we would question their place in grade-school libraries. Our point is that the curriculum is still influential despite the New York vote. The alternative lifestyle movement is advancing unabated in American education under the heading of "diversity appreciation."

Better self-esteem, postmodernists argue, can only come when schools empower those who traditionally had very little power, that is, minorities and women. Efforts to advance empowerment of students is seen in a movement called "critical pedagogy." The goal of critical pedagogy is to empower those who have been pushed to the margins of society, who therefore have had little say about what ideas and practices count as legitimate and worthwhile. Critical educators work not to *remove* politics and ideology from education, but rather to make power relations more equal between the diverse groups in society. Their goal is to equalize the relationships in the education community so that oppressed people have the freedom and the power to overcome oppression and pursue lifestyles of their choosing.

A Biblical Evaluation of Self-Esteem

Postmodern educators hold that self-esteem not only affects educational performance but actually determines performance. Their claim that self-esteem involves unconditional positive self-regard, for example, contradicts the biblical view that humans, though valuable because they are created in God's image, are also sinful. Postmodernists routinely reject the concept of sin as antagonistic to self-esteem, even while chiding majority culture for marginalizing people, apparently a sin.

Research demonstrates a clear correlation between infancy nurture in intact families and later learning ability, which may suggest some relationship between self-esteem and academic capability. On the other hand, children also develop confidence as they gain mastery in performing important tasks, and this confidence helps them tackle new learning challenges in school. A healthy family life is the most important factor for academic performance, and yet this well-established fact gets little or no attention from postmodern determinists.[39]

Postmodern educators are so focused on the role of positive self-esteem as a necessary pre-condition for learning that their educational model becomes *therapeutic*. When self-esteem becomes the be-all and end-all of education, teachers are no longer in a position to insist on performance. Discipline is rejected as dangerous to children's self-esteem. During the past three decades—during which self-esteem has become the holy grail of much of American education—standard achievement test scores have plummeted 73 points, even though spending per student increased more than 200 percent during the same period![40]

Although the U.S. outspends other countries, and teacher-student ratios have steadily improved, academic performance ranks well below other developed countries.[41] Where is the evidence that this approach is accomplishing anything but the disablement of an entire generation of students?

If children can't be corrected for wrong answers because it damages their self-esteem, the only result will be incompetent students who feel good about their ignorance! One well-known study assessed students from many countries in two areas: their estimation of their mathematical competence, and their actual mathematical competence. Not surprisingly, American students ranked first in their assessment of their own competence but they ranked last in actual competence. Conversely, Korean students ranked last in their assessment of their own mathematical competence, but they were first in actual competence.[42] This isn't the kind of positive self-esteem that American educators should be encouraging, if we want to see our children lead meaningful and successful lives.

Conclusion

Postmodern education attempts to address some important issues, but is in general a wrong and even catastrophic direction in American education. The overthrow of truth, the denial of objective reality, the spread of radical constructivism, and the open legitimizing of propagandistic approaches to teaching are all menacing to every aspect of sound education. Unless the trend toward critical pedagogy and radical multicultural education is reversed, our country will continue to slide into a new "Dark Age" of ignorance, racism, and social fragmentation with terrifying possibilities. No one will pay for the errors of postmodernism more than minorities.

Christians should be careful not to align themselves with either modernist or postmodernist education, because neither is aligned with the cause of Christ. But to resist the postmodern denial of knowable truth, we may have to make common cause with modernists on this particular point. After all, Christians generally agree with modernists that transmission of objective knowledge is the centerpiece of education. In the end, only Christ and his Word can guide us as we consider how to educate our own children and redemptively influence public education.

> Ironically, no one is more menaced by multicultural education than minorities.

In Brief

- Postmodernism has appeared as a driving force in American education, often under the label of "Multicultural Education."
- Postmodern educators see knowledge as constructed in the mind of students. Therefore, teachers are not to transmit their own previously constructed knowledge, but are to facilitate students' creation of new knowledge.

- Efforts to teach kids to conform to established rules and practices in various disciplines, such as standard grammar in English or rules of research in social or natural sciences, is considered a form of cultural domination—an imposition of Western enlightenment culture onto minority groups.
- For postmodernists, the mission of education isn't to train students to move ahead in established society, but to empower them to fight for revolutionary social change.
- To respect knowledge created by students, educators should not tell them their conclusions are "wrong." Negating students inhibits the main prerequisite for learning—a good self-image.
- Since knowledge is a social construction, postmodernists favor culturally based schools, where communities can deal with knowledge that is meaningful to their reality.

Notes

1. Quoted in A. Schlesinger, Jr., *The Disuniting of America: Reflections on a Multicultural Society* (Whittle Direct Books, 1992), p. 33.
2. See the discussion of these concepts in Chapter 2.
3. See the discussion of two types of postmodernists in Chapter 4.
4. It is important to note that there are different types of constructivism; Davis and Mason (1989) contrast "simple" constructivism with "radical" constructivism. Both groups accept the idea that people have to take an active role in their learning, but a "radical constructivist goes further, denying that there is necessarily a 'true state of events' which the individuals' stories represent. Instead, people's stories *constitute* the world they inhabit" (p. 160). Radical constructivists are postmodern and therefore we will focus on them. We will use the term "constructivism" for sake of brevity.
5. Ruth Zuzovsky, "Conceptualizing a Teaching Experience on the Development of the Idea of Evolution: An Epistemological Approach to the Education of Science Teachers," *Journal of Research in Science Teaching*, Vol. 31(5) (1994): p. 558.
6. Ernst Von Glasersfeld, an influential radical constructivist, says, " 'to know' is not to possess 'true representations' of reality, but rather to possess ways

and means of acting and thinking that allow one to attain the goals one happens to have chosen." Ernst von Glasersfeld, "Knowing Without Metaphysics: Aspects of the Radical Constructivist Position," EDRS microfiche: ED 304 344, (1989), p. 5.

7. In C. Lankshear, and P. McLaren, *Cultural Literacy: Politics, Praxis, and the Postmodern* (New York: State University of New York, 1993), p. 195.
8. Michael Apple, *Official Knowledge: Democratic Education in a Conservative Age* (New York: Routledge, 1993), p. 195ff. This postmodern view of knowledge affects not just textbooks and classroom instruction but also educational research. Postmodern theory and practice are evident in what is known as *qualitative research.* Compared to modern *quantitative* research methods, the methodologies of this brand of research are much more intuitive, relativistic, and eclectic, including borrowing from the modernists when advantageous. See Glesne and Peshkin, *Becoming Qualitative Researchers: An Introduction* (White Plains, N.Y.: Longman Publishing Group, 1992).
9. Patti Lather, "Critical Frames in Educational Research: Feminist and Post-structural Perspectives," in *Theory Into Practice*, Vol. XXXI, Number 2 (Spring 1992): p. 92.
10. Christine E. Sleeter, ed., *Empowerment Through Multicultural Education* (Albany, N.Y.: State of New York Press, 1991), p. 51.
11. Ibid., pp. 20–21.
12. There is a critical tension (or lack of clarity) in constructivist learning theory between the role of the group and the role of the individual in constructing knowledge. On the one hand, the construction of knowledge is seen to be a social phenomenon; on the other, the individual must mentally construct knowledge inside his or her own mind, which can receive no clear objective inputs from the outside world. Therefore, the postmodern position in regards to radical individualism is ambivalent, though the postmodern theoretical positions tend to explicitly emphasize the role of the social.
13. See, for example, Grayson Wheatley, "Constructivist Perspectives on Science and Mathematics Learning," p. 12.
14. McCarthy (1987), for example, discusses how people learn in different ways. She discusses "concrete experience," "reflective observation," "abstract conceptualization," and "active experimentation" as different preferences for learning; as well as right/left brain processing (not that people *only* learn in one way; rather, people tend to be most comfortable or learn best with a certain method).

    Another important theory in this area is Howard Gardner's theory of multiple intelligences—namely, "musical," "body-kinesthetic," "logical-mathematical," "linguistic," "spatial," "interpersonal," and "intrapersonal" intelligences; these are in contrast to the general assumption of traditional education that there is only one preferable type of intelligence (often thought to be measured with an IQ test). See J. Walters and H. Gardner, "The Development and Education of Intelligences" in F. Link, ed., *Essays on the Intellect* (Alexandria, Virginia: ASCD, 1985), pp. 1–21, for an overview of this theory. Different types of intelligence is a theory not unique to postmodern education. Many modernists also accept the concept.

15. Everhard cited in Christine E. Sleeter, ed., *Empowerment Through Multicultural Education*, p. 52.
16. Judith Renyi, *Going Public: Schooling for a Diverse Democracy* (New York: The New York Press, 1993), p. 122. Likewise, Selase Williams, and many others, argue that AAL (African American Language) is a regular language like Spanish or Asian. He shows that statements like, "Shanita bin pass that tes," means "Shanita passed that test a long time ago." The difference, he argues, is that AAL arises from an African linguistic base. Therefore, inner-city kids should be taught in AAL as their mother tongue, with English as a second language. Selase W. Williams, "Classroom Use of African American Language: Educational Tool or Social Weapon?" in Christine E. Sleeter, ed., *Empowerment Through Multicultural Education*, pp. 205–207.
17. P. Davis and J. Mason, "Notes on a Radical Constructivist Epistemethodology Applied to Didactic Situations," p. 169.
18. Ernst von Glasersfeld, "Knowing Without Metaphysics," p. 137.
19. Rita Kramer, ed., *School Follies: The Miseducation of America's Teachers* (New York: The Free Press, 1991), pp. 29, 95–96, 139.
20. *Constructivism* provides much of the theoretical basis for postmodern multicultural education by providing an explanation as to why the knowledge and values of different cultures should be considered equal (that is, because they are all merely human constructions) and therefore why they should all be treated equally in the classroom.
21. They see power relations embodied mainly in "politics." The postmodern use of the term "politics" is often a very broad one that includes more than what professional politicians do. It frequently includes all relations that involve authority and regulatory principles, including the teacher-student relationship. For example, Stanley Fish says, "All educational decisions are political by their very nature." Dinesh D'Souza, *Illiberal Education: The Politics of Race and Sex on Campus* (New York: The Free Press, 1991), p. 176.
22. Portland Public Schools, *African-American Baseline Essays* (Portland, Oregon: Multnomah School District, 1987), p. SS–4. These essays have also been subsequently inspirational for school systems in Milwaukee, Indianapolis, Pittsburgh, Washington, D.C., Richmond, Atlanta, Philadelphia, Detroit, Baltimore, and others, according to Arthur M. Schlesinger, Jr., *The Disuniting of America*, p. 35.
23. Becky Thompson and Sangeeta Tyagi, eds., *Beyond a Dream Deferred: Multicultural Education and the Politics of Excellence* (Minneapolis: University of Minnesota Press, 1993), p. xx.
24. Lynn Cheney, *Telling the Truth: A Report on the State of the Humanities in Higher Education* (National Endowment for the Humanities, 1992), p. 41.
25. Educators have used theories like that of Kohlberg to attempt to aid in values formation in children. His is a fairly recent and influential modernist attempt to discover some rational structure in morality, as well as a conception of progress. Briefly, he said that humans progress through six stages of moral development starting with the "punishment-and-obedience orientation," where the physical consequences determine whether an action is good or bad, and ending with the "universal-ethical-principle orientation," where "right is

defined by the decision of conscience in accord with self-chosen ethical principles appealing to logical comprehensiveness, universality, and consistency." L. Kohlberg, "From Is to Ought," *The Journal of Philosophy* (October 25, 1973): pp. 164–165.

26. Lynn Cheney, *Telling the Truth: A Report on the State of the Humanities in Higher Education*, p. 7.
27. R. Pratte, ed., *Theory Into Practice: Multicultural Education* (Spring 1984) (Columbus, Ohio: College of Education, The Ohio State University, 1984), p. 88.
28. Biblical ethics are for Christians, not for non-Christians. We run into serious trouble when we attempt to impose the whole Bible's ethical system on society. For example, Christians are not permitted, according to biblical ethics, to worship anyone other than the God of the Bible. In the past, mistaken Christians have tried to prohibit other religions by law. Instead there are features of God's and humankind's character evident through general revelation (Romans 1:18–20; 2:14–16). These form the basis for natural law. See Norman Geisler, "A Premillennial View of Law and Government," *Biblioteca Sacra*, Vol. 142, No. 567 (July-September 1986). For differing views see Bruce Kaye, "The New Testament and Social Order," in Bruce Kaye and Gordon Wenham, eds., *Law, Morality and the Bible* (Downers Grove, Ill.: InterVarsity Press, 1978) and (our favorite), Richard N. Longenecker, *New Testament Social Ethics for Today* (Grand Rapids: Eerdmans Publishing Co., 1984), and Arthur F. Holmes, *Ethics: Approaching Moral Decisions* (Downers Grove, Ill.: InterVarsity Press, 1984).
29. Jesus' parable of the wheat and the tares in Matthew 13 indicates that it is not God's will in this age to separate the righteous from the wicked. They are both to "grow up together" in the same world. Paul argues against enforcing Christian morality on non-Christians in 1 Corinthians 5:12: "For what have I to do with judging outsiders? Do you not judge those who are within the church?"
30. See Arnold Burron and John Eidsmoe, *Christ in the Classroom* (Denver: Accent Books, 1987), pp. 54–83, for some creative and appropriate ways Christian teachers may expose their students to the biblical worldview.
31. John Elson, "History: the Sequel," *Time* (November 7, 1994): p. 64.
32. This is one important similarity between some strands of modernism and postmodernism; that is, both have a tendency to see humans as determined—biologically determined in modernism, socially determined in postmodernism.
33. David Aronson, "The Inside Story," *Teaching Tolerance* (Spring 1995) (Montgomery, Alabama: Southern Poverty Law Center), p. 26.
34. Ibid., p. 28.
35. Aronson claims that along with feeling that your life is important "comes the capacity to get along with others and the desire to conform to the rules of society." David Aronson, "The Inside Story," p. 29.
36. Ricardo Garcia, *Teaching in a Pluralistic Society* (New York: Harper & Row Publishers, 1982), p. 29.
37. Selase W. Williams, "Classroom Use of African-American Language: Educational Tool or Social Weapon?" in Christine E. Sleeter, ed., *Empowerment*

Through Multicultural Education, p. 202. Many postmodernists claim that we all have these types of prejudices and biases and that it's impossible to completely erradicate them.

38. Dinesh D'Souza, "Illiberal Education," *The Atlantic Monthly* (March 1991): p. 54.
39. In her longitudinal study of more than ten years, Mavis Heatherington found that children of divorce, who scored significantly lower on self-esteem inventories, also suffered lower functionality even years later in school. "These boys from divorced families in comparison to boys in nondivorced families showed more antisocial, acting out, coercive noncompliant behaviors in the home and in the school and exhibited difficulties in peer relations and school achievement." Mavis E. Heatherington, "Family Relations Six Years after Divorce," in Mavis E. Heatherington and Ross D. Parke, eds., *Contemporary Readings in Child Psychology, Third Edition* (New York: McGraw-Hill Book Company, 1988). It seems clear from this and many other studies that traumas that reduce security and self-esteem in children also reduce academic capability, although the cause-effect relationship is mainly a matter of speculation. However, the claim that postmodern techniques to increase self-esteem will enhance academic performance have never been proven.
40. The College Board and U.S. Department of Education, cited in William J. Bennett, *The Index of Leading Cultural Indicators: Facts and Figures of the State of American Society* (N.Y.: Touchstone, 1994), p. 82.
41. U. S. Department of Education, cited in William J. Bennett, *The Index of Leading Cultural Indicators*, p. 91.
42. A. LaPuente, N. A. Mead and G. Phelps, *A World of Difference: An International Assessment of Mathematics and Science* (Princeton, N.J.: Education Testing Service, 1989), p.10.

8

Postmodern Method: History

Tom Dixon, Contributor

Few events are as well-documented historically as the Holocaust. The twentieth-century slaughter of six million Jews by the Nazis left a churning wake of historical evidence, and the waves created by the dark ship's passing can still be felt fifty years later. We can still inspect the camps, the gas chambers, and warehouses full of documentation, and many who were directly involved in the gruesome events remain to tell of it. Such are the kind of sources and documentation historians dream of: a vast number of eyewitnesses whose accounts are in agreement, and a huge cache of virtually harmonious evidence. Historically speaking, it doesn't get any better than that.

In the past few years, however, thousands of people have bought into a remarkable suggestion that the Holocaust was a grand hoax. Most historians brush this theory aside as ridiculous, thinking that if the Holocaust isn't historically proven, probably nothing is. Surprisingly, though, the idea has established a firm

About the Contributor:

Tom Dixon is director of student outreach at Xenos Christian Fellowship. He holds a B.A. and M.A. in history from Ohio State University. Tom is known as an exciting lecturer and communicator through the numerous groups he leads in central Ohio.

foothold in the nation's universities and newsrooms, and a Gallup poll conducted in January 1994 showed that 33 percent of Americans think it possible that the Holocaust never happened.[1]

"Holocaust denial is only the most spectacular example of a broader assault on knowledge, facts, and memory that is sweeping through the culture," writes John Leo in *U.S. News and World Report*.[2] He lists several other unfounded ideas that have gained followings, such as the supposedly strong influence of Iroquois thought on the United States Constitution. Some people are convinced the truth about their own history has been deliberately hidden. An HBO-Pepsi poster promoting Black History Month features a picture of the pyramids and the words, "*We are the builders of the pyramids, look what you did . . . so much to tell the world, the truth no longer hid.*"

The Changing Face of Historical Research

The Holocaust did, unfortunately, occur. But increasingly among students of history and even in popular culture, the facts of history are becoming more flexible. They can be bent to accommodate almost any argument. One historian remarked that he preferred a cloud of "great vague ideas" to the dust of "true little facts."[3] History, long held to be an objective field of study like chemistry or physics, is now considered an ever-changing inquiry into subjective viewpoints of past cultures.

Scholars until now viewed "history" as the investigation into what *actually happened* in the past and why. Today's postmodern historians view history more as a study of people's images and thoughts about their society and their past. What actually happened is no longer the historian's primary concern, and in fact, can never be known. Instead, what matters is what people *thought* happened.

This notion is readily apparent in contemporary historical writing: "Societies will rethink and rewrite their history as it changes," writes one historian.[4] Think about that. History changes? Perhaps our studies periodically need revision as new data comes to light—but can we really say that history itself changes? If so, are we not witnessing the creation of a new definition of historical thought that can be twisted to serve almost any agenda?

Such a trend is frightening especially for Christians, whose faith is based on God's character of love and mercy as proven in his actions in history. God repeatedly reveals himself not primarily as the God of inner impressions or even as the God of nature, but as the God of history. "For the Lord our God is he who brought us and our fathers up out of the land of Egypt, from the house of bondage . . ." (Joshua 24:17), and "I am the God of your father, the God of Abraham, the God of Isaac, and the God of Jacob" (Exodus 3:6). Paul stresses that the historical resurrection is the linchpin of the Christian gospel, without which Christianity falls apart (1 Corinthians 15:17). No one has as much to lose from the postmodern approach to history as Bible-believing Christians.

No one has as much to lose from the postmodern approach to history as Bible-believing Christians.

How has history come to such an unstable predicament, in which "knowledge, facts, and memory" are no longer reliable? And how are Christians to defend their faith while standing on such shifting sands?

Historical Research in the Twentieth Century

At the end of the nineteenth century, historians were busily constructing "ultimate history" by compiling and explaining all available historical knowledge. Following the lead of Germans such as Ranke and Burkhardt, these historians sought to gather the facts of history simply to show "how it really was."[5] They sought to methodically locate, examine, and explain every fact of history and eventually construct the great story of humanity's existence on earth.

Although such a task was immense and tedious, historians of the period were optimistic that eventually the story and significance of human history would be clearly and finally laid out for all to see. As Lord Acton, editor of *The Cambridge Modern History*, remarked in 1896, "Ultimate history we cannot have in this generation; but . . . all information is within reach, and every problem has become capable of solution."[6] Such was the *positivist* view at the turn of the century: that all of humankind's problems could and would be solved, and that human history was an unfolding story of people's upward climb toward a glorious destiny.

Events in the first decades of the twentieth century shattered such a positive outlook. The First World War (ironically referred to as "the war to end all wars") and its even more destructive successor vividly displayed the shocking depths to which even modern, enlightened people could sink. The intellectual community lost confidence in human powers of reason and in former understandings of human destiny.

As twentieth-century historians sought to find meaning and purpose in history, they couldn't resort to an appeal to divine purpose or providence; nineteenth-century thinkers had already ejected the concept of God from Western intellectual circles. Neither could they now appeal to humankind's ability to advance positively, given their recent loss of confidence in human progress. As American historian Henry S. Commager remarked,

> In a general way it could be said that the two generations after 1890 witnessed a transition from certainty to uncertainty, from faith to doubt, from security to insecurity, from seeming order to ostentatious disorder. By the 1950s Americans had all but banished God from their affairs. Who or what would they put in his place?[7]

In modern thought, and now in postmodern thought, people have tried to fill this void with forces greater than themselves that act in nature and society and govern the course of human history.

The First Pillar: Marxism

Amid the rubble of the Second World War, two great pillars were erected upon which current historical thought rests.[8] The first of these pillars was Marxism. Although most in the West deemed Marxist thought an evil and cancerous political ideology, on university campuses Marxism as a philosophical system found more fertile ground. Historians and others in the humanities and social sciences yearned for a controlling force by which human history and behavior were guided and could thus be understood. Marxism today may be failing as a governmental system, but its ideology of economic determinism and social class struggle have as much influence as ever at our colleges and universities.

During the cold war years, Marxist historians began to chisel away both at the traditional subjects of historical inquiry and at the modernists' basis for historical knowledge. Traditionally, historians had focused on political events and powerful individuals as the main flow of history. Marxist historians identified this focus as nothing more than the study of the bourgeoisie. They claimed that by studying only the important acts of the bourgeois—the dominant, ruling class—bourgeois historians and their social class sought to control society and thought.

In light of this critique, many historians began promoting an interest in "history from below"—the study of the oppressed proletariat, locked in silence throughout all of history by the powerful few who held control of society, education, and consequently the history books. Marxist-influenced scholars began to turn history's attention from the notable figures of the past to the common, largely unheard community. Instead of always studying what had been seen as crucial events, they searched for deeper, enduring forces that shaped the course of both individuals and events in a given society. In the tradition of Marx, they saw these underlying forces as mostly economic in nature.[9]

Most importantly, Marxist historians in the mid-twentieth century began to undermine the foundations of accepted historical knowledge. The most weighty chunk they dislodged was the concept of *historical fact*. While positivist historians of the nineteenth-century revered facts for their perceived objectivity, Marxist-influenced historians began to question the usefulness and reliability of such facts.

How could this be? It began with a realization that historians are awash in facts, but they include only a few of those facts when they write their history books. By including only certain facts in his writing, a historian designates those particular facts as significant. For instance, George Washington may have crossed the Delaware, but why is his crossing any more significant than the stories of thousands of other people who also crossed that river? What makes one historical fact more important than another? According to Marxist-influenced historians, it is the mind of the historian that makes some events more important than others. And in turn, the mind of the historian reflects the values of his or her own culture.

Marxists and others have demonstrated that selecting what goes into the history books is the first act of interpretation. That point isn't in dispute. Evangelicals, for example, have complained at times that some treatments of the anti-slavery movement have excluded the leading role Christians played in ending slavery. But Marxist historians went further. They argued that all historians *arbitrarily* assign historical significance as they give voice to some facts but ignore others. As British historian E. H. Carr wrote, "The belief in a hard core of historical facts existing objectively and independently of the interpretation of the historian is a preposterous fallacy."[10] Nineteenth-century historians considered facts to be the firm stones upon which the historian's foot might confidently tread to conquer the river of history. But Marxist historians viewed facts as fish: "The historian collects them, takes them home, and cooks and serves them in whatever style appeals to him."[11]

Professor Michael Oakeshott comments, "History is the historian's experience. It is made by nobody save the historian: to write history is the only way of making it."[12] Thus, under the influence of Marxist thought, the historian came to be regarded more as the *creator* of history than its student. The historian controls the facts, selects them, arranges them, and can make them say almost whatever he wants. We see again, as in previous chapters, constructivism. This time history is the construction, or "story" created in the minds of historians.

The Second Pillar: The *Annales*

The second great pillar of historical thought in the twentieth century is the *Annales* (pronounced *än-áll*) school of historians. The *Annales* school revolved around a French historical journal founded by Marc Bloch and Lucien Febvre entitled *Annales d'histoire economique et sociale.* This journal gained prominence primarily in the years between the first and second world wars. The *Annales* school took the study of history one step past the Marxists. They sought to discover and expose the larger forces that act in human history by looking more at the underlying rules that govern social practices than at fleeting events or mere actions of individuals, or even the history of the underclass. *Annales* historians believed that particular events are caused by larger currents in the flow of history, and that these hidden currents should interest the historian more than passing events. Events, or so-called *historical facts*, are of only secondary interest to this school.

The *Annales* approach differed sharply from traditional historical research. Historians—even Marxist historians—had usually centered their study on historical events and the causes of those events. They looked for the causes of events in one era by studying earlier events, suggesting a linear chain of cause and effect. The *Annales* historians, however, displayed little interest in the linear movement of human history through time. Instead, they focused on determining the relationship between the part and the whole of society. They sought to examine how given parts of society function in relation to the larger "social organism."

Put more simply, *Annales* historians viewed history as not necessarily moving in any certain direction, but as characterized more by the continual interaction of different ideas, natural forces, and human caprice. This led them to draw attention to topics previously considered outside the scope of history. Members of the *Annales* school utilized research tools and methods of other social sciences such as economics, psychology, and anthropology when conducting research. By doing so, they, like their Marxist counterparts, sought to establish "total history," a broader study of the various constituents of societies.

The Postmodern Fusion: Social and Cultural History

Thirty years after the Second World War, the ideological forces of Marxism and the *Annales* school had converged and formed what we now know as "social history." By the late 1970s, history departments across the nation and Europe that had long focused solely upon political and church history had fragmented into a plethora of interests. Major schools began to offer black history, urban history, labor history, the history of women, criminality, sexuality, the oppressed, the inarticulate, and so on. Entire new departments were founded for Black Studies, Women's Studies, Hispanic Studies, and more. Much of what these departments taught was in the category that had been known as history.

This new approach to history embraced findings from the social sciences. Examples include works like Erik Erikson's *Young Man Luther*, a psychological study of the sixteenth-century reformer, in which Erikson argued that Luther's religious impulses stemmed from his father's harsh treatment of him as a boy.[13]

Studies of women and their roles in past societies flourished. These studies often argued that the key to understanding history is to realize that women have been victims of enduring patriarchal regimes. The struggle between women and their male oppressors is analogous to the struggle between the proletariat and the bourgeoisie in Marxism. Christian readers can find much truth in these studies, even if in the end we reach conclusions different from those of feminist scholars. The important point for us to note is that feminist and other brands of social historical studies constitute a completely new way to approach the study of history.

Social history, with its emphasis on the more common aspects of human experience through the ages, has been described as "history from below." Instead of studying military campaigns or the lives of great political leaders, social historians examine things like marriage, working conditions, and social organizations. Between 1958 and 1978, the number of doctoral degrees in social history quadrupled and surpassed the number of dissertations written in political history, and studies on these common areas of life increasingly appeared in historical journals.[14]

Social historians are often driven by activist goals. As historian Lee Benson puts it, the primary goal of social history "should be to develop credible, empirical theories about human behavior highly useful to human beings struggling to create a better world."[15] Historical research becomes not an attempt to understand the past but a propaganda tool for use in modern political and social power struggles.

As social historians sought to discover the history of the voiceless masses, they faced a fairly obvious problem: How do we listen to the silenced masses? How can we learn the story of segments of society that left no biographies, no chronicles, no written data? Social historians claim that although such peoples kept no official history, they left tracks that can be detected in their cultural practices and forms. The study of these forms and practices, *cultural history*, consists mostly of studying symbolic behavior among the inarticulate—that is, these illiterate or voiceless people.

In recent years, studies of intellectual and cultural history have overtaken those done in economic and social history.[16] This shift from social history to cultural history has come as a younger generation of historians has reacted against strictly Marxist models. More importantly, the influence of postmodern literary theories has drawn historians' attention away from economic and social matters toward an increasing interest in language as the primary element of social reality.

Ironically, though historians earlier claimed they were seeking to discover the *people* behind the cultural forms and practices of past societies, postmodern historians assert that the cultural forms and practices themselves are the real reason for the existence of their studies. In other words, language and cultural symbols have come to the forefront of historical investigation because postmodern scholars believe that language not only describes but also *shapes* and *creates* reality. Put simply, postmodern historians contend that if there were no symbolic communication there would be no consciousness, no meaning, *no reality*.

Social history had relied on certain universal concepts such as the state, religion, and family to understand societies. Today, postmodern cultural historians like Michel Foucault claim that such institutions are constantly changing, thanks to the fluctuations of language as it shapes a given society's perception of reality. Cultural historians, like postmodern literary critics, tend to view language not as a *reflection* of the world it describes in words, but as *creating* that world. To them, history is simply a subsystem of linguistic signs. The goal of cultural history, therefore, is to decipher meaning rather than to determine causal laws that explain historical events. The following chart summarizes the differences between traditional and postmodern views of history.

Area of historical research	Traditional View	Postmodern View
Usefulness of texts	Texts are the primary tools for discovering what happened in literate societies. While texts can never be taken at face value, by correlating texts (comparing texts on the same event to each other) and assessing the likely bias of authors, we can piece together a relatively reliable picture of what happened and how people felt about it.	Texts never tell us what happened; they only describe the perceptions of their authors. Those perceptions, even if reported faithfully, are not "objectively true" but are the truth as perceived by that person through the bias of his language and culture. Historical texts are interesting for discovering not what happened but how people's view of the world was skewed by their culture. (See chapter 6 on literature.)
Determining which events are important	By gleaning from correlated texts and other sources, we can determine at least the broad outline of what happened during periods of written history. By examining this sequence of events, we discern that certain key people and events had relatively greater impact from the standpoint of cause and effect. These are important issues—issues that must be covered in any complete telling of history. Luther's 95 Theses, for instance, are counted as important because they led to the Reformation.	"Importance" is never knowable, as though it exists "out there" apart from knowers. A thing is always important to some people and not to others. Historians see some things as important and others as unimportant only because they read their cultural bias into the "text" of history. What historians think is important and unimportant tells us nothing about their importance at the time. It only tells us about historians' worldview and cultural values. What they exclude as unimportant, like the daily lives of poor people, are only unimportant to modernist historians.
Writing history surveys	A history survey should have broad coverage of all segments of the society and time under consideration. Historians should give special attention to key events, people, and trends that led to significant change. Different views and groups at the time should all be explained as possible.	Contemporary historians have a responsibility to correct some of the wrongdoings of their profession, particularly the fact that they have excluded entire populations from the telling of history. These silenced ones should now have their chance to speak through a special focus on the voice of the excluded groups in society. Historians should no longer serve the interests of the power elite in today's society by interpreting history as though only people like them—politically powerful, rich, white, and male—matter.

Readers interested in cultural history will quickly find that these changes bring with them a nearly incomprehensible nomenclature. Obscure terms such as "conjuncture," "structure," "deconstruction," and "mentalities" make historical studies increasingly inaccessible to non-experts. Yet some of the basic ideas behind cultural history are easier to understand.

First, as we saw earlier with literary analysis, most postmodern historical studies contain a pungent strain of determinism. Postmodern historians see culture and environment inevitably shaping all aspects of individuals, thus minimizing individuality and freedom. As French historian Francois Furet remarks, "[people] simply express the rules of [society's] operation and reproduction without knowing that they do so, and enjoying no other freedom than the possibility of entertaining the illusion of freedom."[17]

Second, scholars and students are setting aside the linear model of historical thinking. Because of cultural history's influence, topical, comparative studies are in vogue. University catalogues from across the nation list courses, for example, on women in various cultures and periods, radical religious movements in history, attitudes toward homosexuality through the ages, and other culturally relevant topics. Departments emphasizing Western history are increasingly deemed ethnocentric because they threaten to foster animosity between cultures with different ideas and values than our own. Today's history students spend much more of their time learning to understand and appreciate the similarities and differences between cultures in various ages and geographical areas.[18]

History, a Social Construction?

Finally, postmodern historians regard history as the product of personal interpretation, a reflection of the historian's worldview—and ultimately, then, as a social construction.

When ancient peoples looked into the night sky, they saw thousands of brilliant stars and decided that a certain group of these points of light commemorated the mythical figure of Orion. Thousands of years later, when we look at that same group of stars many of us find it difficult to see how they got Orion out of it. We may conclude the grouping looks more like a bale of hay. The stars, of course, are in the exact same arrangement they were when the

Mesopotamians or Greeks gazed at them, but they were never actually placed where they are in the sky in order to outline the figure of Orion. That meaning was assigned to them by ancient observers. We see the same stars, but might see different lines drawn between them.

The same might be said of human history. We can gaze upon an almost infinite collection of historical facts and figures through documents, artwork, and architecture. We can see that the People's Republic of China was established in 1949 (not 1923) as communist forces crushed Nationalist (not Nazi) resistance and declared Peking (not Shanghai) the new capital. These are the "stars" of history. They do not change.[19] They are the same for all who look at them, regardless of the culture in which one grew up, regardless of social class, race, or nationality.

But when it comes to drawing lines between those stars, that is, when we begin assigning patterns and causal ties between the facts of history, we move beyond merely collecting data. At this point, historians become interpreters. They cannot help but look for meaning, lessons, and even laws of life. Such laws and lessons can only be discovered as we place over the facts of history the template of our worldview—a certain set of presuppositions about things such as human nature, God, truth, and reason. These beliefs allow us to interpret the facts of history.

Postmodern scholars point out that each person has her own worldview, her own beliefs and convictions. Therefore, which lines we draw between the facts of history and the resulting picture we develop is ultimately dependent on individual judgment. John Lankford, a historian at Kansas State University says, "The task of the historian is not to discover ultimate truth, but rather to construct a convincing explanation of selected human behavior."[20] In an atheistic universe, it's easy to see how postmodernists arrive at their view of history. Based on their beginning presuppositions, their conclusions are understandable, even though exaggerated.

Evaluating the Postmodern Approach to History

Historians may not always be objective as they survey the data of history, but they *are* aware of the need to keep their biases in check. Moreover, other historians and readers of history can test their findings by studying how they used their sources. These things, taken together, mean we *can* settle many objective facts about human history. Yet even if we accept this conclusion, a question remains: Which facts are more significant than others? This is the question that pesters today's historian. As Furet has stated, "The uncontrollable expansion of what is regarded as the 'historical' field threatens to increase the quotient of insignificance."[21] In other words, when everything is viewed as important, before long nothing is important. Through the scientific research methods developed in the nineteenth century, we are able to locate a myriad of facts and figures about our past. But such scientific methods cannot assign value or meaning to those facts. What makes one fact more meaningful and more worthy of attention than another?

Postmodern historians argue that no fact of history is truly, objectively meaningful but that the choice and attention of the individual reader *bestows* meaning upon a certain event or idea in history. This view contains clear dangers. If facts are essentially meaningless, if they are no more than valueless data, could there not be a growing willingness to tinker with those facts?

This question has already been answered. The chapter on education mentioned cases of tampering with history for the sake of political activism. The recently completed *New York Curriculum Guide* for eleventh grade American history alters history just as clearly. This guide instructs teachers to inform students of the three ideological foundations for the American Constitution:

> Postmodern thinkers tamper with history for the sake of political activism.

1. The Americans' antecedent colonial experience
2. The European Enlightenment
3. The Haudenosaunee political system of the Iroquois tribe.

Although there is no substantive historical evidence that the Haudenosaunee political system influenced the framers of the Constitution, it alone receives elaboration in the *New York Curriculum Guide*. This may be because New York has a powerful Iroquois lobby.[22]

At the least, postmodernists differ from earlier historians in how they view subjectivity in historical interpretation. In earlier times, historians acknowledged and resisted personal bias as antithetical to good historical research. Now, postmodern cultural historians consider bias unavoidable in whole or even in part. As a result we see a growing willingness to arrange and edit facts in a way that supports the message of particular historians.

Thus we find an increasing willingness to value opinion and conviction more than facts and even to change the facts themselves, as in the argument that Iroquois thinking is behind the Constitution: "What we are witnessing is the transformation of facts into opinion," wrote the editors of the *New Criterion*.[23] "We're in a day and age in which I can make any claim I want," says professor Deborah Lipstadt. "I say that it's my opinion and I have a right to it, and you're supposed to back off."[24]

Note the extraordinary example of Professor Leanard Jeffries, head of Afro-American Studies at New York's City College, who declares that blacks are the "sun people" while whites are the "ice people." He teaches that all that is warm, communal, and full of hope in history and society has been brought by the sun people, while everything oppressive, cold, and rigid issues from the ice people.[25]

Professor Mary Lefkowitz informed a scholarly conference recently that some Afrocentric scholars accused Aristotle of "stealing the ideas for which he is best known from the library of Alexandria." She pointed out, however, that the library wasn't built until after Aristotle's death! The same conference heard reports about the findings of UCLA archeologist Mrija Gimbutas that "stone age Europe was the site of a harmonious, peaceful, egalitarian society that worshiped 'The Great Goddess.' " This civilization was purportedly destroyed between 4000 and 3500 B.C. by "violent, male-god worshiping, Indo-European invaders on horseback."[26]

The relativism of cultural history threatens to lead to nihilism and disinterest in the meaning of history. Stoianovich, speaking from the postmodern perspective, argues that

> Relativism need not terminate in nihilism . . . so long as societies continue to react to "the imagined happenings of the past," even if for no other reason than to try to determine what is useful, beautiful, or good in their own imagined experience—to profit from the exemplar function of history.[27]

As hard as this postmodern historian tries, he fails to paint an optimistic picture of the historical profession. Using words like "beautiful" and "good," he presents a picture of hopelessness and isolation—that all human experience is really subjective or imagined, and that we are each alone in our self-conscious world. Despite Stoianovich's claims to the contrary, the final result of postmodern historical analysis remains unchanged: nihilism—a world where nothing matters.

In Brief

- Postmodern historians have rejected the positivist school, which believed in an objective collection of historical "facts." Earlier, supposed facts were really the selective interpretations of the powerful elite of society.
- Postmodern "cultural" and "social" historians now seek to rediscover "history from below"—that is, history from the perspective of the voiceless masses who were ignored in earlier historical research that favored the elite.
- The resulting devaluation of the facts of history opens the door to the reckless manipulation of history.

Notes

1. *The Gallup Poll Monthly*, Princeton, N.J. (January 1994) #340, p. 26. Survey conducted January 15–17, 1994. Quoted in John Leo, "The Junking of History," *U.S. News and World Report* (February 28, 1994), p. 17.
2. John Leo, "The Junking of History," *U.S. News and World Report* (February 28, 1994): p. 17.
3. Michel Foucault, "La Poussiere et le Nuage," in Perrot, ed., *L'Impossible Prison*, p. 29.
4. Traian Stoianovich, *French Historical Method: The Annales Paradigm* (Ithaca, N.Y.: Cornell University Press, 1976), p. 35.
5. "*Wie es eigentlich gewesen*" in Ranke's oft-quoted words.

6. *The Cambridge Modern History: Its Origin, Authorship and Production* (Cambridge: Cambridge University Press, 1907), p. 12.
7. See conversation with Bill Moyers in *A World of Ideas* (New York: 1989), p. 233.
8. For more see introduction in Lynn Hunt, ed., *The New Cultural History* (Berkeley: Berkeley Press, 1989).
9. George Rude's studies of the Parisian crowd and E. P. Thompson's work on the English working class were efforts exemplary of the Marxist spirit during the 1950s and 60s. George Rude, *The Crowd in the French Revolution* (Oxford: Oxford University Press, 1959); E. P. Thompson, *The Making of the English Working Class* (New York: Pantheon Books, 1963).
10. E. H. Carr, *What Is History?* (New York: Random House, 1961), p. 10.
11. Ibid., p. 6.
12. Michael Oakeshott, *Experience and Its Modes* (Cambridge: Cambridge University Press, 1933), p. 99.
13. Erik H. Erikson, *Young Man Luther: A Study in Psychoanalysis and History* (New York: W. W. Norton & Company, 1958).
14. See Robert Darnton, "Intellectual and Cultural History," Michael Kammen, ed., *The Past Before Us: Contemporary Historical Writing in the United States* (Ithaca, N.Y., 1980), p. 334.
15. Lee Benson, "Changing Social Science to Change the World," *Social Science History*, Vol. 2, #4 (1978): pp. 427–441.
16. Darnton, "Intellectual and Cultural History," p. 334.
17. Francois Furet, "Beyond the Annales," *Journal of Modern History*, 55 (1983): p. 405.
18. The comparative cultural historical courses may not be immediately evident when looking at course catalogues because cultural history is increasingly being handled in entire departments set up for that purpose. For instance, Women's Studies, Black Studies, Hispanic Studies, and Hebrew Studies are all special cultural departments at Ohio State University. The courses in these departments are largely made up of cultural history. Also, note the recent appearance of Comparative Studies classes and Departments in Humanities, offering such courses as "Myth and Ritual" and "Themes in World Folklore." *The Ohio State University Graduate Courses Bulletin*, 1991 (Columbus, Ohio: The Ohio State University, 1991).
19. One might argue that such facts can and do change as research continues and new data comes to light. But facts such as these are *rarely* the subject of revision. Revisions usually concern interpretation and our understanding of those facts, not the facts themselves.
20. Cited in Robert L. Park, "The Danger of Voodoo Science," *The New York Times* (Sunday, July 9, 1995), "OP-ED."
21. Furet, "Beyond the Annales," p. 405.
22. Cited in Arthur M. Schlesinger, Jr., *The Disuniting of America*, p. 54.
23. Hilton Kramer, ed., *New Criterion* (New York: Samuel Lipman) (September 1993), Vol. 12, #1: p. 2.
24. Quoted in John Leo, *U.S. News & World Report*, p. 17. See also Deborah E.

Lipstadt, *Denying the Holocaust: The Growing Assault on Truth and Memory* (New York: Free Press, 1993).

25. *Time* (August 26, 1991): p. 19.
26. Both reports given at "The Flight from Science and Reason" conference at the University of Virginia. Reported in *The Wall Street Journal* (Monday, July 10, 1995): p. 1.
27. Traian Stoianovich, *French Historical Method*, p. 35.

9

BEING OF MANY MINDS: THE POSTMODERN IMPACT ON PSYCHOTHERAPY

JIM FIDELIBUS, PH.D., CONTRIBUTOR

- Joseph, a successful thirty-year-old corporate executive who is "into" New Age spirituality, struggles with jealousies in a conflictual relationship with his male lover.
- Phyllis, a single mother and devout Jehovah's Witness, cannot control her seventeen-year-old son, who experiences violent outbursts and recently attacked her physically.
- Warren, a popular middle-age college professor and a professed atheist, regularly awakens on his living-room floor in a pool of urine following the nightly drinking episodes that leave him unconscious.
- Marla, a born-again Christian, questions whether she should

About the Contributor:
Jim Fidelibus, Ph.D., is a Christian psychologist who serves as Director of Research and Program Development at Interact Behavioral Healthcare, Inc. in Columbus, Ohio. His varied field experience in counseling and related fields extends over twenty years at several institutions. His background in philosophy, theology, and counseling psychology, as well as psychological research qualifies him to speak with authority on the new trends in psychotherapy today.

leave her alcoholic husband after years of enduring emotional and physical abuse from him.

These examples are just a glimpse at the caseload a general-practice psychologist or psychotherapist might face. The muddle of problems and life issues reaches even beyond the patients themselves: Each patient carries a set of assumptions about life, morality, and relationships. Each set of assumptions is supported by a particular cultural context. And each set of assumptions is, to some extent, incompatible with the others. New Age consciousness, evangelical Christianity, and secular atheism aren't easily reconciled. They could be viewed, in a sense, as separate "realities." Yet each of these patients seeks help from the same professional.

Therapists, in attempting to be helpful, learn to understand and assist patients within the assumptions of each of these realities. To some extent, a therapist's professional livelihood depends on an ability to switch channels from one patient's reality to another as a typical workday unfolds. Operating within these diverse worldviews—and regarding each as valid within its own frame of reference—is all within a day's work for today's therapist. As a way of adjusting, many therapists adopt what we could call a "many minds" point of view.

> In postmodern client-centered therapies, reality is in the mind of the beholder.

To be of *many minds* means to make room within oneself for diverse ways of thinking, in an effort to relate to each. It means to regard truth as plural and relative rather than singular and absolute. It's saying that what is true for me in my cultural context may not be true for you in yours. To be of *many minds* is to regard each individual's "reality" as valid within its own context, deserving equal affirmation with all other "realities."

This being of *many minds* is by no means an experience limited to the practitioners of psychotherapy. As individuals within a diverse culture, we find that openmindedness and hospitality call on us for an increasingly new way of thinking. Gay love, radical feminism, political correctness, traditional morality, and the biblical worldview do not blend together easily. And so, as a way of coping, we also become of *many minds*, that is, we develop separate compartments in our thinking which can be switched on-and-off as the situation requires. These compartments can be called "paradigms," "frames-of-reference," or "schemata." Psychologist Kenneth Gergen calls the resulting new outlook "multiphrenia."[1]

Coping With Diversity

Think about a time you made personal contact with someone very different from yourself. The difference might have been their mannerisms or way of dressing, their lifestyle or sexual orientation, their religious or political affiliation. At the start you may have sensed a certain discomfort, perhaps an inner resistance, however subtle. Perhaps as circumstances required continued contact, however, you got to know the person and developed an increasing sense of connection and empathy. Despite the fact that this person held values, beliefs, or customs unlike your own, your newfound empathy led you to accept them. What was initially alienating is now okay. You made room inside yourself for something new.

Now multiply that experience five, ten, twenty times over. This is the experience not only of the psychotherapist, but of all of us as we face the world as students, workers, consumers of entertainment, even as churchgoers. As communication and transportation have improved, as immigration has increased, and as a once-strong consensus of thinking has broken down, we brush up against people and ideas of incredible diversity. We necessarily hear within ourselves a need to incorporate points of view not only different from our own, but different—perhaps radically—from each other. We, like the psychotherapist, come to be of many minds.

Being of many minds is the postmodern mind-set. Postmodernism is made for contemporary times. By radically relativizing the concept of truth, it argues for the presence of multiple culturally determined realities, all of equal validity.

In a society composed of diverse and often incompatible worldviews, postmodernism claims it won't discard or marginalize anyone. As people are converted from their fears and resistance to this new way of thinking—often by psychotherapists—they may feel a freedom to explore new experiences. What was once alienating now becomes intriguing. What was once merely tolerable now may be enthusiastically endorsed. There can be, of course, much good in this. But there is also a price.

This price can easily become exorbitant. Postmodernism creates a worldview which is ultimately untenable and unlivable. From a psychological perspective, postmodernism, when lived-out consistently, fragments the individual's personal identity and promotes isolation. We must attempt to ease the tensions between hospitality amid diversity on one hand and a vigorous concept of truth on the other. There is a better way, I believe, than the fragmentation created by postmodernism. But before we consider the biblical answer, let's first understand the essentials of postmodernism and how they apply to our understanding of psychology and psychotherapy.

Essential Postmodernism

To put it succinctly, postmodernism is what we could call a "culturally determined linguistic constructivism." To appreciate what this mouthful means, let's consider each of the terms.

"Constructivism" is the theory that the mind doesn't passively take in reality, but actively "constructs" reality in its process of understanding. Sensations—hearing, seeing, touching, tasting, or smelling—aren't simply received, but actively used to put together meaningful patterns and relationships, paradigms, or constructs. We don't know things as they are in themselves. We only know them as what we "construct" from our sensations in the act of understanding them.

"Linguistic" constructivism implies that this assembly process is determined by language. As explained in Chapter 3, postmodernists believe that the rules of syntax we use to put words together determine the way in which we *construct* and therefore understand reality. They point out that the use of language, including the rules of syntax, are "culturally determined"—a consensus of the people of a society. As a consequence, our way of understanding reality is culturally determined too.

To help illustrate this, consider an experiment conducted at the University of Oregon in which students were asked to assess facial expression. Two groups of students were shown an identical picture of "Kurt Walden." To one group, he was described as a Nazi who conducted barbaric medical experiments on concentration camp inmates. To a second group, he was described as a leader in the anti-Nazi underground responsible for saving the lives of thousands of Jews. The first group assessed the picture as depicting a cruel and sneering expression, whereas the second group assessed the same picture as depicting an expression of warmth and kindness. In other words, identical sensory information—the picture—was used to *construct* vastly different perceptions based on what the students were told.[2]

Many psychological experiments support the influence of culture and language on our perception of reality. They can be found in any standard textbook of social psychology that describes social thinking. It's important to understand, however, that postmodernism goes well beyond the idea of cultural influence on perception. In its purer forms, postmodernism promotes the idea that language *not only influences perception but creates it*. For all intents and purposes, since culture creates language, and language is our only means to perceive reality, culture creates reality.

The Politics of Therapy

The postmodern idea that culture creates reality through the conventions of language means that mental health and mental illness are unreal apart from culture: What one culture regards as sick, another may regard as healthy. For the postmodernist, there is no culturally neutral standard of mental health or illness that applies objectively across cultures.

> For postmodernists, there is nothing "wrong" with homosexuality except an arbitrary cultural prejudice against it.

According to this way of thinking, there is nothing "wrong," say, with homosexuality, other than an arbitrary cultural prejudice against it. By the same way of thinking, there is nothing "right" about monogamy apart from the conventions imbedded within the culture. The language we use when we call something "right" or "wrong" merely reflects cultural convention or prejudice, not a statement of absolute truth.

A postmodern view of psychotherapy emphasizes the need to

understand the patient in the context of culture. The politically correct therapist chooses language carefully. What is right or wrong, true or untrue, isn't for the therapist to decide. Rather, the therapist must operate within the cultural experience of the patient. The only "right" position is that all experiences—all realities—are valid.

But is it really possible for a therapist to remain neutral and switch from one value system to another like some sort of cultural chameleon? Skeptical postmodernists deny this possibility. According to them the very terms "therapist" and "patient" are culture laden. Using this kind of helping-profession language suggests that the "therapist" is in a privileged position with respect to the "patient." The therapist, of course, seeks to understand the patient in the light of the patient's cultural surroundings. But the therapist can never take the *me* out of counseling. The therapist, for example, may understand a patient to be "depressed," or a family to be "enmeshed." But where do these definitions come from? Not from the patient, but from the therapist. Therefore, some radical theorists draw the conclusion that therapy is exploitive: the imposition of one culture—the therapist's—upon another—the client's.[3] While this conclusion seems extreme, postmodern ideas unavoidably lead to such conclusions when applied consistently.

Postmodern Characteristics of Family Therapy

Family therapy has been influenced by postmodern speculation. The beginnings of family therapy can be traced to the mid–1950s with the publication of Bateson's ground-breaking article "Toward a Theory of Schizophrenia." In this article, he proposed that schizophrenia results from an inability to discriminate "Logical Types," a concept borrowed from the philosophy of Bertrand Russell. More importantly for this discussion, he claimed that this inability results from "double-binds" in family communication.[4]

For example, suppose a parent commands, "Be spontaneous!" To obey this command is by definition not to obey it. Behavior can't be a response to a command if it is to be truly spontaneous. Any attempt to obey the command to be spontaneous, therefore, is a violation of the command—a double-bind—since planned and spontaneous behavior are mutually exclusive. According to Bateson's theory, repeated exposure to this kind of communication from childhood onward interferes with a child's ability to discriminate messages and respond appropriately.

Within the "culture" of a given family, more subtle patterns of communication develop than commands such as "be spontaneous." While words may be used, the language in a family can often be nonverbal. A hurt look might stand for the message, "You're supposed to love me." But to love you out of obligation isn't heartfelt love. A frown might be saying, "Think for yourself." But to comply with your demand that I think for myself is to do what *you* think I should do.

A posture of helplessness might mean, "Tell me what to do." But to follow your instruction and tell you what to do means I am actually doing what *you* tell *me*. All of these communications are double-binds. Each is also inextricably bound-up with the reality created by the family culture in its use of language. A number of principles common to most forms of family therapy have been derived from the "double-bind" hypothesis:

- Communication and language patterns are bound with the structure of power within the family system.
- Pathology doesn't reside within the "identified patient," but within the interactional patterns of the family.
- The "identified patient" isn't any more sick than any other family member; he or she merely bears the symptoms of dysfunctional family communication patterns.
- Symptoms are a form of language (that is, they are metaphors).

In each of these assumptions, the centrality of language betrays the influence of postmodernism. Language defines and identifies those in charge as well as those who are "sick." It constructs the "reality" of each individual as it's defined within the family culture.

Postmodern-influenced therapies often use language maneuvers to effect change because of their belief that reality is a language construct. A clear example is paradoxical intervention in which the therapist prescribes the symptom.[5] The intervention first involves the therapist becoming established within the family system as a credible authority. Once this is done, the therapist, using the weight of this authority, characterizes the symptom as a form of language—a way of communicating, or a "text." He then interprets that language to the family in functional terms, as we see in the following example:[6]

Mark has been running into trouble at school during the past several weeks for not completing his homework. First notes, then phone calls come from several of Mark's teachers informing his parents of the problem. As a result, both of Mark's parents begin coming down on him, without any subsequent improvement on Mark's part.

They finally end up in the counseling office. Mark has now rebelled, blatantly refusing to do his homework, and his parents are describing him to the therapist as irresponsible and defiant. Having done the groundwork, the therapist attempts an interpretation of the symptom that eases both Mark and his parents into a new way of thinking about the problem. The refusal to do homework, according to the therapist, is a way of forcing Mark's parents to interact over him with intensity and place him at the center of their mutual concern. It is, "in fact," a communication of need from child to parents. The therapist then requests that Mark again forego doing his homework for the next several days at least, to further impress this need upon his parents. This would "obviously" be more effective, he claims, than merely telling his parents his needs in so many words. The therapist also instructs the parents to speak with Mark each time this happens, and to acknowledge it as a communication of his need for their attention.

The symptom is now understood as a metaphor—a form of language native to the family culture. If the therapist has been successful, the transactional patterns surrounding the symptom will change as a result of the new interpretation. This will free the family from the vicious cycle that is developing and allow room for more functional communication. The symptom will likely clear up as this occurs.

Note that the therapist's reframing of the symptom isn't necessarily "true," despite the fact that expressions like "in fact" or "obviously" may be used. The symptom could have been interpreted in other, equally valid ways, according to this approach. The point is to get the family to buy into the interpretation. If they do, change will occur because their language structure has changed. Only a novel interpretation from a credible therapist, not representation of truth, is required to effect change. In true postmodern fashion, human beliefs and perceptions determine reality.

Modern vs. Postmodern Therapies

The idea that our use of language may not represent objective truth is nothing new to psychotherapy. Modern counseling approaches in psychology have long assumed, as postmodernists do, that the ways disturbed patients see themselves aren't objectively true. This is a central belief in the schools of cognitive and cognitive-behavioral therapy. However, adherents of these schools further assume, unlike postmodernists, that the patient will become well by developing a more objective, more accurate self-appraisal through the process of therapy. The therapist's job is to guide the patient into areas where important information and experiences have been left out or misunderstood. Modern cognitive-behavioral therapists help patients move from an untrue to a more true view of self based on objective evidence.

In postmodern versions of therapy, however, things are different. First, as we have seen, people's lives are considered "texts," in the sense that they are narratives. To postmodernists, we each "live in story," therapists included. To assume that the therapist's construction of reality (or narrative) is superior to or more true than the patient's is arrogant. According to postmodernism, the therapist's views are just as culture-bound as the patient's, and therefore the therapist can claim no superior interpretation. The therapist never tries to "correct" the patient's narrative by comparing it to any standard of "truth." Rather, the postmodern therapist seeks to disrupt the client's personal narrative by switching the frame-of-reference. He seeks to change meanings, and refers to "marginalized subtexts" or alternative interpretations.[7]

To understand the contrast between this approach and the modernist cognitive approaches, consider the case of Madalyn. She describes herself as depressed and provides the therapist with a narrative about her problems. The conventional modern therapist has a number of interventions from which to choose. He might directly confront the content of the patient's thinking. He might point out logical errors in the client's thinking, such as a tendency to overgeneralize from a few experiences, while selectively leaving out contradictory evidence. The patient might be assigned a task as a personal experiment to check the validity of a view she holds about herself. She might also be given homework exercises in an effort to "restructure" or monitor thought patterns.

The postmodern therapist's approach will be entirely different. It will involve no effort to confront or correct the patient's narrative. The therapist might, however, offer alternative language to replace the label of depression: "You feel things deeply." The therapist might encourage the patient to distance herself from the problem by giving it a name.[8] They might discuss how "Lady Blue" has affected Madalyn's friendships or feelings about herself, thus creating a new frame-of-reference. The therapist might also ask Madalyn to describe life when "Lady Blue" has been gone for a while, and to encourage this "marginalized" part of her narrative to be included in how she tells her story.[9]

Both modern and postmodern approaches to treatment have useful applications. For cognitive-behavioral therapies in particular, studies have documented effectiveness.[10] To be effective, however, practice often breaks from theory at some point. While our emphasis is on postmodern approaches, this is true for modernist approaches as well.

For example, cognitive-behaviorists insist that their patients improve because they have succeeded in moving toward a more objective, data-based assessment of themselves than they had prior to therapy. While their patients do often get better, their assumption about why this occurs is questionable. It completely ignores a well-documented phenomenon: depressed individuals have been shown to have more objective assessments of themselves than non-depressed individuals. Studies show that people who are depressed do not show evidence of the self-serving biases characteristic of those we tend to regard as "well-adjusted." Cognitive-behavioral therapy may work in part, then, not by helping patients develop more accurate self-appraisals, but by bolstering rational defenses and supporting self-serving illusions.[11]

Postmodernists might well view this as support for their position. They would claim that it is the patient's construction or narrative *itself* which is important, not whether it represents reality. Notice, however, that in supporting a position against truth and objectivity, postmodernists contradictorily assert their own views as objectively true—and therefore privileged—over other views. They attempt to deny this by describing their views as relative to their own frame-of-reference, and therefore not superior to others. They seem not to notice that the offer of this very statement as "true" is self-contradictory. There is no defense of their point of view that doesn't automatically discredit it.

The therapist who manipulates frames-of-reference and meanings cannot work without believing that this approach works better than, say, confronting the content of a patient's thinking. Without the ability to assert privilege on the basis of some form of truth-claim, a therapist becomes paralyzed and cannot intervene. If therapists act at all, they have taken a stand for truth at some level. But "truth" is inconsistent with postmodernism, and the therapist has therefore acted in contradiction to the very theory that supports his interventions.

Unless postmodern theorists abandon all therapeutic efforts, they are forced into inconsistency. Even when postmodern thinkers produce useful therapeutic strategies, their denial of objective reality undercuts the basis for those strategies. Psychotherapy implies a desire to advance a "better" state of affairs than the current situation. But advancing a better state of affairs requires a value judgment—again, something postmodernism condemns. Yet without this kind of value judgment, psychotherapy, including postmodern-influenced psychotherapy, is rendered meaningless.

Without a foundation of truth, therapy is paralyzed. Moving ahead to a better way of living requires a value judgment.

Identity—Postmodernism's Tragic Loss of Self

The problem of inconsistency for postmodernism isn't just a theoretical issue. To act in denial of truth is to lose self-identity. To lose identity is to lose the possibility of relationship. One of the great lessons of social psychology is just this: The personal and the social are mutually interactive. In other words, our sense of identity and our relationships are dynamically interdependent.

Our identity is the part of ourselves that we experience as constant—the same across a variety of situations—our "true" selves. When we identify ourselves as shy or bold, passionate or sedate, even male or female, we are noting a sense of who we are, a sameness independent of our surroundings.

Being of *many minds* makes defining our own identity increasingly complex. The diversity that surrounds us can become duplicated inside of us as we switch mental frameworks from one situation to another. We find ourselves thinking and acting differently depending on where we are and who we are with, thus losing our sense of identity. We wonder if anything, including our own character, is constant or genuine. Even the most stable part of our identity—our gender—comes into question as we are confronted with feminine-looking-and-acting males, masculine-looking-and-acting females. We might begin to ask what being male or female really means after all.

To be part of contemporary society is to be part of a struggle for self-identity. According to postmodern theorists such as psychoanalyst Jacques Lacan, we never really achieve a stable image of who we are.[12] In a seemingly ever-changing contemporary society with media linkages to our homes, cars, schools, and places of employment, the images we are fed—and with which we identify—are so varied and incongruent that we begin feeling like patchwork. The moment we are sure of ourselves, we hear scores of dissenting voices, no longer just from without, but now from within. To take a stand on any issue, be it related to lifestyle, career or marital choice, sexual orientation, childrearing, religion, or politics, seems arbitrary in the light of so many choices, all of which present themselves as equally valid alternatives. And certainly, claiming "truth" for an arbitrary stand can only be seen as arrogant. So we act without any claim on truth.

Compelled to act without a foundation in truth, we are put in a position of not really knowing why we do what we do, or why we believe what we believe. It's all a matter of where and with whom we happen to be at the moment. Consequently, we lose a sense of who we are—we lose a sense of identity—in a world of equally valid but dissonant alternatives.

One way to reduce the dissonance is to surrender to the culture of the moment—to exchange a consistent self-identity for shifting cultural identity. Thus, coasting through the ebb-and-flow of social change, we yield an independent "I" for an ever-changing "we." This is the direction postmodernists would have us take, as Gergen explains:

> Postmodern psychology argues for the erasure of the category of self. No longer can one securely determine what it is to be a specific kind of person—male or female—or even a person at all. As the category of the individual person fades from view, consciousness of social construction becomes focal. We realize increasingly that who and what we are is not so much the result of our "personal essence" (real feelings, deep beliefs, and the like) but of how we are constructed in various social groups.[13]

Loss of Self Isn't Biblical Self-Sacrifice

But can there be a "we" without an "I"? The postmodern de-emphasis on self may seem corrective, even refreshing, compared to the preoccupation with self promoted by modernism. Don't, however, mistake the postmodern de-emphasis of self for a praiseworthy attitude of self-sacrifice. Postmodernism doesn't see self-sacrifice as anything more than a metaphor—a way of communicating. True self-sacrifice is a distinctively biblical concept. While substituting "we" for "I" might seem self-giving, it can easily produce as much harm as good.

The loss of self-identity has been associated with some of the most unsettling findings in the entire psychology research literature. When people's group experience diminishes their sense of self, people tend to behave in ways less restrained and more indulgent.[14] Individuals are also carried into adopting more extreme positions, and favor more radical action than they would take independently.[15]

Some of the most disturbing findings in this area come from the work of Philip Zimbardo of Stanford University. He conducted a prison-simulation experiment in which college students role-played guards and prisoners over a period of six days. What happened was frightening. Participants increasingly seemed to confuse role-playing and self-identity as the basest, most morbid side of human nature was exhibited. Experimenters were horrified to see "guards" take pleasure in cruelty and "prisoners" become increasingly preoccupied with escape, individual survival, and mounting hatred. The experiment, originally planned for a two-week period, had to be aborted before even one week had been completed.[16]

The loss of self-identity isn't only frightening. It can be tragic. We need to think back no further than Waco or Guyana to see the devastation that can result from the surrender of self-identity to a culture. Perhaps less dramatically, but no less disastrously, the anonymity associated with the loss of self-identity can easily lead to a loss of social conscience, as Rosenau explains:

> The end of the twentieth century is a time when it is more popular, perhaps even more plausible, to deny personal responsibility. The political landscape includes world wars, environmental disasters, the Holocaust, Vietnam, the rise of religious fundamentalism, world-wide poverty, and unanticipated famine. In the absence of cause and effect, the postmodern individual cannot be held personally accountable because these things "just happen."[17]

It's true that societies influence us in more dramatic ways than we might think. But thankfully, individuals also influence society. To deny this not only goes against common sense but a substantial amount of definitive research.[18] It's frightening to speculate where the denial of self-identity—the death of the self—can lead. When "truth" becomes a multiplicity of socially constructed "truths," and individuals become anonymous within the social groups that define them, we have a recipe for potential disaster.

Postmodernism: A Stealth Destroyer

Postmodern eclecticism, or combining different views, may seem to ease the tensions of modern society. But in our need to solve the problems posed by cultural diversity, we may miss the destructive potentials of postmodernism. In embracing a solution that promotes culturally determined identity, we can be opening ourselves to explosive consequences without realizing it.

Michel Foucault, a leading proponent of postmodernism, was motivated to challenge the oppressive conditions in the mental institutions of France, particularly toward women. His concerns, while noble, led to a philosophy that has potential for even greater oppression. Consider these possibilities:

- *Loss of Individual Freedom*: Cultural determinism led to the definition of Jews as non-persons, resulting in their near extermination in Europe. Cultural determinism has led to the definition of the unborn as non-persons, resulting in their destruction by the millions. When society is left to determine who counts, anything is possible.

- *Danger to Mental Health*: With the loss of self, or identity, culture is given enormous power. If I cannot stand apart from my culture, then I am completely controlled by it. Whether I can feel good about myself—whether I really matter at all—is determined by society and those who run it.
- *Mental Illness an Illusion*: If there is no self apart from a social construction, then mental illness is an illusion. Dysfunction must be seen exclusively in the social environment. While this is often the case, this way of thinking can also contribute to a radical sense of victimization in which emotional problems are too easily interpreted as purely the result of past abuse. Such theories ignore the individual's response to abuse.
- *Psychology As an Instrument of Social Control*: Not long ago in the Soviet Union, psychology became the tool of choice for waging war against those who would not conform to the totalitarian standards of the state. From the time of Breshnev on, the Soviets often preferred to put dissidents into psychiatric wards rather than into Gulags. Without the applications of objective diagnostic standards, it could well be that anyone who fails to conform to the status quo (who perhaps is too "intolerant" or "fundamentalist") may be considered insane.

Postmodernism is a stealth destroyer. It may seem open-minded and tolerant on the surface, but with its denial of the individual and its fascination with power, the makings of manipulation are all present. People may not recognize its danger until it's too late.

Where, then, do we turn as we struggle for self-identity in an age of "many minds"? How do we open ourselves to the diversity around us while taking a stand for truth?

The Bible: Another Way

The biblical solution to the tensions between social diversity and objective truth (truth that doesn't depend on our opinions) is just the opposite of the prescriptions of postmodernism. In stark contrast, the Bible teaches us that objective truth exists and is knowable. It teaches that in identifying ourselves as choosing agents, we are capable of influencing our culture for the good, and to do this, we must be rooted in the truth. Postmodernism can help us to see that knowing the "truth" doesn't come naturally to us. We indeed do construct—or, more honestly, misconstruct—the truth more often than we would like to admit. And our misconstructions are usually self-serving.

This self-serving bias is well documented in the research literature. Studies have repeatedly found that we tend to attribute our own successes to positive internal traits, such as ability and effort, and our failures to external factors outside of our control. By contrast, we tend to attribute the successes of others to "luck," and their failures to inability, lack of perseverance, or some other personal shortcoming. We blame our own failings on the situation while taking credit for our successes, and blame others' failings on their personal attributes while discrediting their successes.[19]

> Postmodernism may seem open-minded and tolerant on the surface, but with its denial of the individual and its fascination with power, the makings of manipulation are all present.

To the extent that we "construct" reality, then, we construct it to serve an inflated view of ourselves over others—exactly what we would expect if we accept the biblical notion of fallen human nature. If our attempt to influence culture is based on our constructions of truth rather than truth itself, we are likely to influence culture to our own advantage rather than to the greater social good. If we are in a socially privileged position, we become part of the imperialism that postmodernists rightly detest.

Influencing the culture for good means living and acting on the basis of the truth. Seeing the truth, however, is painful. Because of our tendencies to construct self-serving viewpoints, a commitment to the truth requires self-sacrifice.

Sin, as an indulgence of our self-serving tendencies, blocks our ability to see the truth. The Bible makes strong reference to this in its repeated teaching on the connection between sin and deception. Consider this sampling of verses:

> They conceive mischief and bring forth iniquity, and their mind prepares deception. (Job 15: 35)
>
> Your lips have spoken falsehood, your tongue mutters wickedness. No one sues righteously and no one pleads honestly. They trust in confusion, and speak lies; they conceive mischief, and bring forth iniquity. (Isaiah 59:3b–4)
>
> The light is come into the world, and men loved the darkness rather than the light; for their deeds were evil. For everyone who does evil hates the light, and does not come to the light, lest his deeds should be exposed. (John 3:19b, 20)
>
> Like a cage full of birds, so their houses are full of deceit; therefore they have become great and rich. They are fat, they are sleek, they also excel in deeds of wickedness. . . . (Jeremiah 6:27–28)
>
> "And they bend their tongue like their bow; lies and not truth prevail in the land; for they proceed from evil to evil, and they do not know Me," declares the Lord. (Jeremiah 9:3)
>
> For the wrath of God is revealed from heaven against all . . . who suppress the truth in unrighteousness. (Romans 1:18)

If sin and deception are part of the same package, then so are self-sacrifice and truth. Self-sacrifice isn't merely a pious euphemism or an exhortation to "be nice" or "do good." It's an *epistemological necessity*—a prerequisite to knowing what is true. The renewal of our minds is the outcome when we present ourselves to God as living sacrifices. (See Romans 12:1–2.) This is what Paul referred to when he said,

> Do nothing from selfishness or empty conceit, but with humility of mind let each of you regard one another as more important than himself; do not merely look out for your own personal interests, but also for the interests of others. Have this attitude in yourselves which was also in Christ Jesus, who, although He existed in the form of God, did not regard equality with God a thing to be grasped, but emptied Himself. . . . (Philippians 2:3–7a)

Indeed, we can view spiritual growth as a process of emptying ourselves as Christ emptied himself, of gradually yielding our own self-serving "constructions" of reality to an objective perspective on truth, which is God's perspective.

In our attempt to relate to others, the uniqueness of each person will reveal to us our sinful areas of self-serving. God's advanced guarantee of acceptance, however, supports our efforts to look honestly inward and to act on the basis of Christ's self-giving love, in spite of ourselves. The diversity of persons we encounter is then no longer a threat but our path to freedom: a freedom to take joy and delight in the diversity of others through a deeper, stronger, and more secure identity in Christ.

Christians might succumb to the same error as postmodernists if we decide to define ourselves by reference to our Christian subculture—which only imperfectly reflects God's truth—rather than by the absolute truth of God's Word. When we contentedly rest our self-identity on the foundations of Christian culture, we may be surprised to find ourselves at cross-purposes with Christ. When, on the other hand, we rest our identity on the person of Jesus Christ alone, gradually allowing his character to be imprinted on us, we find ourselves capable of speaking and acting based upon our confidence in him. The real way to maintain a place for objective truth while compassionately opening ourselves to the diversity around us is to develop Christian character through a more radical commitment to the person of Jesus Christ living in us.

In Brief

- Because it supports the validity of diverse points of view, postmodernism is attractive to practitioners of psychotherapy and to others who feel concerns about diversity and cultural pluralism.
- Postmodernism is increasingly influencing approaches to psychotherapy. The notions of culturally determined identity and language drives much of family therapy. Their importance can be seen in recent developments, such as narrative therapy.
- A basic contradiction in postmodernism forces therapists into inconsistency. They work for achieving a "better" state of affairs for clients, while denying that such value judgments are valid.

- Postmodernism erodes self-identity. Such erosion has been associated with a decreased sense of personal responsibility and with the misuse of power. It can contribute to a dangerous victim mentality.
- The Bible promotes an affirmation of objective reality and truth as the basis for personal identity. This implies self-sacrifice, since we feel uncomfortable either when facing the truth about ourselves or when engaging the diversity around us.
- The final biblical answer to cultural diversity and the marginalization of the oppressed is willing self-sacrifice as we grow in our identity in Christ.

Notes

1. Kenneth Gergen, *The Saturated Self* (Basic Books, 1991).
2. M. Rothbart and P. Birrell, "Attitude and the Perception of Faces," *Journal of Personality Research*, Vol. 11 (1977): pp. 209–215.
3. For an understanding of this perspective, see: C. Steiner, et al., *Reading in Radical Psychiatry* (New York: Grove Press, 1975); P. Chesler, *Women and Madness* (New York: Avon, 1972); and Michel Foucault, *Madness and Civilization: A History of Insanity in the Age of Reason* (London: Tivistock, 1977).
4. G. Bateson, D. Jackson, J. Haley, and J. Weakland, "Toward a Theory of Schizophrenia," *Behavioral Science*, Vol. 1: pp. 251–264. Also *Steps to an Ecology of Mind* (New York: Ballantine, 1972), pp. 201–227.
5. This approach is articulated by, among others, Jay Haley, *Problem Solving Therapy* (New York: Harper & Row, 1976).
6. J. Haley, *Problem Solving Therapy*, pp. 67–76.
7. R. Hare-Mustin and J. Marecek, "The Meaning of Difference: Gender Theory, Postmodernism, and Psychology," *American Psychologist*, Vol. 43 (1986) No. 6: pp. 455–464.
8. This is a technique called "externalization." It is based on the postmodern idea that an individual's identity is culturally determined. For an explanation of the technique, see Bill O'Hanlon, "The Third Wave," in *Family Therapy Networker* (November/December 1994): pp. 19–29.
9. For a complete single-volume treatment of postmodern therapeutic inter-

ventions, see S. Friedman, ed., *The New Language of Change: Constructive Collaboration in Psychotherapy* (New York: Guilford Press, 1993).

10. For supportive documentation see S. Hollon and A. Beck, "Cognitive and Cognitive-Behavioral Therapies" in A. Begin and S. Garfield, eds., *Handbook of Psychotherapy and Behavioral Change*, 4th edition (New York: John Wiley, 1994), pp. 428–466.
11. For a review of the literature on this point see D. Myers, *Social Psychology* (New York: McGraw-Hill, 1983), pp. 89–90.
12. For representative material, see J. Lacan, *Speech and Language in Psychoanalysis*; translated, with notes and commentary by Anthony Wilden (Baltimore: Johns Hopkins University Press, 1968).
13. K. Gergen, *The Saturated Self* (New York: Basic Books, 1991), p. 170.
14. S. Prentice-Dunn and R. Rogers, "Effects of Deindividuating Situational Cues and Aggressive Models on Subjective Deindividuation and Aggression," *Journal of Personality and Social Psychology*, Vol. 39 (1980): pp. 104–113; E. Diener, R. Lusk, D. DeFour, and R. Flax, "Deindividuation: Effects of Group Size, Density, Number of Observers, and Group Member Similarity on Self-Consciousness, and Disinhibited Behavior," *Journal of Personality and Social Psychology*, Vol. 39 (1980): pp. 449–459.
15. N. Johnson, J. Stemler, and D. Hunter, "Crowd Behavior As Risky Shift: A Laboratory Experiment," *Sociometry*, Vol. 40 (1977): pp. 183–187.
16. P. Zimbardo, "The Stanford Prison Experiment," a slide/tape presentation produced by Philip G. Zimbardo, Inc. (1972), P.O. Box 4395, Stanford, Calif. 94305.
17. P. Rosenau, *Postmodernism and the Social Sciences* (New Jersey: Princeton, 1992), p. 56.
18. Examples would include the following studies on "psychological reactance": R. Baer, S. Hinckle, K. Smith, and M. Fenton, "Reactance As a Function of Actual vs. Projected Autonomy," *Journal of Personality and Social Psychology*, Vol. 38 (1980): pp. 416–422; S. Brehm, and J. Brehm, *A Theory of Freedom and Control* (New York: Academic Press, 1981); M. Helimann, "Oppositional Behavior As a Function of Influence Attempt Intensity and Retaliation Threat," *Journal of Personality and Social Psychology*, Vol. 33 (1976): pp. 574–578; W. Gamson, B. Fierman, and S. Rytina, *Encounters With Unjust Authority* (Homewood, Ill.: Dorsey Press, 1982).
19. The self-serving bias is a well-documented phenomenon supported by studies too numerous to detail here. For a review of the literature, see a standard text in social psychology, such as D. Myers, *Social Psychology* (New York: McGraw-Hill, 1983), pp. 85–91.

10

POSTMODERN IMPACT: LAW

GARY SAALMAN, CONTRIBUTOR

In a violent confrontation in the streets of Los Angeles in 1992, police severely beat a black man, stunning him with tasers and clubbing him with nightsticks. A bystander with a video camera, however, records the beating of Rodney King for the entire nation to see. Months later, an all-white jury refuses to convict the officers involved, provoking a riot that burns hundreds of buildings and injures and kills scores of people. African-American citizens in Los Angeles and across the country are enraged. Many believe that blacks cannot get justice from a white American justice system. Later, though some of the officers are convicted in federal court of civil rights violations, doubts remain. What if no camera had been running? Would anyone have believed Rodney King's claims that he had been unjustly beaten?

Three years later, again in Los Angeles, O. J. Simpson goes to trial for the murder of his ex-wife and her friend. The racist remarks of an investigating detective fuel defense claims of a police conspir-

About the Contributor:

Gary Saalman received his Juris Doctorate degree from the University of Notre Dame Law School. His B.S. in accounting is from Miami University in Ohio, where he was a merit scholar. He has served as an editor for the *Notre Dame Law Review* and at positions in the U.S. Department of Justice and U.S. Court of Appeals. He is currently a trial lawyer in private practice and attends Xenos Fellowship.

acy. Prosecutors and defense lawyers trade charges of racism and "playing the race card." Defense lawyers accuse the judge of racism in his rulings on the evidence. The media focuses on the racial composition of the jury, and commentators wonder whether the jury put aside issues of race and celebrity status when it considered the evidence. Polls show a marked decline in public confidence in the jury system.

Incidents like these have highlighted questions about the objectivity and neutrality of the rule of law in America.

The Rule of Law

If you asked a hundred people the straightforward question "What is law?" most would respond that law is a set of rules and principles by which a society maintains order and preserves freedom. Most would state that in a democratic society, law is enacted by duly elected representatives accountable to the people. If these representatives enact "wrong" or "unjust" laws, citizens can change the law by electing new representatives or by ballot referendum. Nearly everyone, furthermore, would agree that legal rules and principles should be neutral, that is, they should apply to everyone equally, regardless of race, creed, or gender. Most would also agree that police officers, prosecutors, and judges should be fair, impartial and independent, and that they should treat similar circumstances equally and enforce the law dispassionately. They would also likely agree that judges should base their decisions on the law and the facts of the case, not on the wealth, fame, race, or gender of the person appearing before them.

Most citizens, moreover, probably believe that laws are—or at least *should* be—based on natural and universal "truths" determined through nature, reason, and social experience, and that any laws that violate these principles should be changed.

A legal system that more or less fulfills these ideals is one built on the "Rule of Law."

The "Rule of Law" means that law is capable of constraining human will and behavior. It means that men and women are constrained by fair and impartial rules, rather than the rules being mere devices of power that can be changed at will.

While traditional legal thinkers may disagree on the best foundation for legal principles—whether revelation, legal reasoning, social experience, secular ethics, or the will of the majority—they generally agree that it is possible to create a legal system where law is separate from politics, where neutral principles of law provide correct legal solutions, and where disinterested judges apply these rules fairly. Together, these ideals are often called "traditional legal theory."

Postmodern Legal Theory

In recent years, however, postmodernism has come to the forefront of legal theory. Postmodern theorists, best known as "anti-foundationalists" or advocates of "Critical Legal Studies," claim that law has no objective basis. Like postmodernists in other fields, they argue that we do not *grasp* reality, we *construct* reality. All knowledge depends on social convention, especially language, which provides the building blocks of law. Since we have no foundation for objective knowledge of any kind, law has no foundation but power. Because it has no foundation in truth or reality, law does not deserve our allegiance.

Having discounted our capability to reason and to discern truth impartially, postmodernists focus instead on how each social group develops beliefs and rules favorable to their particular group. Principles of law never reflect universal truths, they argue, only the distribution of power among social groups. According to these scholars, it is senseless to talk about whether a law is right or wrong, moral or amoral. Law is whatever a society's most powerful cultural group makes it. And when the different cultural presuppositions of different groups clash, no group has an objective basis from which to demand another group's obedience to the law.

> According to postmodernists, laws aren't right or wrong. Law is whatever a society's most powerful group makes it.

It isn't difficult to see that postmodernism's influence in the law raises fundamental challenges to the legal system. If law isn't objective—if it doesn't state universal truths to which we all should adhere—then why should we feel bound to obey it? If law doesn't embody principles of right and wrong—if it is merely a naked assertion of power by one social group over another—then why should we not grab whatever we can for ourselves? This chapter will examine the tenets of postmodern legal thought and some of its actual and potential effects on society today. To orient you to our discussion, the following chart compares traditional legal theory to postmodern, or "critical," legal theory.

	Traditional Legal Theory	**Critical (postmodern) Legal Theory**
The rule of law	A society governed by law is better than society governed by men because law is neutral, created and modified by the will of the majority. It is also stable, fair and not subject to the whims of human rulers.	Society is never governed by law, because *people* have to interpret laws and enforce them. Since people can interpret laws any way they want, people not laws are the real rulers. Law is no more stable than its latest interpretation or application. "Fairness" is the rhetorical tool used by majority culture to describe their view of what should happen.
The meaning of laws	Laws can yield a stable and generally agreed upon meaning when interpreted using grammatical-historical hermeneutics and previous case law.	Careful study demonstrates that those in power—judges and governments—can always find a law that backs their interests. The poor and minorities are excluded from interpreting law their way.
The law and society	Everyone is equal under the law. Judges should be impartial, administering law to the rich and the poor according to what the law says, not according to the judges' feelings.	Laws are written by the powerful of society to protect their interests and to describe as "criminal" any action that threatens their property or persons. The poor and minorities will always be arrested more, convicted more and imprisoned more, while crimes of the rich will go unpunished much of the time. Judges should realize this and use their power to even the score.

Postmodernism's Prominence in Legal Theory

Although hard to measure, the influence of postmodern theories of law on the courtroom and the legislature already are *significant.* According to one law professor, postmodernism has become "as dominant in legal theory as any paradigm was in the past."[1] Another authority says that "aspects of postmodern philosophy . . . have by now thoroughly infiltrated academic legal analysis."[2] Yet another claims, "Postmoderns have redefined the benchmark for evaluating . . . reasoning and the validity of the evidence."[3]

Despite the power of this movement, few Americans have any idea what it is.

Origins of Postmodern Legal Theory

Beginning in the late 1970s a loose association of professors spearheaded a challenge to traditional legal theory that became known as the *Critical Legal Studies* movement. Sharing a neo-Marxist political orientation, the professors argued that law was biased in that it reflected the political ideology of a ruling class and protected their interests. These professors maintained that legal principles and rules, though designed to appear neutral, were in fact weighted in favor of the wealthier classes. As the professors explain in an outreach letter,

> If there is a single theme [in Critical Legal Studies], it is that law is an instrument of social, economic, and political domination, both in the sense of furthering the concrete interests of the dominators and in that of legitimating the existing order. This approach emphasizes the ideological character of legal doctrine. . . .[4]

Organizers of the first Critical Legal Studies conference were repelled by the "traditionalist" or "formalist" approach to the law and legal studies. They rejected the notion that neutral and nonpolitical legal reasoning could resolve most controversies. Like other postmodernists, they held that language means different things to different cultures, and that language shapes thinking. Reason, they argued, is never fully reliable because it is never actually objective. What masquerades as objective legal reasoning is actually an assertion of the rights of the privileged.

Critical Legal Studies is indeed both a political movement and a legal philosophy. It's a legal philosophy because it puts forward a theory about law and its function and operation. It's a political movement because it advocates a program for radical political change. When law is reduced to politics, law and politics converge and are indistinguishable from each other.

The Principles of Critical Legal Studies

In traditional thinking, the law is legitimate because it is *objective*—has a basis in our knowledge of reality; *determinate*—it yields a distinct set of answers we can understand; and *neutral*—it does not favor some citizens over others. Critical Legal Students hold that all three claims are false.

Traditionals counter that a major purpose of law is, of course, to legitimize a set of societal norms. As one traditionalist argues, "It would be a sorry and badly functioning social system that did not try to legitimate a dominant set of norms."[5] Admitting that the law legitimates a set of norms, however, is a far cry from stating that the legal system is fundamentally unjust.

Critical Legal Theorists advance several counterclaims:

1. The law seeks wrongful legitimation.

Critical Legal Students argue that the law wrongfully sanctions unjust and illegitimate structures of power and distributions of wealth. Duncan Kennedy, a Harvard law Professor has argued that

> the law as we have chosen to make it through our various law-making institutions, is profoundly implicated in distributional, social injustice in our society . . . the rules we have chosen as the rules of the game reproduce social injustice generation after generation . . .[6]

Legitimacy is achieved, according to Critical Legal Students, through "mystification." The use of black robes by judges, of complicated procedural rules, and of the convoluted language of "legalese" only mystify the law for the public. People conclude that anything so complicated and so well established must be right.

Advocates also argue that the ruling classes create a sense of legitimacy by occasional court decisions and legal doctrines that actually do favor the oppressed classes. These examples, while not the norm, are window dressing to make the oppressed believe the law is neutral.

2. *The law is plagued by contradictions.*

Critical Legal Students cynically believe that for each legal conclusion one can develop an equally plausible argument for the opposite conclusion. The best we can do, then, is to suspend judgment and recognize the law as the naked assertion of power it is. This is the same approach we have seen postmodernists take in other areas: Texts have no meaning in any objective sense; instead, they must be deconstructed to determine how their authors sought to guard their social privileges.

The battle cry of postmodern legal thinkers might be stated as "choose your side, but don't pretend to be objective." Like all postmodernists, legal postmodernists strive to demonstrate the contradictions in traditional legal thinking. They believe that all legal perspectives can be deconstructed into two or more opposite and competing forces, impulses or desires. These contradictions, according to Critical Legal Students, create a freedom, a choice, which renders law "indeterminate," unable to provide binding, meaningful guides to judgment. A judge can therefore favor one principle over the other principle and still be said to be honestly applying the law.

3. *There are no foundational principles.*

For Critical Legal Students, the foundational principles of law and so-called rational thought are nothing more than social constructs. Since they reject these beginning principles, they also reject any conclusions derived from those principles. Neither deductive reasoning nor empirical verification yield valid conclusions.

Critical Legal Studies advocates claim they are engaged in a project of "human emancipation," seeking to demonstrate to all that neither pre-Enlightenment faith in God nor post-Enlightenment faith in reason can supply the principles needed to give legitimacy to our social order. Any attempt to articulate universal principles, theories, and visions of social order is what they call a "contextual political construction." Looking deeper still, they say, we discover that every social construct is a naked assertion of power.

Concerning what most people would regard as relatively well-defined laws and court precedents detailing the meaning of free speech, for example, Stanley Fish, a professor of both Law and English at Duke University, argues that "we have never had any normative guidance for marking off protected from unprotected speech. . . . In short, the name of the game has always been politics."[7] His claim that there are no transcendent norms ultimately leads to nihilism—a belief that we can know nothing, communicate nothing, and that life itself is meaningless. He writes,

> Hearkening to me will lead to nothing. Hearkening to me, from my point of view, is *supposed* to lead to nothing. . . . All I have to recommend is the game, which, since it doesn't need my recommendations, will proceed on its way undeterred and unimproved by anything I have to say.[8]

Skeptics—including Fish—argue that actions in our everyday lives do not require a commitment to normative beliefs that prescribe right and wrong. Our natural needs, wants, and desires, as well as uniquely human customs, laws, and professional training, permit us to act even in the absence of norms or reasons for what we do. Only when we abandon any attempt to derive the "right" choice or the "ethical practice" will we find tranquility and freedom. We should stop searching for the supernatural or logical origins of right and wrong.

From these points it is obvious that once we begin down this road, we cannot confine our argument to law. It applies to morality as well, or for that matter, any practice or discipline or institution that rests upon what we hold to be unchanging structures of what is true and good. Anything that prescribes one choice or one understanding of reality over another must go. There can never be a right answer in morals, just as certainly as there can never be a right answer in law.

4. *Law is not neutral.*

Critical Legal Students scorn the idea that judges are or can be neutral. Judges try to show that their decisions are rendered on the grounds of case precedent, statutes, or equitable principles. Of course, judges pretend to be, or even naively believe that they are unbiased, and that their cultural identity or ideology does not determine their decisions. But this is never possible, according to Critical Legal Students. They claim that underneath a theater of neutrality the legal system uses ideology, legitimization, and mystification to ensure class dominance. It's only to be expected that the legal system would use such tools to ensure that the public believes the laws are neutral, inevitable, and just.

Later Postmodern Legal Thinkers

The first generation critical legal theorists deconstructed traditional legal theory by arguing that law contradicted itself and provided no unchanging objective principles. Today, a second generation of critical theorists focuses on the way law defines and reproduces cultural values in society. They are affirmative postmodernists, seeking to use the law to reconstruct a new social reality.[9] Many second-generation theorists seek to demonstrate the inherent racial, gender, and cultural bias of legal principles that otherwise appear neutral on their face.

Several distinct groups have emerged from the second generation of critical legal theorists. Feminist legal theorists (fem-crits) and critical race theorists (race-crits) have developed their own conferences and symposia to advance themes raised by first-generation theorists.

Fem-Crits

Postmodern feminist legal theorists deny the law is or could ever be a set of universal, gender-neutral policies. They argue that legal principles that are gender-neutral on their face are nonetheless inherently patriarchal and should be reconstructed to take into account the unique perspective of women. The sentiments below are typical of feminist legal theorists' thinking:

> Men have created and named a world in which men have power over women—physical power, political power, opportunity power, silencing power. We must learn how our social and political organizations have been constructed by men in their own image and explore how a world constructed by women and men for women and men would be different. . . . The primary task of feminist scholars is to awaken women and men to the insidious ways in which patriarchy distorts all of our lives. . . . Unearthing each shard of patriarchy is especially difficult because of the powerful assumptions embedded in our language and logic. Western culture teaches us that the patriarchal description of reality is not biased but neutral; that our knowledge and truths are not subjective, intersubjective, relative, or constructed from narrow perspectives but objective, scientifically based, and universal. . . .[10]

Race-Crits

Bill Clinton created quite a stir when he nominated Lani Guinier to a post in the Justice Department. As Congress began to study her background, they found in her writings what they considered shocking criticisms of "majoritarian interests." She argued against majority rule, claiming that democratic rule was often unfair to minorities, and she proposed alternatives to our system of "one-person, one-vote." She proposed that the votes of minorities should count for more than the votes of other citizens, in order that minorities should have greater influence.

Just as feminist legal theorists argue that patriarchy is embedded in our principles, critical race theorists argue that racism is deeply imbedded in our culture and what would otherwise appear to be race-neutral legal principles:

> For race-crits, racism is not only a matter of individual prejudice and everyday practice; rather, race is deeply imbedded in language, perceptions, and perhaps even "reason" itself. In CRT's [Critical Race Theory's] "postmodern narratives," racism is an inescapable feature of western culture, and race is always already inscribed in the most innocent and neutral-seeming concepts. Even ideas like "truth" and "justice" themselves are open to interrogations that reveal their complicity with power. . . . [11]
>
> Long ago, empowered actors and speakers enshrined their meanings, preferences, and views of the world into the common culture and language. Now, deliberation within that language, purporting always to be neutral and fair, inexorably produces results that reflect their interests.[12]

A Fundamental Challenge to the Legal Order

Postmodern legal movements present a fundamental challenge to the legal system. Unlike prior legal reform movements, they hold that the impartial rule of law is a myth. Law, they claim, is politics, and attempts to make it appear otherwise are pure theater. In a legal system where politics and law converge and the participants are thought to be incapable of escaping their own cultural biases, the only right solution is the solution of the mightiest forces in society:

> Must might make right? In a sense the answer I might give is yes, since in the absence of a perspective independent of interpretation some interpretive perspective will always rule by virtue of having won out over its competitors.[13]

Traditional legal theory holds that law and politics are separate. Traditionals maintain that those in the political realm are free to debate what is good and right for the community and then to embody those value preferences in legal rules, usually through a process of compromise. The legal system, however, is then to interpret and apply those rules with impartiality regardless of the race, gender, or culture of the people involved. Postmodern legal theory threatens to politicize the legal system and in turn to rob the system of its capacity for dispassionate decision-making.

Postmodern legal theory threatens to politicize the legal system and destroy its capacity for justice.

> For if one can no longer cogently distinguish between impartial judgment and . . . lobbying, between dispassionate description and partisan propaganda, one can no longer make sense of the moral and intellectual ideals on which society is based. . . . What we see at work throughout is a deliberate attempt to supplant reason by rhetoric, truth by persuasion, using the simple device of denying that there is any essential distinction to be made between them. This would be troubling enough if confined to literary texts; extended to legal texts and basic political concepts such as justice, it is nothing short of disastrous.[14]

Postmodern Legal Theory and Its Effects on Society

What actual effects have postmodern legal theorists wrought on society so far? How will we see the effects in the years immediately ahead?

Destroying the idea of the neutral rule of law could be a self-fulfilling prophecy. If lawyers and judges believe the law is nothing but masqueraded power, professionals will increasingly act accordingly, and use the law as a cynical and manipulative tool. The public will eventually come to believe that law exists only for those who can bend it to their purposes, and the rule of law will be destroyed. As Dean Paul Carrington of Duke University explains:

> Lawyers lacking confidence that legal principles actually influence the exercise of power have no professional tools with which to do their work. In due course they must abandon whatever professionalism they have, to choose between simple neglect of their work or the application of common cunning. . . . A lawyer who succumbs to legal nihilism faces a far greater danger than mere professional incompetence. He must contemplate the dreadful reality of government by cunning and a society in which the only right is might . . . [and] that who decides is everything, and principle nothing but cosmetic. . . . Teaching cynicism may, and perhaps probably does, result in the learning of the skills of corruption: bribery and intimidation.[15]

Rather than being fair and just, law is already becoming politicized by interest-group selfishness and power allocation. Postmodernism undercuts the prospect of nourishing a common morality or civic virtue that holds individuals accountable regardless of their cultural presuppositions. These theories are rapidly gaining support, especially in minority communities, and a legal system that emphasizes our gender, racial, and cultural differences can only foster further divisions.

Racial, gender, and cultural politics have become an integral part of the legal system. Special bias crimes and defenses based on gender and culture have been incorporated into the governing law of many states. Lawyers use jury consultants to evaluate how a juror's racial, gender, and cultural bias might impact their decision on a verdict. In high-profile cases—the trial of the officers who assaulted Rodney King, or the O. J. Simpson murder trial—the media relentlessly focus on the racial composition of a jury, subtly suggesting that the makeup of the jury, not the evidence, determines the verdict. And given the growing postmodern consensus, they may be right. Judges, lawyers, and jurors who hear that they are incapable of escaping their bias may decide to act accordingly, regardless of the weight of the relevant evidence.

Postmodern legal theory trickles down to breed cynicism toward all government and the entire criminal justice system.

This, then, is the real issue. No one questions the fact that law requires interpretation, or that judges or juries may have acted unfairly, sometimes based on race or gender bias. The question is this: How do we view such unfairness? Do we accept that all people must inevitably be unfair and subjective, as postmodernists claim? Or do we recognize such unfairness as the evil it is and resist it? When we accept what postmodernism preaches, we lose all basis for calling the system to fairness. We instead challenge minority populations to pursue power so they can take their turn.

A Prescription for Society

Law is both cause and effect. We need public morality to sustain law. Just as clearly, though, we need law to foster public morality. Evangelical Christian thinkers today argue that natural law—the reflection of the image of God in humans and the structure of the world created by a moral God—is the basis for law in a pluralistic society.[16]

But how do people realize natural law as the basis for public morality? For one thing, they cannot realize moral principles in an atmosphere of anarchy. We need the Rule of Law to create an envelope of security, order, and freedom where people can engage in rational discussion and develop a public consensus about what is right and wrong. Christians would naturally be one important voice in this debate. Pluralism and diversity in our society means that there are more voices in the debate. However, many voices engaging in rational discourse about moral principles can reach a public consensus about what our laws should be and then apply those laws neutrally and fairly to all. Law has been threatened by the disintegration of public values and by divisive cultural politics in society, and its future can only be assured by the reversal of those social processes.

As the postmodern worldview spreads through society, we can only suppose that postmodern schools of legal thought will grow in popularity as well. Already, *radical criminology*, first cousin to Critical Legal Studies, is widely influential. Large numbers of residents in some minority neighborhoods are firmly convinced today that law and law enforcement are nothing but tools of oppression. For too many, law is the oppressor, not the protector. As contempt for the criminal justice system grows and the very concept of fairness and neutrality in law vanishes, we can hardly feel comforted about the future of America's legal system.

In Brief

- Postmodernism is active in American jurisprudence and legal education under the titles of Anti-Foundationalism, Critical Legal Studies, Feminist Legal Theory, Critical Race Theory, and Radical Criminology.
- Traditional legal theorists maintain that it is possible to have neutral and nonpolitical legal principles that reflect "truths," whether those truths are based on revelation, reason, science, or social experience.
- Postmodernists argue that all law is really about politics and power and that it can be deconstructed to demonstrate the power maneuverings and cultural biases behind what a law says and how it is applied.
- They argue that judges cannot separate themselves from their own culturally constructed reality. Therefore, purported impartial application of law is all theater designed to fool the weak in society.
- Feminists and minority activists are using postmodern principles to advance their agendas in classrooms, courts, and legislatures, arguing for race-conscious and gender-conscious laws.
- As cynicism about the rule of law in America spreads in legal circles as well as in popular culture, the prospect looms of a loss of public respect and adherence to the law, manipulation of the law for political ends, the loss of objectivity, universality, and neutrality as ideals for law, and ultimately the replacement of the rule of law with rule by the most powerful.

Notes

1. Peter Schank, "Understanding Postmodern Thought and Its Implications for Statutory Interpretation," *S. Cal. L. Rev.*, Vol. 65 (1992), p. 2507.
2. James Gardner, "The Ambiguity of Legal Dreams: A Communitarian Defense of Judicial Restraint," *N.C. L. Rev.*, Vol. 71 (1993), p. 817, n. 22.
3. Gary Minda, "Jurisprudence at Century's End," *J. Legal Educ.*, Vol. 43 (1993), p. 56.
4. Mark Kelman, *A Guide to Critical Legal Studies*, 1 (Cambridge: Harvard University Press, 1987), p. 1.
5. Clark, "Remarks to the Harvard Society for Law and Public Policy Studies" to Harvard Alumni on May 13, 1985 at The Harvard Club, reprinted in *A Discussion on Critical Legal Studies at the Harvard Law School*, p. 5.
6. Duncan Kennedy, "Remarks to Harvard Alumni on May 13, 1985 at The Harvard Club," reprinted in *A Discussion on Critical Legal Studies at the Harvard Law School*, p. 10.
7. Stanley Fish, *There's No Such Thing As Free Speech: And It's a Good Thing, Too* (New York: Oxford University Press, 1993).
8. Ibid., p. 307.
9. Gary Minda explains: "In advancing a social construction thesis, second generation CLS scholars seek to reveal how various legal categories are constructed by judges and legislatures from cultural and political contexts [i.e., biases]. . . . Crits attempted to show how legal meaning about the world 'comes from within' the interpreting subject and is itself constituted by an external and social cultural environment." Gary Minda, "Jurisprudence at Century's End," p. 41.
10. Leslie Bender, "A Lawyer's Primer on Feminist Theory and Tort," *Journal of Legal Education*, Vol. 38, no. 3 (1988): pp. 7–9.
11. Angela Harris, "Forward: The Jurisprudence of Reconstruction, Symposium: Critical Race Theory," *Calif. L. Rev* Vol. 82 (1994): pp. 741, 743.
12. Angela Harris, "Critical Race Theory," p. 741, quoting Richard Delgado and Jean Stefaniz, in "Hateful Speech, Loving Communities: Why Our Notion of a 'Just Balance' Changes So Slowly," *Calif. L. Rev* Vol. 82 (1994): pp. 851, 861.
13. Stanley Fish, *Doing What Comes Naturally: Change Rhetoric and the Practice of Theory in Literary and Legal Studies* (New York: Duke University Press, 1989), p. 10.
14. Roger Kimble, *Tenured Radicals: How Politics Has Corrupted Higher Education* (New York: HarperCollins, 1991), p. 164.
15. P. Carrington, "Of Law and the River," *Journal of Legal Education*, Vol. 34 (1984), p. 222.
16. See our discussion of natural law versus biblical law as the basis for social ethics in the endnotes of Chapter 7.

11

Postmodern Impact: Science

Lee Campbell, Ph.D., Contributor

Science isn't the wonder we once thought it was. No, we admit, science hasn't cured cancer or the common cold. The optimistic belief in the power of science that not long ago launched men to the moon and sought a vaccine for everything that ailed us has been tempered in many of us by a more sober realism. Gratitude for the comforts and conveniences produced by decades of research mixes with an awareness of the price of science gone awry: pollution of land and sea and sky, workers rendered obsolete by industrial robots, a proliferation of bacteria resistant to antibiotics, a frenetic pace of life enabled by technology. The supreme symbol of scientific progress—a man in a white lab coat—might scare some of us as much as impress us.

Postmodernists are quick to exploit our concerns. They remind us that science isn't as trustworthy as we thought. Moreover, they tell us, science isn't even as rational as we think. Postmodernists claim that other disciplines or cultures may have equally valid descriptions of reality, one no better than the next. Consider this statement by P. K. Feyerabend, who rejoices we are free to reject Chris-

About the Contributor:

Lee Campbell, Ph.D., is chair of the Division of Natural Sciences at Ohio Dominican College. In addition to being the author of numerous technical papers, Lee is known as a dynamic speaker on apologetics and biblical issues.

tianity, yet fumes we still must submit to the equally oppressive worldview of modern science:

> The rise of modern science coincides with the suppression of non-Western tribes by Western invaders. The tribes are not only physically suppressed, they also lose their intellectual independence and are forced to adopt the bloodthirsty religion of brotherly love—Christianity. . . . Today this development is gradually reversed. . . . But science still reigns supreme. . . . Thus, while an American can now choose the religion he likes, he is still not permitted to demand that his children learn magic rather than science at school. . . . And yet science has no greater authority than any other form of life.[1]

Today, Feyerabend's complaint that parents can't choose to have their children educated in magic isn't altogether true. Times are changing. We have entered a new age in which postmodern skepticism poses a mounting challenge to science.

New Sciences Are Confusing

Strangely, postmodernists turn to science itself for support for their worldview.

When scientific disciplines are young, as are modern physics or cognitive neuroscience, the meaning and significance of their findings aren't always clear. This lack of clarity invites apologists who seek grist for their ideological mills. Lately, no one has been more guilty of this than postmodernists and religious mystics. They often treat science like a variety store where they can pick and choose the interpretations that best serve their particular beliefs.

In earlier years, modernists often laughed at theists who appealed to the divine as an explanation for every scientific mystery. They mocked this approach as the "God of the gaps." Yet in a similar way, postmodernists and their allies—mystical scientists—are each inserting their own worldviews into the scientific mysteries created by new sciences. Traditional scientists are less than approving. While postmodernists and mystics today use science and math to back their views, in my experience, most practicing physicists deny that modern physics supports any of their conclusions; a fact even some proponents admit.[2]

Modernism and Science[3]

As you have read about the impact of postmodernism in the past several chapters, you might have concluded that modernism is over the hill, *passé*. But especially in the sciences, modernism is alive and well. And one social psychologist estimates that thirty-five to forty percent of the American public identify themselves as modernistic.[4]

But mark this well: Modernism is quite distinct from science. The originators of modern science and many leading scientists after them have been theists, not modernists. Modernists, however, like to identify themselves with science. Many people have bought the modernist notion that science and modernism are identical, and as a result modernism has gained undeserved credibility through people's lingering respect for science.

Modernism and postmodernism are antagonistic philosophical viewpoints. Modernists hold that reality is composed of matter/energy in a closed universe of space/time. They believe reality should be *discovered* through observation, forming hypotheses, and testing those hypotheses experimentally. Brian Swimme expresses the modernist view:

> I am convinced that the story of the universe that has come out of three centuries of modern scientific work will be recognized as a supreme human achievement . . . a revelation having a status equal to that of the great religious revelations of the past.[5]

As you can see, modernists are also often arrogant. In a current general biology text, for instance, the authors employ inept philosophizing to equate the modernist worldview with rationality and all other worldviews with irrationality:

> Darwin knew that accepting his theory *required* believing in philosophical materialism, the conviction that matter is the stuff of all existence and that all mental and spiritual phenomenon are its by-products. . . . In Darwin's world we are not helpless prisoners of a static world order but, rather, masters of our own fate. . . . And from a strictly scientific point of view *rejecting biological evolution is no different from rejecting other natural phenomenon* such as electricity and gravity.[6]

This extreme modernist position is all too typical of the arrogance that has earned the ire of postmodernists as well as many others in society, including Christians. To these modernists, people who reject atheistic materialism are so ignorant that they might as well deny gravity! Modernists claim an omniscience that says that nowhere in the universe can the supernatural exist. They make assertions requiring data their methods can't supply. They leverage the real discoveries of science—like gravity and electricity—in an effort to win converts.

Modernism remains a potent enemy of theism and other supernaturally based beliefs. Our purpose in this chapter, however, isn't to decry modernism. But as we move ahead to examine the validity of science, be aware that our aim isn't to defend modernism.[7] Instead, we will show how various postmodern ideas arising inside and outside the sciences attack the undergirding principles of traditional science at the same time that they claim science supports their views.

Postmodernism and the Sciences

We will only be able to briefly survey how postmodernists and their mystical allies are challenging the validity of science in Western culture. In doing so, we will follow this chart.

Subject	Traditional Scientific Principle	Postmodern Critique
Scientific Progress	Science should be a quest for truth about the universe, ignoring all voices who deny truth and defend superstition.	Science actually arrives at its "truths" in response to social forces both inside and outside the scientific community. Their periodic shifts in outlook come as a result of the irrational conversions of influential scientific leaders, not from systematic searches.
Scientific Objectivity	Scientists are supposed to be *objective* observers. They study nature through direct observation, indirect observations, or controlled experiments intended to rule out bias.	Observations do not interpret themselves. They are interpreted by a mind, filtered through the biases of the person or group conducting the experiment. Human minds are affected by their culture and language to such an extent that the "actual" nature of things may be unknowable.

(Continued)

	Traditional Scientific Principle	Postmodern Critique
Scientific Rationality	Science is supposed to be rational. Scientists use inductive or deductive logic to outline a problem or question, interpret an observation, formulate an hypothesis, articulate the logical implications of an hypothesis, and test an hypothesis.	Some postmodernists question not whether science is rational but whether rationality provides any real insights into the world. They argue that there is no such thing as reason in the sense Europeans use the word. All agree that the rules of logic only apply within a given cultural paradigm or language/ thought system.

The Progress of Science

When postmodernists criticize the sciences, they often include the influential work of science historian Thomas Kuhn.[8] Kuhn criticizes what he sees as modernist misrepresentation of the nature of science. Modernist definitions of science claim that science is objective because it is *empirical*—based only on the data of our senses; *rational*—reasonable, or logically defensible; and *reliable*—its presuppositions are obviously true. Kuhn claims, though, that science is a social enterprise and as such is also quite subjective. He argues that "every individual choice between competing theories depends on a mixture of objective and subjective factors."[9]

Kuhn calls a scientific consensus a *paradigm*. He claims that each succeeding paradigm carries no more weight than the preceding one. Paul Feyerabend, a prominent and more radical postmodern theorist, uses the same word but takes the point one step further: When scientists operating in one paradigm change their minds to another paradigm, they undergo an irrational conversion experience in their thinking. Because the meaning of the words used in the first paradigm can't be translated into the language of the second, the paradigms can't be related to each other (they are "incommensurable"). And since these theories can't be directly compared to each other or to any objective reference point, we can't say that one more exactly describes objective reality than the other.[10]

Kuhn, Feyerabend, and others draw much of their thinking from theorists in the field of sociology of knowledge.[11] These radical critiques of science have eroded the confidence of many in the certainty of scientific findings, particularly among non-scientists.[12] Popular culture is increasingly skeptical about the reliability of science.[13] In movies of the 1950s, for example, science was usually the hero. In most movies today, science is the villain—a discipline run amok.

Can Observation Be Objective?

Scientists are supposed to be objective observers. In other words, they claim to see what is actually "out there," not what they want to see. They aim to study nature by direct or indirect observation using experiments designed to minimize bias.

> Science, postmodernists argue, isn't as rational as we think.

Postmodern objections to this claim are too complicated to cover here in depth, but we will mention the areas and footnote additional reading for those interested:

- From *neuroscience*: Postmodernists claim recent research shows that the nervous system can't be trusted to provide accurate impressions of nature.[14]
- From *philosophy*: They point out that observations do not interpret themselves, but must be interpreted by a human mind. Therefore, they are subject to the biases of the particular person conducting the experiment.[15]
- From *psychology*: Studies of perception[16] and belief formation[17] seem to confirm the concerns raised by philosophers. Studies show that people's beliefs affect what they notice through their senses. Also, the formation of false beliefs can be entirely hidden from the one who forms them.
- From *sociology*: If we accept that observations are affected by beliefs, sociology carries the argument a step further, by arguing that beliefs, in turn, are substantially influenced by culture[18] and language.[19] Therefore, our observations, including those of scientists, are biased by our culture.
- From *the history of science*: An analysis of the history of science shows that dominant theories have often had a controlling influence upon what scientists notice and what they don't.[20]

So what are we to make of this? Observations obviously don't interpret themselves. They are interpreted by a human mind, through the observer's biases, perhaps based on his culture—or even where the research dollars are coming from—and this may prevent him from knowing the actual nature of things.

Of course, such gloomy views of observation ultimately are self-defeating. How can those who claim that observations are entirely shrouded by perceptual error and mental bias hold that their own observations are true? But science also uses a number of techniques to limit the influence of bias in research. We can name some of these here:

- *Experimental Design*: When scientists prepare to investigate a phenomenon or test a hypothesis, they structure their experiment and determine how they intend to assess their results *in advance*. The experimental design should be such that the number of factors that could affect the outcome are limited and should include "control" groups that are exposed to all of the same experimental conditions except the one being tested. Also, by deciding upon an appropriate statistical method before experiments begin, scientists are less likely to pick a statistical test that casts the results in the most favorable light.
- *Replication*: When scientists do research, they disclose not only what they found but how they found it. If the research involved experiments, those are described along with the controls used. Other scientists try the same experiment. If other scientists get different results, the findings are falsified or at least weakened pending futher tests. However, if different scientists all over the world can do the same experiment with the same results, it seems clear that the findings are real and objective—not just a matter of personal interpretation.
- *Double-Blind Testing*: When scientists wonder about the effectiveness of, say, a drug, they arrange for blind testing. Under blind testing, a control group and an experimental group are administered pills that look identical. One group takes the real drug—the other takes a so-called "placebo." Most importantly, neither the subjects nor the scientists administering the drugs and measuring the effects know which group is which. They are "blind" as to who took the real drug. Therefore, their measurements cannot be affected by their desire to see the drug work. These kinds of controls

are especially useful when the data analysis requires some subjective assessment on the part of the subject or the scientist.

- *Peer Review*: When scientists think they have discovered something, they submit their findings to scientific journals. Then the material is sent to other qualified scientists. These other scientists study the research and look for possible errors or leaps in logic. They study the methods of experimentation to determine whether the designs of the experiments were valid and whether they really show what the authors claim. Only when scientists from different areas agree the research is valid is it published. Not only does peer review minimize bias, but over time accumulated data tends to overthrow erroneous theories and expose fraud. The very historical evidence cited by postmodern critics to show that the scientific community has at times held to false theories demonstrates science's ability to refute those false theories in the long run.
- *Falsifiability*: Well-conceived hypotheses are falsifiable—that is, their authors suggest conditions that would negate them. If someone claimed they were being visited by aliens who only appeared when no one was looking, he would be making an unfalsifiable claim. Within the constraints of the scientific method, we could never know if such a claim is true because it can be neither proven nor disproven. Scientists, however, would never accept such a claim because it fails the test of falsifiability.

Postmodern critics haven't demonstrated why these safeguards against subjectivity are invalid. Even in cases where safeguards have failed, it usually isn't for long. Moreover, when results are unclear, responsible scientists hold their conclusions tentatively. It seems that the sciences try and often succeed in being unbiased and objective in what they observe. This is particularly true when the areas studied are not too far removed in space and time from those conducting the investigation.

Is Reason Valuable in Discovering Truth?

Modernists claim the sciences are rational. They use logic to outline problems, interpret observations, and formulate and study hypotheses. Postmodernists deny that science is rational in the way modernists claim. They also deny that rationality offers any hope for objectivity. As earlier chapters have noted, postmodernists believe logic itself is an invention of Western culture. Therefore, some question not *whether* science is rational, but whether rationality offers any insights into the world better than, say, intuition or feeling. They also argue that there is no such thing as purely objective reason in the sense Europeans use the word.[21]

Again, as we have noted before, the postmodernist's arguments are self-defeating. Postmodernists depend on a number of *reasons*—ironically—to express their view.

Do Scientists' Hypotheses Ruin Their Objectivity?

Other postmodernists claim that even if reason shows us reality, that doesn't mean science operates rationally. These psychologists and historians of science argue that once scientists form hypotheses they lose objectivity.[22] Also, some statisticians have argued that scientists must acknowledge "the role of subjectivity in the interpretation of data."[23]

Further, as previously mentioned, philosophers have long observed that hypotheses do not merely rise up from raw data. Instead, they originate in the mind of the observer, who then imposes the hypothesis upon the data as a way of organizing it.[24] The world is full of physical data, much of which goes unnoticed by the casual observer. How does a scientist decide which information is useful and which isn't?[25] In order to collect data she must first decide what is important. But once that is done, she has introduced subjectivity into her reasoning process. In other words, the act of selecting what data to study is the first act of *interpretation*. This is how, according to postmodernists, scientists impose an artificial and subjective order upon their observations. Because the order is being applied *before* observation and testing rather than as a *result* of testing, it cannot be considered a product of rational scientific methodology.

Postmodern criticisms are of some value in that they unmask and correct the extreme modernist idea that the sciences are supremely rational. We should probably say that science *tries* to be rational through its methods and procedures, and this is a good thing. Postmodernism, though, would abandon all effort to be objective.

Surely we can hold that science provides a reasonable guide to large portions of the natural realm. All humans, modernists and postmodernists alike, base their actions upon beliefs they take to be true because of reason. In that sense, everyone is a scientist. Professional scientists simply attempt to introduce more rigor and thus more certainty into these processes.

Are the Assumptions of Science Obviously True?

All rational disciplines take certain things for granted, things considered true even though they can't be proven from within that particular discipline. Such beginning points are called *presuppositions*. For instance, we assume our eyes see things that really exist, and that our ears hear real sound. We have no way to prove these assumptions, because any machine or experiment we concoct to test them would also depend on our senses to gather measurements. Therefore, all knowledge has beginning points that we accept as an act of reasonable faith.

Since the assumptions of science are impervious to scientific methods, modernists can't on the one hand claim to be scientists and on the other hand argue that the truth of their presuppositions is irrefutable. This is a contradiction within modernism: Their conclusions are supposed to be based on reason and observation, not on faith. Yet confidence in things like observation require, as their base, a commitment of faith. Modernists end up using faith even as they argue against it.

For example, scientists suppose that nature is understandable. The practical successes of science and technology over the past century is powerful evidence that this assumption is usually valid. On the other hand, there may be limits to our ability to understand nature. Current cosmological theory, for instance, holds that the laws of physics as we understand them did not operate until a few moments after the "Big Bang." How, then, can we claim the universe is comprehensible?

Likewise, scientists assume that nature is uniform, yet they have not and cannot analyze every discrete event in the cosmos to see if this is true. Scientists design experiments to *sample* nature and then they *extrapolate* principles from that sample. They believe such extrapolations hold true for the rest of the universe, although this has not been proven.

These are only two of many presuppositions underlying science. But they should suffice to demonstrate that scientific assumptions aren't undeniably true.

Quantum Physics and Scientific Mysticism

Postmodern critics of Western science have a powerful and popular ally in their attacks—scientific mystics. These mystics generally seek to demonstrate that science backs up the great religions of Asia: Buddhism, Hinduism, and Taoism. They attempt to draw support for their beliefs primarily from the field of quantum physics—the branch of physics concerned with the behavior of sub-atomic particles.

Scientific mystics are not explicitly postmodern. Their origins are different and unlike strict postmodernists, who tend to deny all doctrines, they espouse a doctrine. They do, however, use postmodern rhetorical techniques and attacks on rationality to prove their points, and postmodernists in turn draw on the mystics to sustain postmodernism. For instance, Anderson, in his postmodern treatise, uses Capra's points on physics as proof of postmodern rejection of reason.[26]

Therefore, the mystics should be seen as new, slightly different allies within the postmodern fold. Like militant feminists, race theorists, and other ideological groups, they are the heirs of the postmodern method. Many have suggested that postmodernism's critique of reason has paved the way for mysticism to assert itself.[27] As time passes, the distinction between mysticism and postmodernism grows increasingly dim. Both oppose the traditional view of theism and modernism that a real physical universe exists and can be studied using the tools of observation and reason to discover reliable knowledge. Both find that science leads to contradictory data, suggesting that the rules of logic don't square with reality. For all practical purposes, then, while technically different, postmodernism and mysticism have made common cause today in their struggle against Western modernism and theism, including Christianity.

Mysticism and Science in the Past

Attempts to connect science and mysticism aren't new. Prominent scientists, including some of the key figures involved in creating the atom bomb, have claimed a connection between science and the anti-rational traditions of the East, as these statements from some of this century's most prominent scientists show:

J. R. Oppenheimer, 1954:

> The general notions about human understanding . . . which are illustrated by discoveries in atomic physics are not . . . new. Even in our own culture they have a history, and in Buddhist and Hindu thought a more considerable and central place. What we shall find is an exemplification, an encouragement, and a refinement of old wisdom.[28]

Niels Bohr, 1958:

> For a parallel to the lesson of atomic theory . . . [we must turn] to those kinds of epistemological problems with which thinkers like the Buddha and Lao Tzu [the founder of Taoism] have already been confronted, when trying to harmonize our position as spectators and actors in the great drama of existence.[29]

Werner Heisenberg, 1958:

> The great scientific contribution in theoretical physics that has come from Japan since the last war may be an indication of a certain relationship between philosophical ideas in the tradition of the Far East and the philosophical substance of quantum theory.[30]

From the period after World War II until the present, mystically minded scholars have drawn upon the work of theoretical physics and mathematics to justify their beliefs. Typically, mystical scientists argue that science and math show that nature isn't like a machine—the modernists' view—but fluid and ethereal, as the religions of Asia claim. In their mystical view of nature, all distinctions disappear. They are *monists*, who believe everything is ultimately one. Mathematician Rudy Rucker, one of their own, explains:

> The Irish philosopher George Berkeley (1685–1753) advocated an idealistic philosophy called *immaterialism*. . . . It is surprising to learn that such a seemingly perverse worldview is embraced by modern physicists. . . . I propose that we stop trying to explain our mental experiences in terms of invisibly tiny objects arranged in patterns in 3-D space. Instead let us take our actual thoughts and sensations as the truly fundamental entities.[31]

Notice the progression in Rucker's comments: Once we accept the "evidence" for monism, the source of authority rapidly changes to nothing more than personal experience. Renee Weber, a postmodern philosopher, agrees, and takes the argument one step further:

> Unlike science, which turns to the world outside the seeker, mysticism turns within, to the laws that govern the seeker himself. . . . Both scientist and sage are transformers of energy, involved in the dance of Shiva. The scientist makes the dense matter dance to produce pure energy, the mystic—master of subtle matter—dances the dance of himself. . . .[32]

Fritjof Capra and Friends

Like postmodernists, mystical scientists view traditional science negatively. In contrast, however, these thinkers believe a more enlightened science is possible. Enlightened science, as usually defined, is "inclusive," "holistic," and nurturing of life. Fritjof Capra, the best-selling apologist for postmodern mystical science, explains in his book *The Tao of Physics*:

> This book aims at improving the image of science by showing that there is an essential harmony between the spirit of Eastern wisdom and Western science. It attempts to suggest that modern physics goes far beyond technology, that the way—or Tao—of physics can be a path with a heart, a way to spiritual knowledge and self-realization.[33]

We see the same themes in the words of Renee Weber, mystical apologist: "Science as it is used in this book stands for the attitude of Einstein rather than of Bacon: an attitude of kinship with nature rather than of exploitive power over her."[34]

Quantum Physics and Reality

Mystics use quantum physics to claim nature is more mystical and irrational. Mystical apologist Fritjof Capra explains how he sees the relationship between Eastern religion and quantum physics:

> The basic oneness of the universe is not only the central characteristic of the mystical experience, but is also one of the most important revelations of modern physics. . . . As we study the various models of subatomic physics we shall see that they express again and again, in different ways, the same insight . . . [that all things are] interconnected, interrelated, and interdependent; that they cannot be understood as isolated entities, but only as integrated parts of the whole.[35]

How does he arrive at this? Mystics base their views on three major findings of quantum physics:

- *Complementarity*: Physicists have found that light or electrons behave paradoxically under some experimental conditions. At times they behave *as if* they were particles, yet under other conditions they behave *as if* they were waves.

  Mystics believe that because one thing behaves like two different things proves that language and reason are inadequate to describe reality. Reality is actually a fusion of opposites, just as good and evil are part of the same whole in mysticism. Traditional scientists argue that their findings support no such mystical conclusion. They charge that the mystics take an analogy—that light behaves *like* a particle, and that light behaves *like* a wave—as solid reality. Moreover, the mystics confuse paradox with contradiction. In this instance, the analogies each describe one aspect of the behavior of light. These descriptions are no more contradictory than it is to say a motorcycle is similar to both a bicycle and a car.
- *Indeterminacy*: Heisenberg's uncertainty principle says one can't measure a subatomic particle's position and momentum simultaneously with perfect precision. In other words, if a physicist can determine the location of a particle, he can't find its exact momentum. The very act of observation is what causes uncertainty.

  Mystics claim that such uncertainty shows that the observer and the observed are inseparable, and that the universe is a unified whole—"all is one and one is all." Scientists respond that at least eight different theories have been developed to explain Heisenberg's uncertainty principle, none of which has won the day. Where science is without a definitive answer, the mystics have inserted an unprovable philosophical view, a sort of "Tao of the gaps" approach.

- *Action at a distance*: Physicists have found that if a pair of particles are created then separated, changing the spin of one particle instantaneously changes the spin of its mate. Again, mystics see this as proof of the interconnectedness of all things. Traditional scientists charge that mystics are taking a small piece of data from the physical universe and stretching it to apply to a non-physical concept. The meaning of such experiments is simply not clear at this time.

To summarize, traditional scientists believe the mystics are flawed in taking the tentative findings of quantum physics—a young, developing scientific field—and claiming to find proof for philosophical arguments. When we look at all the data and possible interpretations, we discover that the mystical claims laid upon quantum physics aren't justified. Efforts to back up Eastern religious doctrine by reference to physics are really rhetorical rather than scientific.

Where Postmodern Critics Are Wrong

Postmodern criticism of science is, as in other areas, mainly a grand exaggeration. Postmodernists begin by successfully showing that scientific conclusions often include ambiguity at some level. Yet they exaggerate that ambiguity to suggest that no scientific findings are rational or true in the objective sense.

> Christians have nothing to gain from a return to the "dark age" of pre-scientific superstition.

They also commit the same error we have seen in other areas: They use observation and logical inference to reach the conclusion that observation and logical inference tell us nothing. They argue in a circle, only defeating themselves. By using the tools of science, they demonstrate that they too believe these tools work. Some postmodernists play fast and loose with the findings of the sciences to a level that seems patently hypocritical.

After considering all the postmodern observations of fringe examples and selected scientific error, the fact remains that science attains the goal of discovering objective, rational truth much of the time. The methods used in the sciences have produced powerful explanations about how things work and innumerable useful applications, including technology even its harshest critics would never be without. Geison's words still ring true: "No serious student of modern science will deny that it represents the closest thing we have to consensual, objective, international, 'universal' knowledge. The claim to a special epistemological status for modern science . . . has been under assault for a generation or more, but no better alternative is yet in sight."[36]

Christians have suffered from scientific subjectivity in the past, as in modernist propagandizing about naturalistic theories of evolution. Yet the rise of modern science would have been impossible without Christian presuppositions that the universe is rational because it was created by a rational God. Christians have nothing to gain from a return to pre-scientific superstition, and we may well be headed into a new dark age of ignorance in the scientific realm. Christianity has rightly critiqued instances where science has acted more like a religion. However, we can't turn away from critiquing the postmodern onslaught on reason and truth, including the truth in the sciences.

Can there be a position somewhere between modernism's boasts of omniscience on one hand and postmodernism's denial of reason on the other? We believe so. We can welcome some of the postmodern critiques of so-called objectivity in science—most of which have been argued by Christian thinkers in the past—without reaching the postmodern conclusion that scientific objectivity is a pointless goal.

In Brief

- Postmodernists see science as the ultimate example of Western arrogance. They attack the scientific method, denying that science can deliver the objectivity it claims.
- They argue that the progress of science has come not through a process of gradual application of reason, but through periodic

shifts in paradigms when all theories are rethought based on the new view. The transitions between old and new paradigms are irrational conversion experiences often caused by social pressures.

- Postmodernists deny the objectivity and the rationality of science in a way similar to their denial of objectivity in other disciplines—that language determines one's interpretations, that individuals can never remove themselves and their impressions from their study, and that reason itself cannot guide us to an objective knowledge of truth.
- Mystical scientists are now making common cause with postmodern critics to argue that science proves monism, and that reason and language cannot explain reality. Both mystics and other postmodernists argue against rationality and objectivity.
- None of the conclusions of either group have been demonstrated, although some points raised by postmodern critics helpfully check modernists' overconfidence in reason.

Notes

1. P. K. Feyerabend, *Against Method: Outlines of an Anarchist Theory of Knowledge* (London: New Leaf Books, 1975), p. 299. Feminist philosopher Sandra Harding suggests that Newton's "Principles of Mechanics" should be called, "Newton's Rape Manual." Cited in Constance Holden, "Reason Under Fire," *Science*, Vol. 268 (June 30, 1995).
2. Renee Weber, *Dialogues with Scientists and Sages*, ". . . most scientists want to dissociate themselves from mysticism . . . ," p. 4.
3. For the purposes of simplicity I will use the term *modernism* to refer to various ideologies including materialism, naturalism, logical positivism, rationalism, and empiricism. These are metaphysical beliefs about the nature of reality or epistemological beliefs about how reality can be discovered.
4. Raymond Eve presented this and other research at the convention of the American Association for the Advancement of Science, 1995. His research also showed that twenty to twenty-five percent of those interviewed held distinctly mystical views.

5. Connie Barlow, ed., *Evolution Extended: Biological Debates on the Meaning of Life* (Cambridge: MIT Press).
6. Joseph S. Levine and Kenneth R. Miller, *Biology: Discovering Life*, 2nd edition (D.C. Heath and Company, 1994), p. 161 (emphasis added).
7. Other authors have devoted considerable effort to critiquing modernism and its use of science. See, for instance, J. P. Moreland, *Christianity and the Nature of Science: A Philosophical Investigation* (Grand Rapids: Baker Book House, 1989); D. Ratzsch, *The Natural Sciences in Christian Perspective*, from C. S. Evans, ed., *Contours of Christian Philosophy* (Downers Grove: InterVarsity Press, 1986); Phillip E. Johnson, *Reason in the Balance: The Case Against Naturalism* (Downers Grove: InterVarsity Press, 1995).
8. T. S. Kuhn, "The Structure of Scientific Revolutions," R. Carnap, P. Frank, J. Joergensen, C. Morris, O. Neurath, and L. Rougier, eds., *International Encyclopedia of Unified Science*, Vol. 2, No. 2 (Chicago: The University of Chicago Press, 1962).
9. From J. Kourany, *Scientific Knowledge* (Belmont, Calif.: Wadsworth Publishing Co., 1987), p. 200.
10. P. K. Feyerabend, *Science in a Free Society* (London: New Leaf Books, 1978), p. 70. This same point is made by Kuhn in his 1969 postscript to *The Structure of Scientific Revolutions*, p. 198ff.
11. There are many such critics (e.g. Marx, Nietzsche, Max Scheler, Emile Durkheim, Marcel Mauss, and Karl Mannheim). Mannheim argued that social relationships influence the actual form of thought in P. Kesckemetic, ed., *Ideology and Utopia: An Introduction to the Sociology of Knowledge* (London: Routledge & Kegan Paul, 1952). See our explanation of sociology of knowledge in Chapter 3. Beyond Kuhn and Feyerabend, sociology of knowledge has energized even more radical critiques of traditional science. See, for example, Jerome Bruner, *Actual Minds, Possible Worlds* (Cambridge: Harvard University Press, 1986), who writes, "The moment one abandons the idea that 'the world' is there once for all and immutable, and substitutes for it the idea that what we take as the world is itself no more or less than a stipulation couched in a symbol system, then the shape of the discipline alters radically. And we are, at last in a position to deal with the myriad forms that reality can take—including realities created by story, as well as those created by science." See also B. Latour and S. Woolgar, *Laboratory Life: The Social Construction of Scientific Facts* (Beverly Hills: Sage, 1979); B. Barber, *Resistance by Scientists to Scientific Discovery*, Science 134, #3479 (1961), pp. 596–602, or to some extent David Bloor, *Knowledge and Social Imagery* (London: Routledge & Kegan Paul, 1976).
12. Actually, Feyerabend complains about this when he says, "Never before has the literature on the philosophy of science been invaded by so many creeps and incompetents. Kuhn encourages people who have no idea why a stone falls to the ground to talk with assurance about scientific method." In E. D. Klemke, R. Hollinger, and A. D. Kline, eds., "How to Defend Society Against Science," from *Introductory Readings in the Philosophy of Science*, Revised Edition (Prometheus Books, 1988).
13. See Robert L. Park, "The Danger of Voodoo Science," *New York Times*, OP-

ED (Sunday, July 9, 1995), and Christina Hoff Sommers, "The Flight From Science and Reason," *The Wall Street Journal* (Monday, July 10, 1995): p. 1.

14. See Walter Anderson, *Reality Isn't What It Used to Be*, Chapter 3 for the use of neurophysiology research to undermine the notion of objective perceptions; some examples of this kind of evidence might include the following: 1. Kittens raised in environments devoid of vertical visual cues have brains that are devoid of regions that respond to such cues, and behaviorally these kittens cannot be conditioned to respond to reward triggers that are vertically oriented. 2. Subjects who've lost or never had neuronal connections between their right and left cortex have behaviors that indicate they don't know why they are doing what they are doing. See the work of Roger Sperry on split-brain patients, for which he received the Nobel Prize, e.g. Kandel, Schwartz, and Jessell, *Principles of Neural Science*, 3rd edition, (Appleton & Lange, 1991), pp. 833–835. Subjects with damage to the visual cortex are essentially blind, yet they can react to things in their visual field while denying that they see anything—a phenomenon called "blind-sight." These are all used to illustrate the possibility that we might be perceiving things that are different from "objective reality" and different from what other people see because our brains are wired differently.
15. This critique has a long tradition reaching back to Kant. Even if we detect reality through our perceptions, how can we be assured that our *beliefs* about those perceptions are "true" in an objective sense? N. R. Hanson in his book *Patterns of Discovery* (Cambridge: University Press, 1958) emphasizes the dependence of seeing upon theory. See especially pp. 8, 17–19. See also Nelson Goodman, *Fact, Fiction, and Forecast* (Boston: Harvard University Press, 1983), pp. 59–83.
16. Perceptual illusions, be they optical, tactile, aural, olfactory, kinesthetic, are evidence that the senses can be fooled. Perceptions may produce beliefs but they do not, necessarily, produce true beliefs. See E. H. Grombrich, *Art and Illusion* in The A. W. Mellon Lectures in the Fine Arts, 2nd edition, Bollingen Series XXX.5 (New York: Pantheon Books, 1960), p. 204. See also D. C. McClelland and J. W. Atkinson, "The Projective Expression of Needs: I. The Effect of Different Intensities of the Hunger Drive on Perception," *Journal of Psychology*, Vol. 25 (1948): pp. 205–222. This research is not new, but the conclusions postmodernists draw from it is more recent.
17. Subjects in one study tended to initially accept propositions as true regardless of the *prima facie* evidence they were false. If they were distracted while considering those propositions, they tended to retain the belief that these propositions were true regardless of evidence to the contrary. See Bower, Bruce, "True Believers: The thinking person may favor gullibility over skepticism," *Science News*, Vol. 139 (January 5, 1991): pp. 14–15.
18. For example, Bloor writes, "Psychologists, historians, and sociologists have provided fascinating examples of social processes interacting with perception, or perception and recall. . . . Unexpected events then take place before their eyes and are not seen—or if they are seen, they evoke no response. . . . Conversely, where some observers see nothing . . . others do have experiences . . . which fall into line with their expectations." David Bloor, *Knowledge and Social*

Imagery, Second Edition (Chicago: The University of Chicago Press, 1991), p. 25. Collins and Pinch cite several such examples including Eddington's use of Einstein's theory to distinguish "real" data from "noise," while at the same time using his results to confirm Einstein's theory. H. Collins and T. Pinch, *In the Golem: What everyone should know about science* (Cambridge: Cambridge University Press, 1993); Barber argues from several case studies that particular paradigms had the effect of blinding researchers to the evidence right in front of their eyes because those paradigms did not anticipate the evidence they encountered. Kuhn, Lakatos, Feyerabend, Bloor, Latour, Barber, and others deal extensively with the influence of culture upon beliefs.

19. See L. Wittgenstein, *Philosophical Investigations* (Oxford: Basil Blackwell, 1953), pp. 193ff, and W.V.O. Quine, *From a Logical Point of View* (Cambridge: Harvard University Press, 1953), pp. 131ff, for critiques of objectivity based on linguistic problems.
20. In Kuhn's *The Structure of Scientific Revolutions*, he argues that theories are required for meaningful observation to take place. But this makes the observation selective and subjective because it depends on a model of reality rather than on reality itself. He says that fact collecting without the context of an operant model, theory, or as he terms it *paradigm*, "produces a morass." "Only very occasionally . . . do facts collected with so little guidance from pre-established theory speak with sufficient clarity to permit the emergence of a first paradigm," p. 16.
21. See Andrea Nye, *Words of Power: A Feminist Reading of the History of Logic* (London: Routledge, 1990). She claims that logic has meant different things in different eras, and that the rules of logic are constantly changing.
22. As mentioned previously, Feyerabend and Kuhn view paradigm shifts as essentially irrational processes. Bloor doubts that efforts to correspond theories with reality are fruitful and suggests that correspondence of a theory with observations and predicted outcomes is more relevant for a scientist to consider. Kuhn and Bloor cite Priestly's experiments to demonstrate "phlogiston" as an example of faulty theories controlling the direction and interpretations of experimentation. In a well-known example, Lister found it very difficult to convince his fellow physicians to wash their hands between the dissection room and the operating table in spite of overwhelming evidence that the physicians were causing the spread of a deadly disease. His notions of infection were not the current view or *paradigm* of how disease was caused and so the data was ignored.
23. J. O. Berger and D. A. Berry, "Statistical Analysis and the Illusion of Objectivity," *American Scientist*, Vol. 76 (March-April, 1988): pp. 159–166; Berger and Berry are professors of statistics at Purdue University and the University of Minnesota, respectively; Bayesian statistics is an effort to make the subjective elements in inferential analysis explicit.
24. This concern dates back to Hume and Kant, but see Michael Polanyi, *Personal Knowledge* (Chicago: The University of Chicago Press, and London: Routledge & Kegan Paul, Ltd., 1958; revised edition 1962) where he argues that adoption of new theories is an intuitive, therefore subjective event.
25. For instance, suppose you wanted to study the cause(s) of light emission by

certain fungi. What data would you collect and what data would you ignore? Is the time of day relevant; the ambient temperature; the cycle of the moon; the presence of dog urine; the orientation of the planets; the presence of cellulose in the fungus?

26. Walter T. Anderson, *Reality Isn't What It Used to Be*.
27. See Park and Sommers, above.
28. J. Robert Oppenheimer, *Science and the Common Understanding* (New York: Oxford University Press, 1954), pp. 8–9.
29. Niels Bohr, *Atomic Physics and Human Knowledge* (New York: John Wiley & Sons, 1958), p. 20.
30. W. Heisenberg, *Physics and Philosophy* (New York: Harper Torchbooks, 1958), p. 202. Interestingly, all three citations (of Oppenheimer, Bohr, and Heisenberg) are found in Capra's *The Tao of Physics* (Boston: Shambhala Publishers, 1991).
31. Rudy Rucker, *The Fourth Dimension. A guided tour of the higher universes*. (Boston: The Houghton Mifflin Company, 1984), pp. 193–195.
32. Renee Weber, *Dialogues With Scientists and Sages: The Search for Unity* (London: Routledge & Kegan Paul), pp. 7, 16, 18–19.
33. Fritjof Capra, *The Tao of Physics* (Boston: Shambhala Publishers, 1991), p. 25.
34. Renee Weber, *Dialogues With Scientists and Sages: The Search for Unity* (London: Routledge & Kegan Paul, 1987), p. 7.
35. Fritjof Capra, *The Tao of Physics*, p. 131.
36. Geison and Holmes, eds., "In Research Schools: Historical Reappraisals," (Osiris, Vol. 8) as cited in *Science*, Vol. 263, February 4, 1994.

12

Postmodern Impact: Religion

Jim Leffel and Dennis McCallum, Contributors

Religion has sustained centuries of attack from modernists. Yet people today are as interested in spiritual things as ever. Recently, sociologists have shown that 95 percent of adults believe in God or a Universal Spirit.[1]

Books on angels, near-death experiences, the New Age, Christianity, and the occult top the best-seller lists. While people are still tuned in to spiritual things, in recent years the *kind* of spirituality commanding interest has changed vastly.

In this chapter, we will investigate the impact of postmodernism on American religious thought. In the next chapter we will examine several case studies that illustrate the shifts this chapter describes.

New Attitudes Toward Religion

Not long ago, the *Dear Abby* column tackled the issue of family quarrels over religion. A reader told Abby,

> Your answer to the woman who complained that her relatives were always arguing with her about religion was ridiculous. You advised her to simply declare the subject off-limits. Are you suggesting that people talk only about trivial, meaningless subjects so as to avoid a potential controversy? . . . It is arrogant to tell people there are subjects they may not mention in your presence. You could have suggested she learn enough about her relatives' cult to show them the errors contained in its teachings.

In response, Abby wrote this:

> In my view, the height of arrogance is to attempt to show people the "errors" in the religion of their choice.[2]

Abby's reply captures a growing sentiment about spirituality today. The grossest possible sins one could commit in the religious arena are showing *intolerance* and claiming *objectivity*. You don't have to think long to recognize these as the cardinal sins reviled by postmodernism in general. Those who differ with others based on reason are using "truth claims" to exclude other cultural groupings. Those who think they are objective are naive, and dangerous.

The First Cardinal Sin: Intolerance

Abby complains that the reader was arrogant to try to discuss errors in someone's religious beliefs. The point is clear: Offering objections to an article of faith is morally offensive.[3] To Abby and the majority of Americans below the age of fifty, questioning the truthfulness of another person's religious view is showing intolerance.

In the past, intolerance meant bigotry or prejudice—that is, judging someone or excluding them because of the color of their skin or their country of origin, or because of a superficial understanding of what they believe. It also usually implied a desire to use force to oppose other points of view. Intolerance, in the old sense, offends most of us. Evangelical Christians have suffered bitterly from intolerance—persecution ranging from social ridicule to martyrdom. At other times they have perpetrated crimes of intolerance against others. But in postmodern usage, intolerance has come to mean simply disagreeing with anyone else's beliefs. It's off limits—"arrogant," to use Abby's word.

This prohibition against challenging the ideas of others is clearly postmodern. To question another's view is to invade and pillage a different cultural context—or a different "reality"—than our own. Given postmodern assumptions, such judgments are naive. If we can't communicate cross-culturally or even interpersonally without seeing things from our own subjective context, how can we critique another view?

The Lone Exception to the Rule of Tolerance: *Fundamentalism*

Strangely, it turns out that postmodernists grant one exception to this universal prohibition against intolerance. For some reason, it's okay to question and even denounce the religious views pejoratively labeled "fundamentalism." Today, when people refer to *fundamentalists* they no longer just mean religious extremists, like the Shiites waging holy war against the West. Today, "fundamentalism" can refer to anyone who claims to know truth or who charges another religion with falsehood. Postmodern analyst Fredrick Turner, for instance, calls for tolerance and syncretism (mixing different religions together). Yet in the same article he calls evangelical Christianity a "junk religion"![4]

Where is the tolerance? Where is the inclusiveness?

Postmodernists argue that those they label fundamentalists are unacceptable because they subscribe to universal truth claims, what postmodern thinkers call *metanarratives*. Metanarratives are overarching explanations of reality based on central organizing "truths." Those who believe in universal explanations for reality are considered to be *totalistic* or *logocentric* in their thinking. Instead, postmodernists believe each group tells its own story or narrative, their own understanding of reality—understandings that others should never discount, exclude, or marginalize. *Totalistic* thinkers such as *fundamentalists* want their story to dominate all other stories.

How do postmodern thinkers reconcile their attacks on so-called fundamentalist religious belief with their insistence that no one should ever differ with another's religious views? By now you should be able to predict the answer—any need for rational consistency is a Western cultural construct! In fact, any who point out this inconsistency are simply trying to use so-called reason to gain power over cultural groups that dare to question the status quo. Besides, postmodernists say, Christians and other fundamentalists are never consistent with their own truth claims either.

Abby's judgment that her reader was arrogant turns out to be profoundly intolerant, even though asserted under the guise of hypertolerance. Abby thus becomes a spokesperson for postmodernism, the most *totalizing* of all views because it completely discounts all alternative understandings.

Abby may or may not realize she reflects postmodern analysis. She may be like many who fell into Transcendental Meditation in the 60s and 70s without realizing they were practicing Hinduism. Nevertheless, they were. The same is often true in the field of popular American religion. The attitudes are postmodern no matter what labels are attached.

The Second Cardinal Sin: Objectivity in Religion

Abby implies that because a person has chosen a religion, others should accept its validity without assessment. Remember her words: "The height of arrogance is to attempt to show people the 'errors' in the religion of their *choice*." Postmodern thinkers have two problems with criticizing religious choice: First, questioning another's beliefs implies that we can discover an external, objective reality, when reality in fact is a social construct. By trying to apply rationality to religion, we are actually trying to impose European Enlightenment culture on others. Also, according to postmodernists, people "construct" reality—that is, something is true *because* I believe it. Therefore, by challenging the truth claims of another's religion, we devalue the person, who is the source of his or her own truth. Rejecting the *content* of belief is assumed to be the same as rejecting the believer.

According to postmodernists, fundamentalists are those who believe religious teachings are true or false not just within their own paradigm but over all paradigms. Fundamentalists view religious truth as objectively true, and therefore subject to rational scrutiny. Evangelicals—those who strive to hold to a biblical faith as expressed in the early church and the Reformation—certainly fall within this circle because we believe that if something is true, its opposite cannot be true at the same time, regardless of what paradigm a person holds.

You may have noticed that evangelicalism, like modernism, insists on consistency. Both evangelicals and modernists have historically believed in the use of reason, beginning with the law of noncontradiction: "A is not non-A." So, for instance, the Creator can't be a personal God and an impersonal force at the same time.

By taking the same stand as modernism in this particular area—though not in others—evangelical Christians have placed themselves in the direct line of fire of the growing postmodern consensus.

Let's be clear: Postmodernists aren't against religion. They are only against religious teaching that holds to objective truth and the usefulness of reason. Religion based only on personal experience and "what's true for me" is perfectly compatible with the postmodern worldview.

> Most postmodernists aren't against religion. They are only against religious teaching that holds to objective truth and usefulness of reason.

But once reason is rejected, truth in the objective sense must be automatically rejected as well. What use is a "truth" if the opposite, or "antithetical," position is also true? In place of truths that make sense or truths that can be backed up in some way, postmodernism again leaves its adherents with two things: experience and power. My experience is the basis for my beliefs, and those beliefs exist to empower me.

Postmodernism and the Shift in American Religion

From this brief discussion of a *Dear Abby* column chosen for its common sentiment, we see obvious parallels between academic postmodernism and popular American religious views. Certainly it is impossible to trace the spread of postmodern faith to popular culture through any single entry point. Neither is postmodernism the sole explanation for why this religious shift has occurred. As with most major cultural swings, people are never fully aware of the exact source of their beliefs. They seem to gradually accept a consensus arising from a number of sources. Aside from formal postmodernism, the following factors have also played a part in the religious shift in America:

- In the 60s, *the drug culture* expanded into the vacuum of meaning created by naturalism and sterile church traditionalism. Along with drugs came *Eastern religious views*. Through hallucinogenic drugs young people experienced states of "altered consciousness" they couldn't explain in rational terms. The early years of the drug culture should be seen not only as a rejection of middle-class American values but also as a departure from modernism's cold objectivity. Popular books such as Carlos Castineda's *Don Juan* and the teachings of Alan Watts, Timothy Leary, the Maharishi Mahesh Yogi, Krishna Consciousness, and Alan Ginsberg, among others, helped bridge hallucinogenic drug experiences and mysticism, both Eastern and Native American. We shouldn't overlook the fact that many of the apostles of postmodernism were part of this period's countercultural movement.

- During this same period, *the church was experiencing substantial decline*. Reports that people have since been returning to church are largely untrue.[5] A huge number of Americans have been lost to the church during our lifetimes. For instance, of those born between 1945 and 1962 and raised in a religious environment, 33 percent never left the church, 25 percent have come back, but a walloping 42 percent are still away.[6] As analysts like Os Guinness point out, the decline of Christianity is a major factor in the growth of Eastern mysticism and the occult.[7]
- In an age where *relativism* is a measurable consensus, even those remaining in the evangelical church have shown little discernment. According to Gallup, while 88 percent of evangelicals believe that "the Bible is the written word of God, accurate in all it teaches," 53 percent of the same respondents believe "there is no such thing as absolute truth."[8] The impotence of the evangelical church in helping even its own members resist postmodern thinking must be a major factor in the rise of this irrational outlook.
- A number of *liberation movements* have focused attention on the plight of minorities—blacks, the poor, women, gays and lesbians, the handicapped, and so on. Religious outlooks identified with such liberation movements, such as native spiritualities and goddess spiritualities, have risen along with the others being "liberated." Those who oppose liberation movements have come to be characterized as intolerant and repressive. In some cases, Christians have been viewed as intolerant—sometimes deservedly, as in the case of churches that fought against equal rights for blacks, or out of faithfulness, as when resisting gay liberation movements.[9]
- *New Age spirituality and occultism* are on the rise, partly because they have been championed by popular figures in the media.[10]

In many cases, these people are unaware of postmodernism. They simply adopt these views based on the word of a celebrity and their own sense that it "rings true" to them.

None of these movements descended directly from postmodernism. However, they share some views identical to those advanced by postmodernists, and they gather together under the umbrella of postmodern culture. Postmodernism has provided the philosophical framework that lends intellectual respectability to views and practices that once were considered superstitious or weird.

The coexistence and growth of these cultural and religious forces is worrisome, but their confluence into a single cohesive worldview is downright alarming. As such separate streams unite into the river of postmodernism and related outlooks, they gain a scholastic, institutional, and governmental credibility they never had as grassroots movements.

Borrowing or Coincidence?

Observers of religion are aware of a relativism that is part and parcel of Eastern mystical traditions such as Hinduism, Buddhism, and Taoism. These religions teach that everything is part of one essence, a belief system known as "monism" ("one"-ism). In Hinduism, the one divine essence is *Brahman*. In China it's the *Tao*, the *Way*. All these traditions reject reason as a tool for discovering truth. The central proposition of monism, that "everything is one," is no more rational than saying 1=1,000,000. They even utilize contradiction to drive learners to a deeper or higher plane of understanding. Zen Buddhism, for instance, offers *koans* such as "What is the sound of one hand clapping?" The Hindu *Brahman* is "always and never." With its rejection of rationality, such paradoxical thinking is naturally compatible with postmodernism.

Also, neither Eastern religions nor postmodernism accepts the reality of the world we observe in any objective sense. In Hinduism, the material world is *Maya*, which means *illusion*. What seems real to us—the material world—is an illusion.

The similarities between some central features of Eastern mysticism and postmodernism are so striking that many wonder whether there is a cause-and-effect connection between them.[11] Are postmodern scholars simply Hindus or Taoists who read their religious thinking into other disciplines?

Although this thought is tempting, and although a number of prominent postmodern thinkers are also Eastern mystics, the answer is, "Not exactly." Careful analysis shows that postmodern thinking didn't flow in any *direct* way from Eastern mysticism. The origins of postmodernism are the philosophies of Nietzsche, Heidegger, Marx, and Freud. This isn't to say that the religions of the East and tribal religions have played no part in the formation of postmodern analysis, particularly as it has recently evolved. Many postmodern students of culture have observed that in other worldviews (such as those of India, China, and aboriginal cultures) reason as the West defines it holds no important place and may indeed be virtually absent as a source of knowledge, especially in religion. This observation has supported postmodern scholars' claim that reason is nothing but a Western European construct. Confidence in rationality is, according to postmodernists, a religious doctrine based on faith, just like the religious view of other cultures.

Because postmodern analysis is in harmony with Eastern religion, postmodernists also may have hijacked Western interest in mysticism as a vehicle for propagating their views. The cultures that spawned Eastern religions as well as animistic mysticisms are also among the oppressed, non-European cultures championed by affirmative postmodernists.

Another possibility is that the Eastern, mystical climate in the West preconditioned people to accept the anti-rational postmodern arguments. Perhaps most likely is the theory that the influence has moved both ways. If this is true, then postmodernists may themselves be the very thing they describe: merely a construct of their—our—culture!

Anti-Rationalism in Religion

Animists and Eastern mystics aren't the only ones holding to an anti-rational worldview. According to a recent study, only 26 percent of progressive Catholic priests affirmed the statement "We are utterly dependent on God and should completely submit ourselves to His will for us." And at the same time, 65 percent of the same priests affirmed that "God is the Divine Presence in this world whom I discover through people, things and events."[12] The established church is awash in postmodern religious attitudes.

As mentioned earlier, tribal religions, or *animism* (such as Native American religion), also have no place for rationality. Faith in these systems is blind faith—reason cannot confirm or deny any aspect of their spirituality, according to adherents. Most tribal religious views are accepted from early childhood as part of what it means to be a member of the tribe. Under postmodern analysis, their religion is a construct of their culture, just as our confidence in enlightenment rationality (and Christianity) is a construct of ours.

Whether it's pantheism, animism, or theism, we search in vain for any safe haven from postmodern religious thinking.

Postmodernism lends intellectual respectability to views and practice that used to be considered superstitious or weird.

Today we face an American religious cafeteria. According to one postmodern religious leader, we "take the best and leave the rest," without any thought as to whether any of it is true in any objective sense. The question isn't whether shamanism, Zen Buddhism, or goddess spirituality is true, but whether "it works for me."

From Worship of God to Worship of Self

Postmodern religion seeks to bring together and appreciate elements from all religions. While the religions of oppressed (non-Western) cultures are particularly popular, even Christianity gets to make a contribution, as we shall see. The religious strands are sewn together with the thread of individual mystical experience.

In both pantheistic religion (where God is in everything) and animism (where the natural world is inhabited by spirits, or gods) people naturally reach conclusions different from those of theism, especially about our place in the cosmos. In pantheism, people are identical to god because all things are part of the One.[13] In animism, people gain control over spirits through shamanistic spiritual practices. In theism, God is distinct from creation. Faith centers on obeying and loving God.

New Age consciousness is an effort to affirm the good parts of all religions and develop a new meaning for spirituality. New Agers generally follow postmodern assumptions, and should therefore be viewed as within the postmodern fold.[14] Among other things, they argue that because humans are part of the cosmos, we are gods too. This is one reason contemporary spirituality focuses on the self, discovering our divinity within. New Age thinking is explicitly concerned with the journey toward realizing our essential divinity. Consider this statement from a popular New Age magazine:

> All paths lead to God. The true path finally becomes self empowerment: the path of self-love. Then one demonstrates that they can manifest God and no longer need to look outside themselves for this information. They have become the path themselves.[15]

Through meditation, hypnosis, "creative visualization," and "centering," we are taught that we can become conscious of our "higher self," our god within. Worship, then, becomes self-love. New Age spirituality is narcissism in the extreme!

This focus on self is strangely contradictory to academic postmodernism's denial of the self. Clearly, postmodern denial of self is primarily a denial of the modernist self and its complete autonomy and rational freedom. Apparently, room remains for a self based on these cultural, religious constructions. Eastern religion displays the same contradiction when it denies the self (*Atman*—the self is *Brahman*—the all) yet focuses attention on self-centered disciplines that seek self-consciousness.

The basically inward and self-oriented focus of postmodern spirituality is also pervasive outside New Age mysticism. For example, consider some branches of the self-help movement based on the Twelve Steps. Within many evangelical churches, these groups explicitly acknowledge that the "higher power" of twelve-step literature is none other than God and Jesus Christ. These responsible groups cast "unmanageable" (step 1) in terms of personal sin, and have adapted the twelve-step model to Christian teaching. Many secular programs and some church programs, however, use the literature of the movement without this clarification.

The handbook for the twelve-step movement, *Twelve Steps and Twelve Traditions*, teaches that recovery is based on entrusting ourselves to "God as we understand him." The vague but ever-present message of these branches of the recovery movement sharply distinguishes between "religion" and "spirituality." Spirituality is preferred over religion. "Spirituality" relates to whatever people choose to be their god (higher power). "Religion" refers to formal religious doctrines and institutions. Faith in our higher power exists primarily for the purpose of recovery. Such spirituality becomes an expedient to achieve what the believer wants or needs.

Christians have rightly welcomed the good fruits born in the secular recovery movement, such as people getting off drugs, and even many turning to Christ. But we haven't always considered the price paid for such fruit.

What do we communicate if we merely urge group members to give themselves to "God as you understand him" or to a "higher power" of your own making?[16] Ultimately, such vague and subjective formulas suggest that the *content* of belief is irrelevant. A higher power could be the God of the Bible, but it could also be anything from the recovery group itself (which is often encouraged) to a New Age concept of "the god within" to the gods of Buddhism.[17] People might have a religious experience with such a higher power, but one thing is discounted: the importance of propositional truth—statements of fact that can be confirmed or denied by reason and evidence. Or to put it differently, postmodern worshipers are like postmodern readers: They are the *source* of truth—because truth is true if they really believe it—not the *discoverers* of truth, which is true whether they realize it or not.

The literature of the secular recovery movement teaches that it's inappropriate to question another person's higher power, because recovery is tied to their belief in the power of the God of their understanding.[18] These branches of twelve-step spirituality are distinctly postmodern in the way *personal interpretation* or *experience* and *personal empowerment* are substituted for *truth* about God.

Postmodern religion in all its forms is marked by a placing of self and experience at the center. Once self occupies the center, a whole new world opens up. In New Age thought, we are gods able to *create* our own reality. How similar this is to the secular postmodern notion of "constructivism," where people construct knowledge or reality from within themselves or their belief community![19]

Reality has no objective meaning in postmodern religion. It's a projection of consciousness. As our consciousness changes, so too does our reality. Reality outside the mind is ethereal, without definition, until shaped by consciousness. By directing our consciousness through "creative visualization" or "imaging," we can make our future whatever we want it to be. Note the comments of Gary Springfield, New Ager and entrepreneur:

> The visualization process creates out of etheric matter something in fact. That is the beauty and power of visualization—we are creating out of etheric matter. As we create that powerfully enough within etheric matter, it becomes reality.[20]

New Age religion rests on the premise that reality is contingent on consciousness and that through directing individual consciousness, reality is shaped and molded.[21] In practical terms, adherents can use the power of visualization and imaging to enhance physical and emotional health, and not surprisingly, their financial situation. Springfield continues,

> If we still have issues with money, they are only a symbol for our lack of self-empowerment. Money is a symbol of power. When we don't have money, it is a symbol that we're not powerfully knowing of who we are.[22]

What is the relation between New Agers seeking to create reality through imaging and mind power and the Affirmative Postmodernists constructing new realities? Postmodernists start with the goal of a socially constructed reality, while these religious schools begin with the deity of self and the power of the mind. For both, the originator of reality is humankind. In both, people don't merely try to understand and respond to reality. They are the source of reality. And in both the reason for creating reality is personal empowerment.

From Truth to Experience: Authority in Postmodern Religion

Spirituality in postmodern religion puts the individual at the center, as we have seen. Authentic worship ends up being self-worship and self-empowerment. The self also becomes the integration point for spiritual truth: "It's true for me because I believe it." Organized religion with its creeds and statements of faith are out. Vague, individualistic spirituality is in.

We can characterize postmodern spirituality as a flight from the pursuit of historical and propositional truth to a preoccupation with mystical experience. For example, the claim "Christ rose from the dead" is an assertion of historic fact. It either happened or it didn't, and reason and evidence can shed light on whether or not the claim is true. The claim that "Jesus arose in my heart" is, on the other hand, a mystical experience. Reason and evidence are useless in assessing such a claim. To postmodern mystics, reason and evidence are deemed unnecessary, and even viewed with suspicion.

These views are very similar to postmodern assertions that truth and reality are cultural constructions. Remember, when postmodernists say our ideas are all social constructions, they are arguing that our experience determines truth. The whole point of formal postmodern analysis is that nothing is ever objective, that all we think is the result of our cultural experiences. Our beliefs never really result from rational analysis of evidence—though as members of a modernist society we may be the last to realize our own subjectivity.

> Postmodern worshipers are like postmodern readers: They are the *source* of truth, not the *discoverers* of truth.

Such subjectivity makes traditional approaches to Christian apologetics, with its emphasis on evidence and argument, less effective with many people. Of course, there are still millions of modernists who will listen to reason, and even the most committed postmodernists must eventually see reason if they are ever to see truth.[23] Postmodernists, in fact, use reason all the time. Their whole position is based on the complicated arguments found in this book. They only reject reason when it becomes inconvenient, and religion is one area where it's an absolute nuisance!

The more we study and understand postmodern culture, the more we will see how desperately people still need absolute, objective truth. In a world where everyone's position is true, nobody's position matters. The result is a lonely vacuum waiting for answers that matter to fill it. The loneliness and despair of the postmodern world will open new opportunities for evangelicals who take the time to understand the new consensus.

In Brief

- Our culture can be characterized as postmodern because the basics of modernism—confidence in reason, personal autonomy, and human progress—are rejected on a wide scale.
- Christianity shares with modernism a confidence in reason. Still worse—from a postmodernist point of view—Christianity claims we can know right from wrong even beyond our own culture. Christianity, therefore, comes under attack by postmodern thinkers who seek either to eradicate it or to reinterpret it along postmodern lines.
- According to postmodernists, just as rationality and objectivity are naive illusions in other fields, they are in religion the mark of crass Eurocentrism—and even worse, of fundamentalism.
- The inherent relativism and mysticism of Eastern and tribal religions are compatible with postmodern assumptions. These movements have developed independently, but now support each other and are virtually merging into one cultural consensus.
- Under postmodern influence, our culture is increasingly adopting religious views that transfer the focus of worship from God to the worshiper himself.
- In postmodern religion, reality is not fixed or objective. It is the construction of the religious faithful. Propositional truth is out. In its place is personal, subjective mystical experience. And in the postmodern view, any claims about the "authority of God" are really the thinly veiled power demands of religious leaders.

Notes

1. Andrew Greeley, *American Health* (January/February, 1987): p. 49. These statistics have been confirmed by Gallup and others.
2. "Deciding Whether to Discuss Religion Prompts Debate," in "Dear Abby," Tuesday, September 19, 1989.
3. The moral tone of Abby's comment is made more forcefully by W. C. Smith. "It is morally not possible to actually go out into the world and say to devout, intelligent fellow human beings: We believe that we know God and we are right; you believe that you know God, and you are totally wrong." Wilfred Cantwell Smith, *Religious Diversity* (New York: Harper and Row, 1976), p. 13.
4. Fredrick Turner, "The Future of the Gods: Notes Toward a Postmodern Religion," in *Rebirth of Value* (Albany, N.Y.: State University of New York Press, 1991), p. 83. Junk religion, in this context, means religion that is like junk food—it gives people what they want (like sweetened cereal) but little or no nutrition.
5. George Barna's surveys indicate that in spite of spending nearly three-quarters of a trillion dollars since 1982 on domestic missions, evangelical church attendance has dropped one percentage point during those years—from 40 percent to 39 percent of all Americans. George Barna, *What Effective Churches Have Discovered: New Insights on Ministry in the Late Nineties* (Glendale, Calif.: Barna Research Group Ltd., 1995), p. 11. Of the widely held belief that baby boomers are returning to church in large numbers, he reported at a conference in Columbus, Ohio, in June 1995, that "Nothing could be further from the truth . . . except for a short upturn from 1985–1991, boomers have been leaving the church in record numbers."
6. *Christianity Today* (March 8, 1993): p. 57, citing a survey by Wade Clark Roof of UC Santa Barbara.
7. Os Guinness, "The Encircling Eyes" and "The East No Exit," in *The Dust of Death* (Downers Grove: InterVarsity, 1973), pp. 277–278.
8. Gene Edward Veith, *Postmodern Times* (Wheaton, Ill.: Crossway Books, 1994), p. 16. Barna's figures are even higher. See Chapter 15, note 4.
9. Postmodern observers of course make no such moral distinction.
10. Greeley's survey indicates that over one half of Americans believe they have experienced ESP (extra-sensory perception). Sixty-seven percent of widows believe they have contacted the dead, and 42 percent of the general adult population claims to have had contact with the dead, while 31 percent have experienced clairvoyance. Andrew Greeley, *American Health* (January/February 1987): p. 49.
11. Some well-known postmodern thinkers are Eastern mystics, such as Walter Truett Anderson, a practicing Buddhist. See *Reality Isn't What It Used to Be* (New York: Harper Collins Publishers, 1990).

12. Michael P. Hornsby-Smith, Michael Procter, Lynda Rahan, Jennifer Brown, "A Typology of Progressive Catholics," *Journal for the Scientific Study of Religion*, Vol. 26, #2 (1987): pp. 234–248.
13. In Hinduism, for instance, the classic formulation is "Atman is Brahman." Atman, the individual soul, is Brahman, the universal spirit of god. Any sense that we are distinct from the universal "All" is an illusion.
14. They agree with postmodernism in these key areas: (1) They reject the modern view of nature as a physical machine. (2) They reject modern rationality, replacing it with intuition and mystery. (3) They reject the notion that humans are the pinnacle of evolution and somehow stand apart from the rest of nature. They are concerned with the unity of humans with the rest of the natural order. (4) So-called "primitive" cultures are not primitive, as modernists claim; they are simply different, and often more pure and deeper than ours.
15. Mitchwel Heril, "Grounding the Spirit," *Meditation* (Fall 1988): p. 47.
16. The third step states, "Made a decision to turn our will and our lives over to the care of God *as we understood Him*."[emphasis added] *Twelve Steps and Twelve Traditions* (New York: Alcoholics Anonymous World Services, Inc., 1981), p. 34.
17. AA's co-founder, Bill W., states, ". . . the designation 'God' [does not] refer to a particular being, force or concept, but only to 'God' as each of us understands that term." *Al-Anon's Twelve Steps and Twelve Traditions* (New York: Al-Anon Family Group Headquarters, 1981), p. ix. Alcoholics Anonymous doctrine also teaches explicitly that the support group can act as one's "higher power." See *Twelve Steps and Twelve Traditions*, p. 25.
18. See Stan Katz, *The Codependency Conspiracy*, pp. 22–23.
19. We explained this term in Chapter 7. p. 99.
20. Mitchwel Heril, "Grounding the Spirit," p. 45.
21. This assumption finds its primary support from postmodern interpretations of relativity and quantum theories in physics. See for example, Frijof Capra, *The Tao of Physics* (Boulder: Shambhala, 1975). See Chapter 11 on science for a response to this illicit use of quantum physics.
22. Mitchwel Heril, "Grounding the Spirit," p. 46.
23. We will explain why reason and truth must go together in Chapter 14.

13

The Postmodern Religious Shift: Five Case Studies

Jim Leffel and Dennis McCallum, Contributors

In this chapter, we will take a closer look at five prominent examples of postmodern religious thinking, each with a short assessment at the end. If we want to speak effectively to our neighbors in the postmodern age, we need to grasp the emerging religious consensus. Therefore, we should take the time to hear in their own words the ideas of postmodern religionists. Our five cases are:

1. *Christianity as Gnosticism*: Elaine Pagels illustrates how postmodern "subversive" readings are used on the Bible and other ancient writings to produce a radical, postmodern version of Christianity.

2. *Religion as Myth*: Joseph Campbell, made extremely popular through books like *The Masks of God* and the TV series *The Power of Myth*, argues that spiritual truth is metaphor, and discovering God is really discovering ourselves.

3. *Feminist Theology*: Feminist spirituality uses postmodern methods to deconstruct Christianity and the Bible, only to substitute their own new "metanarrative" in place of the old.

4. *Psycho-Spirituality*: John Bradshaw, whose number one bestsellers are among the most popular books in recent years, illustrates how the postmodern method can be eclectic—gathering insight from Eastern mysticism, the recovery movement, and the Bible.

5. *Ritual in Place of Truth*: Fredrick Turner illustrates the surprising postmodern affinity for ritual and ceremony. In the vacuum left by the death of truth, contentless ritualism carries the postmodern religionists away to sacred rapture.

Christianity as Gnosticism

In 1979, Elaine Pagels published *The Gnostic Gospels*. It was an immediate hit, earning Pagels the National Book Critics award.[1] Prior to Pagels' work, the Gnostic gospels were considered to pose only a marginal challenge to the authenticity and authority of the New Testament. According to most scholars, this Gnostic literature, written well after the New Testament documents, had nothing to do with the origin of biblical Christianity. But in postmodern fashion, Pagels took these essentially mystical and unorthodox second- and third-century writings and spun a new *story* of Christian origins.

Following a predictable postmodern scenario, Pagels holds that Gnosticism represented a valid Christian tradition but was oppressed by the powerful orthodox church. She claims that because Gnostic beliefs directly challenged the authority of the emerging hierarchical church, church leaders concluded—for primarily political, rather than doctrinal reasons—that they must squelch Gnostic spirituality.

As Pagels "deconstructs" the New Testament and the post-apostolic writings, she claims the orthodox church used apostolic authority and teaching as an instrument of repression against Gnostic Christians. She argues that once we understand the *politics* of orthodoxy, the *doctrine* of orthodoxy loses its force. Truth claims turn out to be politics. Gnosticism emerges as a valid, even desirable alternative to biblical Christianity.

We see Pagels' postmodern approach to Christianity especially in her analysis of the doctrine of Christ's bodily resurrection. According to Pagels, the doctrine of the resurrection is at the heart of orthodoxy's stranglehold on Christianity. She states her thesis this way:

> When we examine its practical effect on the Christian movement, we can see, paradoxically, that the doctrine of the bodily resurrection also serves an essential political function: it legitimizes the authority of certain men who claim to exercise exclusive leadership over the churches. . . .[2]

Pagels discounts the testimony to Christ's physical resurrection.[3] She thinks their stories were calculated to aid in the exercise of ecclesiastical power. The authority of the apostles is tied to their witness of the resurrection. The early church restricted apostolic authority to those who saw the resurrected Christ. This meant that official doctrine was permanently rooted in a small band whose members had incontestable authority.

Gnostics claimed a different source of authority—direct mystical union with Christ. Consequently, Gnostic faith wasn't mediated through an official body of doctrine. The experience of *gnosis* gave individuals their own apostolic authority. As Pagels explains,

> The resurrection, they (Gnostics) insisted, was not a unique event in the past: instead, it symbolized how Christ's presence could be experienced in the present. What mattered was not literal seeing, but spiritual vision.[4]

If the authority of individual experience was equal to the testimony of the apostles, as the Gnostics contended, then no body within the church had greater authority than any other. Orthodox leaders, therefore, had to suppress the Gnostics in order to justify their own claim to power. In the end, the apostolic teaching of the bodily resurrection is all political.

Under postmodern analysis, the reason the early church insisted Christ arose from the dead was to establish its leaders' authority over the oppressed Gnostics.

Pagels' revision of church history accords well with the general spiritual sentiment of our day. By proclaiming biblical authority to be rooted in political self-interest, she urges a return to Gnostic-style spirituality, where mystical experience stands over and above truth. She also creates sympathy for the Gnostics by portraying them as a sect oppressed by the totalistic system of emerging orthodoxy, but all the while closer to the center of authentic spirituality.[5] When the totalizing postmodern method takes on theology, all orthodox views are discounted as political oppression, and radical mystics turn out to be the persecuted heroes.

Assessment

When Pagels links the biblical text to later church politics, she implies that first-century church teaching lacked a clear consensus on doctrine. While this may have been true in some areas, scholars are virtually unanimous that belief in the physical resurrection of Christ was the earliest, most central teaching of the New Testament era. So the question of what the original—and orthodox—Christian message was is quite distinct from later theological and ecclesiastical controversies.

By linking New Testament teaching with second- and third-century writings, Pagels paints a grossly distorted picture of Christian origins. She implies that the doctrine of the resurrection was rolled out and featured at a late date in order to solidify power for church leaders. The politics of the early Roman Catholic church were related to apostolic authority and apostolic succession, but this fact is completely distinct from the doctrine of the New Testament. With Pagels, as with other postmodern historical commentators, history must be distorted to fit the ideological model, or grid, they impose.

Religion as Myth

Joseph Campbell's very popular PBS series *The Power of Myth*[6] presents us with a view that all religions are essentially the same, if we understand them properly. The unity of religion rests on the fact that they speak to deep human need and experience. Once we see that every religion is simply a mythological framework for self discovery, all final distinctions between religions evaporate.

According to Campbell, all religion, including Christianity, is myth. Myths are metaphors that reflect primal longings in the human psyche. The psyche, as Campbell describes it, is the personal experience of our bodily functions—that is, our instincts, drives, biological processes, fears, and conflicts.[7] Basic physical drives produce both conscious and *unconscious* thought.[8]

The unconscious is a largely repressed set of impulses linking the body and mind. Borrowing from psychologist Carl Jung, Campbell teaches that the unconscious is shaped by *archetypes*. Archetypes are the underlying structure of the self. They are the psychic echoes of our evolutionary past. In religious myth, these archetypes come to the surface as metaphors. Therefore, he reasons, myths are the vehicle by which we come into contact with our archetypes—our true but unconscious selves. Rather than disclosing ultimate truths about reality, myth is really a way of getting to the true self.

Campbell warns that the primary problem in religion is that we interpret religious images literally, as though they relate to transcendent personalities: gods, angels, and so on. He states,

> All of these wonderful poetic images of mythology are referring to something in you. When your mind is simply trapped by the image out there so that you never make the reference to yourself, you have misread the image. . . . Now you can personify God in many, many ways. Is there one god? Are there many gods? Those are merely categories of thought.[9]

Once we see that every religion is simply myth—a framework for self-discovery—all final distinctions between religions evaporate.

What do we discover behind the veil of myth? We discover our essential unity with the "ground of all being." Campbell is advocating pantheism—that all reality is one impersonal, indescribable, undifferentiated Being. Campbell sounds like a Buddhist or Hindu when he says,

> The ultimate mystical goal is to be united with one's god. With that, duality is transcended and forms disappear. There is nobody there, no god, no you. Your mind, going past all concepts, has dissolved in identification with the ground of your own being, because that to which the metaphorical image of your god refers is the ultimate mystery of your own being, which is the mystery of the being of the world as well. And so this is it.[10]

So in the end, we find there is no "me," just impersonal, indescribable "being." As Campbell concludes: "Everything that's transitory is but a metaphorical reference. That's what we all are."[11]

How does Campbell see Christianity as part of this pantheistic world mythology? First, he claims that the authors of biblical myth deliberately told stories as metaphors.[12] But he thinks the metaphorical sense was lost when first the Jewish and then the Christian orthodox communities naively interpreted symbols such as the virgin birth and the resurrection literally.

The Gnostics, according to Campbell, correctly recognized the metaphorical nature of Christian beliefs:

> To say, "I and the Father are one," as Jesus said, is blasphemy for us. However, in the Thomas gospel [Gnostic] that was dug up in Egypt some forty years ago, Jesus says, "He who drinks from my mouth will become as I am, and I shall be he." Now, that is exactly Buddhism. We are all manifestations of Buddha consciousness, or Christ consciousness, only we don't know it.[13]

For Campbell, the Gnostics reflect the authentic spiritual message of Christianity.

Joseph Campbell weaves a creative tale of the religious quest. Unfortunately, from the outset he is committed to the belief that spiritual truth is subjective and experiential, never objective or rational. He is like other postmodern thinkers in this regard. On truth, Campbell says,

> The person who thinks he has found the ultimate truth is wrong. There is an often-quoted verse in Sanskrit, which appears in the Chinese Tao-te Ching as well: "He who thinks he knows, doesn't know. He who knows that he doesn't know, knows. For in this context, to know is not to know. And not to know is to know."[14]

As with other strains of postmodernism, Campbell rejects all categories of rational thought and truth. The only remaining absolute truth is that we cannot know truth. Like other postmodern religionists, Campbell puts self at the center: "The mission of life is to live that potentiality. How do you do it? My answer is, 'Follow your bliss.' There's something inside you that knows when you're in the center, that knows when you're on the beam or off the beam."[15]

In postmodern religion, we cannot trust any rational conclusions but we can always count on self and experience to give us the right answer. Campbell has fully imposed his postmodern grid onto all religion.

Assessment

If we start with the assumption that all religion is myth, then we are forced to overlook what the Bible itself teaches. Campbell never gets around to talking about the New and Old Testament's profound concern for *history* and *fact*. Peter says, "We did not follow cleverly invented stories [from the Greek *muthos*, "myths"] when we told you about the power and coming of our Lord Jesus Christ, but we were eyewitnesses of his majesty" (2 Peter 1:16). Why would Peter emphasize eyewitness empirical evidence?

Campbell is also silent on passages where Paul roots the teaching of Christ's resurrection in eyewitness and fulfilled messianic prophecy. Indeed, Paul was aware that the meaning of the resurrection was tied directly to its historicity. He writes, "If Christ has not been raised, then our preaching is vain, your faith also is vain" (1 Corinthians 15:14). Biblical spirituality is the furthest thing from Campbell's vision of ethereal religion with its contempt for objective truth.

Feminist Spirituality: Liberation From the Text

Scholars debate the relationship between feminism and postmodern ideology. While many feminists today would define themselves as postmodernists, even feminists who object to some aspects of postmodernism often use literary deconstruction and related assumptions about the social construction of knowledge. In our view, most of feminism today has taken its place as part of the postmodernist shift in thinking, specifically in the affirmative faction of postmodernism (see Chapter 4).[16] They are among those who conclude that we can construct new realities based on the notion of socially constructed reality. Some of the strongest voices in feminist postmodernism are theologians, and we will consider their approach to the Bible.

We saw earlier that postmodern literary theory focuses on the reader, rather than the author, as source and judge of a text's meaning (see Chapter 6). We also mentioned the idea of an interpretive community. For feminist analysis, "women's experience" is an interpretive community. They share the experience of oppression by males and male-dominated society. Rosemary Radford Ruether, one of the best-known feminist theologians, puts it this way: "By women's experience as a key to hermeneutics or theory of interpretation, we mean precisely that experience which arises when women become critically aware of these falsifying and alienating experiences imposed upon them as women by a male-dominated culture."[17]

In other words, feminist theology begins by recognizing that women are history's victims. Susan Brooks Thistlethwaite asserts, "All women live with male violence."[18]

Feminist theology attempts to legitimize women's experience by approaching the Bible as an artifact of male oppression. Feminists point out that common interpretations of the Bible demean and oppress women. They show how Western culture, shaped by biblical literature, makes sexism appear just and sacred. On this point, we cannot, for the most part, disagree with feminist theologians. Even the most superficial reading of church history and the writings of many prominent theologians give shameful testimony to sexism.

But many feminist theologians go beyond the "patriarchy" of theologians and church history to the Bible itself. Feminist scholars argue that biblical narratives commonly portray women as property, and that they are consistently accorded second-rate status in biblical literature, especially in the Old Testament. The Abraham narrative (Genesis 12–25) is a good example. Abraham possessed concubines, bought Isaac's wife, and ruled with complete authority over his family.

Most evangelical Bible scholars recognize a lower place for women evident in the patriarchal narratives of the Old Testament. They argue, however, that through *progressive revelation* God made his intent for male-female relationships increasingly clear. Thus the New Testament argues against polygamy, and even goes as far as asserting that "There is neither Jew nor Greek, slave nor free man, neither male nor female; for you are all one in Christ Jesus" (Galatians 3:28). The lower place accorded women in the early history of the Old Testament was never *prescribed* by God, but merely *described.* On the other hand, even the New Testament clearly continues to teach that marital roles are the will of God (Ephesians 5:21ff). We might say the Bible affirms both equality and distinctions in marriage roles based on sacrificial love and leadership.[19]

But feminists claim that sexism remains a part of the scriptural narrative throughout. While some biblical perspectives on women may be progressive, they argue, such views cannot erase other, blatantly exploitative ones. Nor can we minimize the influence of such texts within the church and in Western culture, which has been exploitative of women. Therefore, feminist theologians call for a "liberation from the text."[20]

Liberation from the text means identifying sexist passages and rejecting or reinterpreting them. Ultimately, all valid interpretation must be seen in light of the feminist paradigm. Women's experience is the inviolable rule in hermeneutics. Margaret Farley asserts,

> Whatever contradicts those convictions cannot be accepted as having the authority of an authentic revelation of truth. It is simply a matter of there being no turning back. We can be dispossessed of our best insights, proven wrong in our judgments. But as long as those insights continue to make sense to us, and as long as our basic judgments seem to us incontrovertible, there can be no turning back. So it is with feminist consciousness and the interpretation of scripture.[21]

We see here the discounting of reason in favor of the authority of the oppressed interpretive community. Whether these interpreters call themselves postmodern or not, their reliance on the postmodern method is unmistakable.

Under these marching orders, feminist interpreters challenge, rework, or reject much of scripture based on its patriarchal content. But feminist theologians also deconstruct passages that don't *seem* to challenge their views. Postmodern "subversive readings" uncover hidden elements of patriarchy that they believe unconsciously create a climate of repression for women. Consider the creation of woman out of man (Genesis 2:21–24). Feminists argue that since woman's origin is in man, this text legitimizes male authority over woman's body. Consequently, "feminist interpretation must also recognize that the history of control of women's bodies is at stake in this text and must become part of its interpretation."[22]

Finally, following the lead of Marxist liberation theologians, many feminist theologians find the cause of women part of the message of the Old Testament prophets. Often the prophets denounced economic and social exploitation of the poor. Feminists identify women's experience with that of the poor and oppressed. In this way, prophetic confrontation of the rich turns out to be a denunciation of sexist patriarchy as well. Feminists are aware that including sexism in the prophetic attack on social injustice goes beyond the clear meaning of the text.[23] Ruether states,

> In responding to such a justified objection, one must be clear about the *sociology of consciousness* of all critical prophetic culture. One cannot *reify* [elevate cultural beliefs or practices to the level of the sacred] any critical prophetic movement . . . simply as definitive texts, once and for all established in the past, which then set the limits of consciousness of the meaning of liberation. . . .[24]

Ruether justifies expanding the prophetic message to include sexism based on what she terms the "sociology of consciousness." Ruether is referring here to the "sociology of knowledge" we discussed in Chapter 3. According to postmodern interpreters like Ruether, readers are tied to their culture, and as cultures change so does the meaning of the text. That is why she cautions, "One cannot *reify* any critical prophetic movement. . . ." No text, in other words, is ever definitive or final. As social conditions give rise to new thought forms, we should expect fresh meanings to be drawn from the same scriptures. Thus, the Bible is meaningful only as it speaks a liberating word to women. Where the Christian message no longer *resonates* with feminist experience, it is rejected as false or irrelevant. Ruether states, "Traditions die when a new generation is no longer able to reappropriate the foundational paradigm in a meaningful way; when it is experienced as meaningless or even as demonic: that is, disclosing a meaning that points to false or unauthentic life. Thus, if the cross of Jesus would be experienced by women as pointing them only toward continued victimization and not redemption, it would be perceived as false and demonic in this way, and women could no longer identify themselves as Christians."[25] This is a perfect illustration of how the new so-called "ideological readings" are indeed postmodern in their method, even though they embrace an ideology that is an offense to hard-line postmodernists.

In the final analysis, whatever fits the feminist paradigm is truth at least for women. Only a change in social consciousness can produce a new paradigm—a new set of truths. Social consciousness, not rational objectivity, holds the key to truth. This is why feminists call for a "conversion experience"[26] in which women embrace the feminist paradigm of abuser/victim. In the end, feminist theology is dependent on the consciousness-raising ability of the women's movement.

Assessment

In one way, feminist theologians have brought needed insight into biblical study. It's easy to interpret scripture in terms of dominant cultural values and norms, which often has included contempt for women. Prior to the women's movement, the contributions of women in the church were largely ignored. Women's roles in the culture are changing. More women attend universities than men. Women occupy an increasingly influential place in the work force. Clearly, the church needs to carefully address the legitimate concerns of women as they struggle to find a new place in the culture.

However, the feminist subversive reading of the Bible goes beyond these concerns. Feminists raise their experience as women above Scripture as the standard of truth and authority. For many feminists, the Bible is simply a pragmatic tool to further a highly politicized ideological agenda. When Scripture and ideology conflict, Scripture is either radically reinterpreted or rejected outright.

In the final analysis, truth is whatever agrees with feminism.

Feminist theology is gaining wider influence in many seminaries and denominations. Many evangelicals are troubled by the divisiveness of feminist theology. Today, raising critical concerns about feminist methodology or theology is considered sexist or insensitive to the legitimate concerns of women. In higher education and in many seminaries, there is a code of silence that inhibits any substantial analysis or critique of feminist critical method. Such intimidation is an example of what can happen when postmodern ideologies are permitted to substitute power for truth. Instead of refuting the other position, we forbid anyone to mention it. In these cases ideas are monitored and managed for their political correctness, not rationally weighed and assessed.

Psycho-spirituality: John Bradshaw

One of the most popular teachers of postmodern religion and self-help is John Bradshaw. His books have dominated the *New York Times* best-seller lists as number one sellers for months at a time, and his TV lecture series have aired nationwide. In Bradshaw's writings, readers find a mixture of Eastern mysticism, recovery movement self-help theories, and family systems psychological theories.[27]

Bradshaw's postmodern convictions are evident when he discusses notions of inclusion and the need to reject absolutes in the area of truth and morals. He explains that religion is commendable as long as it has no authority to judge morality: "For me, one of the surest ways to know that a given style of spirituality is not true spirituality is to apply the following criteria to it: How blaming and judgmental is it?"[28]

Bradshaw insists that we abandon all truth and all moral norms by which we could judge. Moral norms are the product of the worst enemy of humankind: patriarchy—the rule of the father. We started out well enough as children, he explains, but,

> One of the major consequences of a patriarchal upbringing is that we lose our ability to direct ourselves through our own willpower. In strict patriarchy children are not allowed to express any form of self-will. . . . Children are considered good if they learn to obey and conform to the will of authority figures.[29]

For Bradshaw, nothing could be worse than conforming to the will of authority figures, including God. What takes the place at the center of religion once serving God and doing his will are junked? Here Bradshaw shows his postmodern orientation. The key to entering religious truth, according to him, is to get out of cognitive categories, or rational thought. Where reason ends, spirituality begins:

> Prayer allows you to dialogue with the source of union. And meditation allows you to be united to the source of union in a relationship of bliss. . . . The techniques range from simple breath awareness to the activity exercises of the whirling dervishes. In between there are mandalas, mantras, music, manual arts, mental imaging, and massage exercises. The choice of a technique depends on your personal preferences. Each technique aims at distracting your mind and absorbing all your conscious attention.[30]

Why distract your mind with these techniques? Because your mind, your rationality, stands between you and God. You must leave rational categories behind on your journey to the sacred: "After much practice you can create a state of mindlessness. This state is called the silence. Once the silence is created, an unused mental faculty is activated. It is a form of intuition. With this faculty one can know God directly. Spiritual masters present a rather uniform witness on this point."[31]

After we achieve irrationality and mindlessness we can know God. The rational law of non-contradiction no longer troubles us once we understand the unity of all things.

> In a state of bliss you no longer see things in opposites. There is no "us" and "them." You experience unity. The mystics and physicists tell us that in the state of bliss, we have a *Higher Power* available to us. Being connected to all consciousness gives us resources of insight and knowledge that are more powerful than any we've ever imagined. The only condition required for such knowledge is the letting go of all ego control. A slogan in 12-step groups says, "Let go and let God." Another one reads, "Turn it over."[32]

Part of the knowledge we gain in the mindless state includes the realization that the key to everything is *me!* Bradshaw writes, "Each of us came into the world in order to manifest that unique part of God's reality. We do that by being ourselves. *The more we are truly ourselves, the more we are truly Godlike. . . .*"[33]

Bradshaw reaches the same conclusions as other postmodern religionists. Rationality, authority, and moral constraints must be left behind before we can lay hold of the key to spiritual depth—*being ourselves*. He also reflects the common postmodern view that all religion uses different words to describe the same thing. Only *patriarchal religion* (his word for fundamentalism) is out.

Assessment

Postmodern spirituality places human interpretation and experience at the center, unlike biblical spirituality, which recognizes at the center an authoritative God who declares truth and morality through his Word. Yes, Christianity is patriarchy—the rulership of our heavenly father. It is not, however, the capricious and selfish dominance of one who wants to hold us down, but the loving care of one who knows best. Like Satan, who suggested to Eve that God was trying to hold her down with phony slogans about his will being "for her own good," Bradshaw suggests that authoritative (patriarchal) truth is holding us down by moving the seat of authority away from me to someone else.

Bradshaw is more individualistic than most postmodernists, but he fits perfectly into the postmodern view of truth. Religious truth is never *learned* from an authoritative or objective source outside ourselves. It is *created* by the worshiper once he or she takes leave of all rational categories and enters the mystical religious experience. As biblical Christians, we don't abandon our senses to know real spiritual experience. We are commanded to remain alert and sober, not entranced (1 Peter 5:8; Ephesians 6:18). We are aware of mysteries and things about God beyond our understanding, but these are never incompatible with the objective truths of God's word. On the contrary, the Bible tells us to "test the spirits" on exactly that basis—whether or not they contradict biblical truth (1 John 4:1–4; 1 Timothy 6:3–4). God's Word is prepared to judge both falsehood and moral evil.

Truth does not rob our freedom; it protects our freedom. By knowing the truth we avoid coming under the domination of false teachers and the foolish, self-centered thinking of this world system (Ephesians 4:14). We need truth to keep from becoming captives, as Paul warns: "See to it that no one takes you captive through philosophy and empty deception, according to the tradition of men, according to the elementary principles of the world, rather than according to Christ" (Colossians 2:8).

Ritual in Place of Truth: Frederick Turner

We might assume that postmodern religion would rebel against the constraints of ritual just as it has against truth, but we would be wrong. Most postmodern religionists seem to thrive on ritual, no doubt partly because of the mystical experiences associated with ritualistic religion. Ritual can at times produce dissociation, a mindless, confused state. Once God and truth are removed, nothing is left but the empty shell of religious forms.

Listen to the words of Professor Fredrick Turner, a postmodern scholar of arts and humanities, in his essay subtitled, "Notes Toward a Postmodern Religion":

> We are beginning to discover that . . . the guts of a religion are its rituals. By all means change the theology; this won't do any harm. . . . Theology and ethics are discursive and subject to revision. . . . But where a religion really stands or falls is in its ritual. If it has good old rituals, carrying in them the inherited traces of our early evolution—the great psychic technologies of mythic storytelling, chant, sacrifice, body decoration, music, dance, the fresco—and if the best and most imaginative spirits have continuously been at work embodying the liturgy in new and inventive poetic performance, the theology and ethics will take care of themselves.[34]

Like some even in the evangelical camp today, Turner discounts the importance of truth and theology in favor of ritualistic experience. The final goal, he argues, of postmodern religious studies is a unified new religion: "What should the new religious synthesis look like? . . . First, obviously, it should be syncretic [mixing the teachings of different religions]. It should contain the best of the world's religions. . . . What do we have brains for but to reconcile the irreconcilable?"[35]

This is the postmodern rejection of reason and its unavoidable discounting of truth. The second component of a new religious synthesis is no less interesting:

> The new religion should, moreover, exploit to the full the ancient psychic technologies deployed in traditional ritual practice . . . so that the moments of holiness and ecstasy should have a sure foundation in the sensuality and critical intellect of our species. . . . At the same time that the ancient texts and liturgies are revived, a new playfulness should enter our ritual observance. The energy of performance . . . should be renewed.[36]

Assessment

The guts of biblical Christianity is *not* its rituals. The guts of Christianity is Jesus Christ—a Savior who is real, objective, and who did his work in space and time whether we realize it or not. The reality of Jesus and his work doesn't depend on what we might hold to be true. The person and work of Christ and the revelation in God's Word—these are the things Turner thinks are discursive and changeable at will. On the contrary, these are the things that are non-negotiable. These are truth.

Turner thinks truth doesn't matter, but ritual does. How far this is from biblical Christianity! While the Old Testament had a thorough commitment to rituals, most were explicitly set aside in the New Testament, seen especially in the book of Hebrews. Students of comparative religions are fascinated at how little ritual the New Testament prescribes compared to the sacred texts of other religions. The rituals practiced in the New Testament church could be counted on the fingers of one hand, and most were quite simple. Only two rituals are practiced by all Christians, and one of those—baptism—is practiced only once in each Christian's life. Even the lone remaining ritual Christians are to practice regularly is the *antithesis* of Turner's vision of zoned-out, contentless ritual. Communion is rich in truthful content—not truth I create, but truth I am supposed to *remember*—the historical fact of Jesus' death for my sin (1 Corinthians 11:24–26). Christians should be wary of any suggestion that we come together on the basis of ritual and mystical experience and ignore the question of truth.

> The guts of Christianity is Jesus Christ—a Savior who is real, objective, and who did his work in space and time whether we realize it or not.

The Big Picture

In the future we may be compelled to come together around the shared elements of postmodern religion: self, ritual, mystical experience, and symbols. To some, it's a beautiful dream. To others, a nightmare.

If the Western world ever reaches religious consensus, it won't be on the basis of evangelical Christianity. As postmodern thinkers continue to gain influence and power in society, we will see whether irrationality really leads to tolerance. Turner, for instance, clamors for tolerance but calls evangelical Christianity a "junk religion." We suspect that those who continue to be so bold as to judge unbiblical ideas or behaviors as wrong, who continue to reject things they think are false, will likely earn the ire of postmodern religionists, and possibly the violence that goes with it. Membership in religious consensus is rarely optional.

In Brief

- Postmodern religious analysts take special aim at Christianity and the Bible. Christianity is the seat of Western patriarchy and the Bible a cultural artifact of a power struggle in the early church.
- Christianity can still be serviceable if interpreted properly: its content as mythology (Campbell), its ritual as a door to mindlessness (Turner and Bradshaw), and its emphasis on knowing and doing God's will as the heart of Christian practice replaced by mystical experiences such as those advocated by the Gnostics (Pagels and Campbell).
- Feminist Theology is an example of postmodern interpretation of the Bible through the reader-centered grid of feminist experience.
- While some postmodern thinkers have no place for religion, others want to form a religious synthesis—similar to New Age Consciousness—that draws all religion together, avoids the use of reason, and majors on personal mystical religious experience. In our next chapter, we examine the effect of this emerging synthesis on evangelical Christianity.

Notes

1. The Gnostic gospels are ancient manuscripts discovered near Nag Hammadi in Egypt a few years before the discovery of the Dead Sea Scrolls. They include the *Gospel of Thomas* and other writings. For more on the background of these texts, see A. T. Wells, "Gnosticism," in J. D. Douglas, *The New Bible Dictionary* (Grand Rapids: William B. Eerdmanns Publishing Co., 1975), pp. 473–474. Also, J. N. D. Kelly, *Early Christian Doctrines* (New York: Harper and Row, 1960), pp. 22–51.
2. She is referring to the apostles' claim to be eye-witnesses of the resurrection, which gave them legitimacy (1 Corinthians 9:1). Elaine Pagels, *The Gnostic Gospels* (New York: Random House, 1979), p. 6.
3. In discussing the biblical claim of the resurrection of Christ, Pagels states, "The conviction that a man who died came back to life is, of course, a paradox. But that paradox may contain the secret of its powerful appeal, for while it contradicts our own historical experience, it speaks the language of human emotions. It addresses itself to that which may be our deepest fear, and expresses our longing to overcome death." Elaine Pagels, *The Gnostic Gospels*, p. 26.
4. Elaine Pagels, *The Gnostic Gospels*, p. 11.
5. Pagels states, "The concerns of gnostic Christians survived only as a suppressed current, like a river driven underground." Elaine Pagels, *The Gnostic Gospels*, p. 150.
6. *The Power of Myth* is a series of interviews in which he and journalist Bill Moyers discuss the main conclusions of Campbell's scholarly career.
7. Joseph Campbell, *The Power of Myth* (New York: Doubleday, 1988), p. 51.
8. Campbell thinks it is important to reject the common notion that consciousness is something that goes on in the head. He states: "There is a consciousness here in the body. The whole living world is informed by consciousness. I have a feeling that consciousness and energy are the same thing somehow. Where you really see life energy, there's consciousness. Certainly the vegetable world is conscious. And when you live in the woods, as I did as a kid, you can see all these different consciousnesses relating to themselves. There is a plant consciousness and there is an animal consciousness, and we share both these things." Joseph Campbell, *The Power of Myth*, p. 14.
9. Joseph Campbell, *The Power of Myth*, pp. 57, 62.
10. Ibid., p. 210.
11. Ibid., p. 230.
12. Moyers asks, "You think that the first humans who told the story of the creation had some intuitive awareness of the allegorical nature of these stories?" Campbell responds, "Yes. They were saying it is *as if* it were true. The notion that somebody literally made the world—that is what is known as artificial-

ism. It is the child's way of thinking: the table is made, so somebody made the table. The world is here, so somebody must have made it." Joseph Campbell, *The Power of Myth*, p. 54.

13. Joseph Campbell, *The Power of Myth*, p. 57.
14. Ibid., p. 55.
15. Ibid., p. 229.
16. See correctly John McGowan, *Postmodernism and Its Critics*, who says, "Feminism is so intimately linked to postmodernism because it pursues a similar strategy of showing that the hierarchical pair masculine/feminine depends on the social construction of the two terms as polar opposites . . . ," p. 20.
17. Rosemary Radford Ruether, "Feminist Interpretation: A Method of Correlation," in Letty M. Russell, ed., *Feminist Interpretation of the Bible* (Philadelphia: The Westminster Press, 1985), p. 114.
18. Susan Brooks Thistlethwaite, "Every Two Minutes: Battered Women and Feminist Interpretation," in Letty M. Russell, ed., *Feminist Interpretation of the Bible*. (Philadelphia: The Westminster Press, 1985), p. 96. The factual nature of feminists' claims of male violence is not the subject of this chapter. However, we point out that many researchers have challenged both the research methodology and findings often cited by feminists relating to the physical abuse of women by men. In surveying a growing body of sociological evidence, John Leo concludes, "The radical view of domestic violence (it's the patriarchy in action, oppressing women) simply doesn't fit the accumulating evidence. It's a highly ideological overlay, dividing the world unrealistically into brutish males and innocent, passive females." John Leo, "Is It a War Against Women?" *U.S. News and World Report* (July 11, 1994). Leo's article is a review of Murray Straus and Richard Gelles' study, *Intimate Violence*.
19. See our views on this question in Dennis McCallum and Gary DeLashmutt, *The Myth of Romance* (Minneapolis: Bethany House Publishers, 1996).
20. Susan Brooks Thistlethwaite, "Every Two Minutes: Battered Women and Feminist Interpretation," in *Feminist Interpretation of the Bible*, pp. 104–107.
21. Margaret A. Farley, "Feminist Consciousness and the Interpretation of Scripture," in Letty M. Russell, ed., *Feminist Interpretation of the Bible* (Philadelphia: The Westminster Press, 1985), pp. 49–50.
22. Susan Brooks Thistlethwaite, "Every Two Minutes: Battered Women and Feminist Interpretation," p. 106.
23. Ruether makes it clear that feminists need to go beyond the text to expand the prophetic message: "It may be said that this correlation between the biblical critical principle and the feminist critical principle is insufficient, because biblical prophecy does not clearly include sexism and patriarchy in its critique of social injustice. Women, in expanding the prophetic process of denunciation and annunciation to include sexism, do so without biblical authority." Ruether, "Feminist Interpretation: A Method of Correlation," p. 118.
24. Ruether, "Feminist Interpretation: A Method of Correlation," p. 118.
25. Ibid., p. 112.
26. "Women's experience, then, implies a *conversion experience* through which women get in touch with, name, and judge their experiences of sexism in

patriarchal society." Ruether, "Feminist Interpretation: A Method of Correlation," p. 114.

27. Bradshaw also illustrates the tension evident in some authors who embrace postmodern analytical practices and theories, but retain some Western notions of individuality. As such, he is not a pure postmodernist, but one of the many eclectic thinkers who use the postmodern method to support the bulk of their concepts—especially to defend their concepts when they don't make sense. The family systems school of psychology places the nuclear family in the place where other postmodernists place culture, as the shaping source of reality and personhood. Just as feminism falls today within the postmodern fold in spite of their insistence on strong moral categories, many recovery thinkers and family systems thinkers are postmodern in their basic assumptions, in spite of their affirmation of self. It is the modernist *autonomous* self that postmodernists *and* family systems thinkers deny.
28. John Bradshaw, *Healing the Shame That Binds You* (Deerfield Beach, Calif.: Health Communications, Inc., 1988), p. 219. Notice that Bradshaw pronounces a judgment even as he condemns judgmentalism!
29. John Bradshaw, *Creating Love: The Next Great Stage of Growth* (New York: Bantam Books, 1992), p. 227.
30. John Bradshaw, *Healing the Shame That Binds You*, p. 221.
31. Ibid., p. 222.
32. Ibid., p. 231. We saw what physicists are saying in our chapter on science (10).
33. Ibid., p. 223 (emphasis original).
34. Fredrick Turner, "The Future of the Gods: Notes Toward a Postmodern Religion," *Rebirth of Value* (Albany, N.Y.: State University of New York Press, 1991), pp. 85–86.
35. Ibid., p. 89.
36. Ibid., p. 89.

14

EVANGELICAL IMPERATIVES

DENNIS MCCALLUM, CONTRIBUTOR

> The United States government had little direct involvement in Native American education before the 1880's. Instead, missionaries were encouraged to go into areas populated by Native Americans, to enculturate them to European ways, and to convert them to Christianity.[1]

Which was worse? Enculturating Native Americans to European ways or converting them to Christianity? In postmodern culture, these are two ways to say the same thing. Enculturating and converting a native group to Western ways, particularly to Christianity, is one of the few acts postmodern America would agree is sin. Christian popularity is at an all-time low in the West. And yet our neighbors and friends need Christ more than ever.

During the past thirty years, society has progressively thrown off every moral constraint. First in the realm of sexual conduct, then in the use of drugs, now in many other areas, people have been on a frenzied quest for unqualified freedom from all moral norms. The result is frightening to many Christians and non-Christians alike.

Our culture hasn't yet cast off all restraints. Yet today, with help from powerful intellectual arguments advanced by world-class scholars, people are casting off even the final constraints of reality, truth, and reason itself. We are witnessing the complete abandonment of reason and truth.

The Lesson of Theological Liberalism

During the Enlightenment, thinkers were excited about their new freedom from "superstition," which included—in their view—any belief in the supernatural. Before long, Christians were startled to learn that some of their own leaders didn't want to be viewed as unscholarly or superstitious by their secular colleagues. These Christian leaders were suddenly embarrassed by the supernatural elements of Scripture. Leaders began to form their own enlightenment "Christian" religion, free of "superstitions" such as miracles, angels, demons, and a supernatural Christ. These were the old-line liberal theologians.

More and more local churches were pastored by liberal leaders eager to curry favor with an increasingly secular culture by accepting unbelief as inevitable. Surely, they felt, no one in the modern world is going to believe in things like the earth splitting open to swallow those in rebellion! Modern people can't be asked to believe in a literal hell!

In a similar way, when existential philosophy began gaining popularity, Christian theologians promptly developed Christian existential theology, or "encounter" theology, largely under the banner of "Neo-orthodox" theology. Theologians like Bultmann concluded "that the [enlightenment] quest for the historical Jesus was unnecessary and illegitimate, since the object of Christian faith is not the historical Jesus. The real Christ event is the proclamation of the Church."[2] In other words, what happened in Jesus' life is unimportant. All that matters is a personal encounter with the *kerygma*, the preaching of the church, or the "Christ of faith." Again, Christian leaders had developed a form of Christianity that bore no relation to biblical Christianity, yet was, they thought, more palatable to the secular world of their day, especially their existentialist colleagues.

To the natural mind, these arguments seemed plausible enough. After all, nobody wants to be left behind during a time of cultural change.

Liberal churches, however, failed to gain the acceptance of the culture. On the contrary, liberal and neo-orthodox-influenced denominations have experienced a steady and accelerating decline in attendance as the culture they sought to appease and imitate rejected them. The evangelical churches that refused to compromise morality or truth never experienced the same losses. In fact, they continued to grow even during the 60s, 70s, and 80s.

The liberal leaders should have realized that a church without the supernatural God of the Bible had nothing to offer a lost culture. A church that abandoned moral revelation had no authority. Such a church couldn't look to the power of the Spirit of God to bless its work.

> A church that abandoned God's moral revelation had nothing to offer a lost culture.

Evangelicals may have had their own problems, but no one was more mistaken than the liberals. Their solution to modernity—the abandonment of biblical morality and the supernatural—was a bankrupt, wicked solution if ever there was one.[3]

Standing for the truth often appears risky to the natural mind, and even to the converted mind. When the truth directly opposes beloved convictions held by the majority of our contemporaries, only the courageous dare speak it. But we, as Christians, are to minister with the power of God, not with frightened promises to sinful humanity that they need not repent. We find our faithfulness challenged when the Word of God tells us something we know might offend our culture. But the alternative is even worse: becoming cultural prostitutes, prepared to jettison God's revealed truth for the sake of imagined popularity. When we take this course, we lose any voice we might have had. Our imagined new "friends" from the academic world and popular culture will never love us anyway, and the power of the Spirit of God will be quenched pitifully.

Accommodation Temptation

Evangelicals today are being tempted to make the same mistake liberal and neo-orthodox leaders earlier made with modernism. They are tempted to jettison or at least to minimize the importance of propositional truth—statements of fact that can be confirmed or denied by reason and evidence. In a day when propositional, objective truth is considered "fundamentalist," "intolerant," and "exclusive," Christians are enticed to view it as a nuisance, especially if they crave popularity from the rest of our culture.

At the same time that Christian leaders are being tempted to soft-pedal or apologize for truth, others appear willing to place too much confidence in politically based power. Although no one—ourselves included—can deny the need to fight for just laws in our increasingly godless culture, how much hope do we put in this strategy? Some calls to "take back" America today seem to imply that if we can just impose the right political framework on the country, people will return to God. Doesn't this sound similar to the postmodern belief that we can construct new realities through the application of political power?

Some evangelical calls for empowerment today sound similar to postmodern thought, even though they originate from a different ideological source. Evangelicals need to be alert to this development, because nothing would be easier than for the church to once again adopt secular thinking as its own. Our aspirations for a better society cannot take the place of evangelism. Change in our society must come from the individual hearts of people as they are transformed by the love of Christ. Moreover, for the Christian voice to be credible, we must demonstrate genuine and sacrificial concern for the real needs of the poor and the weak in our culture. We will otherwise sound like little more than cheerleaders rooting for our own interests.

No one would suggest that evangelicals have arrived at their agenda by the same path as postmodernists. Neither can we afford to abandon the political process while anti-Christian forces try to legislate us out of existence. But postmodernism may have an indirect effect on Christian thinking unless Christian leaders exercise discernment.

Pollsters have already given us ample evidence that postmodern attitudes are rampant even among evangelicals. One researcher, for instance, finds that although 88 percent of those in evangelical churches say the Bible is the infallible Word of God, 53 percent also say there is no such thing as absolute truth! The proportion doubting that absolute truth exists is even greater among evangelical church youth—actually approaching the same ratio as that of society as a whole.[4]

Evangelical and Postmodern Flirting

We saw earlier that the central outcome of postmodern thinking is the rejection of the "enlightenment project," a major part of which was the notion that people can be reasonable and objective. In place of rational discourse come two things: *cultural experience* and *power/*

rhetoric. Since one's language and thought processes are constructs of culture, postmodernists argue that when people think they are being reasonable, they are actually just expressing their personal *experience* of enlightenment culture. Thus, *experience* is all we know or ever can know. Our *experience* becomes our *reality*. Those who try to apply reason to the world have naively missed the fact that all their reasonings are nothing but cultural language constructs.

Today, evangelicals should be concerned not only because the secular world has opted for the centrality of experience and power over and above truth, but because some evangelicals are being tempted to do the same! If we think we can offer an experience that will compete effectively with other postmodern religious experiences, we tread ground alien to the New Testament. Paul never argued that Christ could top the mystery religions and other ecstatic cults in terms of religious experience. He offered the truth—Jesus Christ and him crucified. This was the power of God to which he wanted them exposed (1 Corinthians 2:1–5).[5]

Our age is eager to hear a gospel based on experience, but they will abandon it just as quickly when another gospel—or counselor or psychic group or spirituality book—offers them more experience. Evangelicals who teach on the role of experience in faith need to exert special effort to guarantee they are communicating biblical truth, not aping secular culture as the church has done in the past.

Experience and Power in Christianity

One trend is particularly disturbing: a growing call to abandon "head-knowledge" in favor of "heart-knowledge." Stanley Grenz is typical when he argues that in his new "postmodern evangelical theology" we must affirm that "a 'right heart' takes primacy over a 'right head.' "[6] I couldn't disagree more. Those with right hearts and wrong heads might very well be among the ones who burned to death in Waco, Texas, with David Koresh. Their heart was inclined to follow God, to obey, but their heads were wrong—they had the wrong Christ! Those who seek to dichotomize the heart and the head are doing something alien to biblical teaching.

Head-knowledge *can* puff up, as Paul warns in 1 Corinthians 8:1. And we need to reflect on the role of experience, both negative and positive, in the Christian life. These points we don't question. The real problem comes when heart-knowledge and head-knowledge are viewed from an "either-or" perspective instead of a "both-and" perspective. Such a division between our "hearts" and our "heads" is dangerous. What we know in our heads and our hearts should be *the same, not different.* Head-knowledge and heart-knowledge must always be compatible. Neither is dispensable. Those who wish to deprecate one or the other create a dreadful caricature of real biblical Christianity.

Some parts of the church today are afflicted with a rampant experientialism only superficially related to the Bible. The "Word-Faith" movement in particular seems to suggest that mind power creates reality, a doctrine compatible with postmodern assumptions but incompatible with the Bible.[7]

Similarly, postmodern victimology has a strong foothold—though certainly not a consensus—in evangelical thinking today. Within the framework of Rogerian counseling, therapists listen to clients using positive regard without judgment. The assumption is that the counselor should never label as "wrong" anything a client shares. Postmodern victimology goes one step further: The client's reports not only cannot be judged as being morally wrong, but *neither can they be judged as real or unreal.* If the victim feels victimized, that is his or her reality. There is no reason to question whether the victimizing event actually occurred.[8] Victims' "stories" *are* their reality.

How different this is from days when those who reported imaginary events were considered delusional or paranoid!

Again, any reaction that discounts all claims of victims is heartless. But do we have the discernment to cast out thinking that is deterministic—in the sense that victims can't help what they are—and retain only those findings demonstrated biblically, scientifically, and rationally?

In still another arena, postmodern rhetoric today emphasizes the need for "respecting" others. We are to respect the diversity in culture. Teachers are to respect the literacy of even first grade students. Parents are even to respect their children's alternative ideas about how the household should run. Discerning observers realize that in our postmodern world, respect is a code-word for "never criticizing my views or actions." Respect is positive regard *without* judgment. "Respecting diversity," for instance, means never trying to change anyone from the way they are, even if they are behaving self-destructively. Any criticism of others indicates disrespect.

No sooner had our postmodern world propounded this doctrine than the church began to echo this call to show respect. We see an emerging literature of respect, and most authors and pastors, myself included, feel the need to at least tip our hat to the notion.

Interestingly, while there is nothing inherently wrong with respect, the Bible seldom calls on us to respect one another, especially not in the postmodern sense. God calls us to *love* one another. And love *can* confront others with their error. Love *does* call for change from *your* way to the *other* way—to God's way. Like the postmodern concept of respect, love involves positive regard. But unlike postmodern respect, love doesn't tiptoe around human pride. It does what is good and right for another, not what the other demands. Postmodern respect is positive regard *without* judgment. Christian love is positive regard *with* judgment, in a constructive sense.

We could argue that in order to speak with our culture in its own language we should pick up concepts such as respect and use them in Christian communication, just as Paul did for the Greeks.[9] But will we have Paul's discernment and strength when it comes to declaring the *differences* between our mandate to love and the postmodern mandate to respect others? Will we have the courage to point out the damage we do to our children and others when we passively and amorally respect them instead of calling for repentance and helping them to change?

To understand where we should stand as evangelicals, we must carefully define what is right and what is wrong in postmodernism.

What Is Right About Postmodernism?

Postmodern thinkers have pointed out some important and useful things. Among the most helpful are the following:

1. Without the infinite-personal creator God of the Bible, knowledge and reason do indeed become uncertain. Many of us have read books by Francis Schaeffer such as *He Is There and He Is Not Silent*. In such works, Schaeffer showed why people couldn't have objective morals if an infinite personal God did not exist. Many of us skipped sections like "The Epistemological Necessity." The words were so long and the concepts so abstract that it seemed the article could wait for later. But Schaeffer, following the lead of his teacher, Cornelius Van Til, called attention to an important point: Apart from the existence of an infinite personal God, we can't know anything for sure, and we can't rely on reason to tell us about the universe.[10] As Dr. Campbell pointed out in his chapter on science, assumptions such as those underlying science (that natural laws, for example, are consistent throughout the universe) can't always be proven, and depend on the idea that the universe was created by a rational God. Also, we have no assurance that the data of our senses can be trusted apart from theistic assumptions. Postmodernists are saying something very similar to Schaeffer. They are, in fact, more consistent than many of their critics.[11] They have gone far enough to see the real implications of a world without the God of the Bible.

2. *Modernists' faith in human "progress" is misplaced.* Modernists believe Western society is "progressing" toward a glorious future based on technology and advanced learning. Postmodernists scoff at this notion and dwell on the harmful effects of so-called "progress." Biblical Christians have never believed the progress myth—because we know that no matter how much people learn, nothing has changed in their fallen hearts until Jesus comes in. As C. S. Lewis said, education merely makes man a more clever devil.

3. *People are more subjective than they like to admit.* All people, including scientists and other scholars, will at times import their own particular prejudices into their supposedly "objective" discipline. No one has cried foul with the natural sciences more than evangelical Christians. Christian critics believe naturalistic scientists have been willing to ignore contradicting data and even to deceive when it comes to claiming that the fossil record supports naturalistic macro-evolution. In literary analysis, evangelicals have rightly cried foul when modernist scholars applied a double standard to history in the Bible. Their zeal for demonstrating the falsehood in the Bible has intrigued even secular scholars.[12] The Bible declares that in their wickedness, people have often "suppressed the truth in unrighteousness" (Romans 1:18).

4. *Our culture can, and often does, blind our eyes to truth obvious to other cultures and which, in retrospect, may also be clear to us.* Tourists in the desert southwest marvel today that frontier Americans have felt justified driving Native Americans into the desolate areas used as reservations. We don't need to believe that native peoples are sinless or pristine to admit today that white frontier Americans used their power to subjugate a technologically weaker people, often

without ever realizing they were doing anything wrong. The same is true for the American slave trade and wage slavery in some companies in the north—a dominant culture exploited another for its own ends.

Are we certain today that our constant calls to guard American interests and American jobs never cloud our ethical judgment regarding the poor in other developing countries? Can those who spend as much every year going to movies as average families in some countries make during that same year ever understand the situation in those countries? Can middle-class whites ever fully understand what it means to grow up as an African-American girl or boy in a poverty-stricken inner-city project?

It won't be easy, but Christians need to lead the way in developing such understanding or we will lose our debate with postmodernism. If we don't, we will be unable to weigh in with a convincing alternative, and instead we will be first-rate illustrations of the very cultural blindness postmodernists claim is unavoidable. We should see compassion for the plight of genuinely oppressed or disadvantaged people as important common ground between ourselves and postmodernists. We, after all, have in the Bible the moral basis for fair treatment of others.

5. *People are social beings, and our social or cultural setting shapes and informs our values and thinking*. The Bible is much closer to postmodernism than modernism in its portrait of members of the Christian community. The Bible never treats Christianity as something we do as individuals, but a faith we live out together as members of the Body of Christ. True, our decision to follow Christ must be individual, and Jesus declares that he "calls his own sheep by name" (John 10:3). The Bible stresses both the individual and the community, unlike modernism with its radical individualism or postmodernism with its social determinism.

But remember: Even when postmodernists agree with biblical Christians about the importance of community, the agreement is superficial. When Christians stress the importance of community, we do so because we want to build healthy relationships and draw on common strengths and giftedness to build up one another. In other words, for Christians, community is redemptive and open. There is never a suggestion that we are determined or controlled by the Christian community. When postmodernists stress community, they do so mainly as an excuse. Social determinism is the supreme reason why none of us can help the way we are—we're victims of oppression. It provides us with a rationale for separating from one another, not for coming together as the Bible teaches.

6. *Blind faith in our legal status quo is unwarranted.* Within the lifetime of most of us, laws were on the books designed explicitly to exclude Blacks from voting. I still remember living in a neighborhood where "zoning laws" prohibited Blacks from moving in. The power of money can and does produce unjust laws or prevent passage of laws that would promote justice. Claims that America is a "Christian nation" or that American laws are somehow automatically of God are every bit as naive and ethnocentric as postmodernists claim. Instead of perpetuating such mythology, Christians should be in the vanguard of those who stand apart from existing culture, passing judgment on what is right and wrong, not primarily on the basis of a constitution crafted by human beings, but from the Word of God. Reality doesn't yet match the high hopes of our democratic legal code. God doesn't call us to simply screech and bark for our team in the world. He wants us to put the truth first.

The Death of Truth

But even if we admit postmodern scholars have demonstrated some valid points, we dare not become confused. Seen in the larger picture, postmodernism is nothing less than the death of truth!

This is why as biblical Christians we should *never* compromise with postmodernism. At its heart, postmodernism rests on a belief not just in cultural bias, but in culturally constructed reality. At the heart of postmodernism is a denial of the real world, or at least of any knowable, objective truth about that world. This denial automatically implies a rejection of *all objective truth*—that is, truth that exists apart from my thought processes. The existence of the one, unique God and the person and work of Christ are examples of crucial objective truths postmodernists deny as objective or knowable. Indeed, Christianity is exactly the sort of "metanarrative," or overarching explanation of reality, that postmodernists fight against.

Biblical Christians can never admit postmodern assumptions. Although you have already picked up our criticisms in bits and pieces throughout earlier chapters, here, briefly, are our criticisms of postmodern thought:

1. *The postmodern attempt to deny the validity of reason is itself based on reason.* They defeat their own view. They claim no one can know objective truth, but *this itself is a statement of objective truth.* In other words, postmodern preachers declare that if we find anyone claiming to know truth, that person we should ignore. By their own test they should be ignored! This isn't just an unimportant scholastic critique. Internal consistency is the first test of any worldview's validity. And postmodernism flunks.

2. *They exaggerate when they claim people are prisoners of culture and language.* People are *influenced* by their cultures, but examples abound of individuals who have turned against the views of their own culture, thus demonstrating a level of individual freedom. Think how depressing the postmodern message of hopelessness is to people in poverty. Postmodern determinism renders all struggle for good in society pointless.

3. *They exaggerate the difficulties involved in scientific objectivity and neutrality.* Isolated problems in observation and a few unsolved mysteries are taken to show that all observation is subjective. Their exaggerations in this area threaten to turn an entire generation away from studying science. The consequences for our society are dreadful, not only from the standpoint of sheer economics but also the health and well-being generated by scientific research.

4. *They exaggerate the difficulties of translating and interpreting texts.* They focus on the outer fringe of textual interpretation, the five percent we cannot readily convey, and take that to mean we cannot trust *any* of our interpretations. As people lose confidence in every area of knowledge, including our ability to know anything from the Bible, from history, or from philosophy, postmodernists are fomenting a revolution of militant ignorance.

If this trend continues, all of the social and spiritual ills common in ignorant environments can be expected to rear their heads. Ignorant populaces are notoriously vulnerable to manipulation and exploitation. People who lose the ability to generate income in a technological world will soon suffer the well-documented problems always present with poverty. Superstition and conspiratorial fear are always lurking, ready to captivate the passions of the ignorant. Ironically, though the formulators of postmodern philosophy are intellectuals and highly educated professors, their followers in popular culture are drawing the natural conclusion that education in objective fields like science and math is a waste of time. High school students today are turning away in record numbers from hard sciences and math to study art, photography, and music.[13]

Attacks on the usefulness and objectivity of language are also automatically attacks on biblical revelation.

5. *Postmodernists exaggerate the difficulty of understanding other people's "realities."* Their delight in differences between communities leads to division and increased fear and hate. While supposedly giving us a new way of coming together in the world based on relativism and "respect," postmodernists actually foster division. After all, if different communities live in different realities and can never understand each other's lives or language, what reason is there to *try* to understand each other? People who become convinced that their problems are the result of oppression by others develop a murderous rage as a result. Notwithstanding their confident assertions, postmodernists have never shown that their divisive armchair speculations have ever done *any good for anyone* on the material, educational, psychological, or spiritual level.

6. *They try to deny the self, but this is always self-contradictory.* Who is doing the denying? Besides being self-defeating, this denial has terrible social implications. Tyrannies and oppressive regimes always share the conviction that the individual lives of their people are unimportant. The freedoms we have gained under modernistic democracy is clearly one of the best fruits of the Enlightenment. Postmodern thinkers have placed little value on individual freedom.

7. *They claim those who believe in absolutes are oppressive, exclusive, and violent. But they have produced some of the most oppressive and controlling codes of language and conduct ever seen in America.* For instance, the University of Connecticut rules with one great sweep that "Every member of the University is obligated to refrain from actions that intimidate, humiliate, or demean persons or groups or that undermine their security or self-esteem."[14]

We do not believe the central postmodern claim that figures such as Hitler, Stalin, and Mao were violent because they believed in absolutes or metanarratives. They were violent because they shared a willingness to settle social problems via the application of power—something postmodernists *also openly advocate.* Modernists may have been violent, but we see no proof that leaders steeped in postmodernism won't be just as violent.

Biblical Christians know that people are violent because they share the violent human nature that resulted from the fall of the human race. To think that people's ideologies alone make them violent is a superficial explanation of the human condition. Even reputable evangelical thinkers, however, have accepted this view. "Our Western collective hunch has turned out to be a largely destructive wager," comment well-known Christian authorities on postmodernism. "Our 'reality' is one of holes in the ozone layer—rampant environmental destruction, debilitating poverty, worldwide inequity, oppression, and terror. It is a reality of abuse, loneliness, fear, and perpetual threat."[15] In other words, problems with poverty, abuse, violence, and the environment stem from the Western "hunch" about progress—not from fallen human nature as the Bible describes it.

Postmodern analysis points the finger of blame at certain belief systems—at an acceptance of metanarratives. God says the problem goes much deeper than that. Think about it. Are poverty, exploitation, imperial domination, and suppression of the weak unique to modernist times and cultures? An honest student of anthropology or history knows this is absurd! Women are marginalized in virtually all cultures, now and throughout history. Empires like the one cast across Asia by the Mongols were brutal, savage, and sometimes genocidal. Yet the Mongols had never been instructed in modernist thought. How naive it is to think that if we can rid society of modernist metanarratives, then violence, greed, and thirst for power will go away!

The Bible is correct when it says, "There is no one righteous, not even one . . . their feet are swift to shed blood . . ." (Romans 3:10, 15). In another passage James asks, "What causes fights and quarrels among you?" Strangely, his answer doesn't highlight the role of totalizing narratives in producing violence. His answer, though, is more believable: "Don't they come from your desires that battle within you?" (James 4:1). It is the wickedness of our hearts that causes us to war and fight.

8. *The postmodern substitution of power for truth contains a threat of future oppression, especially for minorities.* If the only thing that matters is power, how long will it take majority culture to apply this amoral standard in their favor without any reference to the rights of the weak? Postmodernists like to picture contemporary culture as a power struggle between minorities and the dominant culture. But their vision may be fulfilled at the expense of minorities. Minorities' only hope for fair treatment is that society becomes convinced that right and wrong exist in the objective sense—the very thing postmodernists deny! Only then will majority culture place upon itself the restraints that guarantee safety and fairness for minorities. If society instead opts for the sort of power struggle postmodernists picture, minorities and the weak stand to suffer terrible oppression. As we have said before, no one should be more opposed to postmodern theory than minorities.

9. *Postmodernists contend that racism and bigotry are sins only of dominant groups.* While we share the postmodernists' concern for racism and sexism, the similarity of our views is superficial. Postmodern race and feminist theorists characterize racism and sexism as failings only of whites and men. Yet minorities can be racist, just as women can practice sexual jingoism. Cross-cultural workers know well the prevalence of these problems throughout the world. And again, the Bible is clear that the fall has affected all people. This is identical to the error made by the communists, who argued that aristocrats and the bourgeois were the villians and the proletariat more or less sinless victims. Unfortunately, the dictatorship of the proletariat turned out to be more violent than any of their predecessors. Christians should adhere to biblical teaching on human nature and refuse to buy into faddish explanations of evil based on power relations. Though those who wield power and authority may be more culpable for their deed because they possess greater freedom to act for good and suppress evil, sin is a problem for all people.

10. *Postmodern calls for humility are phony.* To the postmodernist, humility means we avoid claiming to know anything for sure. People who think they know better than someone else are arrogant. People who think their country or their church or their culture is great are arrogant. It's easy to see how postmodernists arrive at their conclusion; if I am the constructor, or source, of my own knowledge, then claiming I know better than another would be arrogant.

But claims to knowledge aren't unavoidably arrogant. Jesus held to absolutes and knew infinitely more than others—and told them so—but he was the essence of humility. When we freely admit that our knowledge has come from the outside—either from experience in the real world, or from revelation—we claim only to be *learners*. Nothing could be more arrogant than claiming with postmodernists that we are *constructors* of unquestionable truth, or even of reality itself. In this sense, postmodern humility is a false humility. Real humility is when we submit our views to testing, refutation, and God's authority.

All these criticisms make sense for non-Christians as well as Christians. But, as Christians, we should have some special complaints with postmodernism.

Complaint 1: Truth Is Not Dead

Our first and most important complaint is that postmodernism is the death of truth.

Christians should never minimize the importance God places on all truth. The object of our faith is our real and truthful God. Without truth, Christianity itself will vanish or be swallowed up in an ocean of subjective religious experience. Remember, Christian experientialists offer nothing unique. Those who engage in tantric Hinduism dissociate—zone out—so completely that people can have nails driven through their flesh without pain! Even the most far-out Christian "experience" will find it hard to compete with a drug trip for pure ecstasy. We aren't here to offer the world the premier rapturous experience. We are here to declare the truth about Jesus Christ and call on sinful people to fall on their knees and repent—often an experience more painful than pleasurable.

Jesus said that when we are his disciples the truth will set us free (John 8:32). Please notice that this truth isn't just a subjective "knowing" of Christ's person. To know the truth in this context means that "you abide in my word" (v. 32). God commands that we "speak the truth in love," and warns of the damnation of those who "did not receive the love of the truth so as to be saved" (Ephesians 4:15; 1 Thessalonians 2:11).

Thank God that exciting experience is also a part of the Christian life. Those of us who walk faithfully with the Lord will periodically experience the thrill of spiritual power moving through us and the joy of a grateful heart. But we may also be called on to experience acute suffering and sorrow, like Jesus, Job, Paul, and the other saints in Scripture. Pain is just as much a part of the Christian life as is excitement. Just look to the Psalms to see how their writers approach God in sorrow and agony more often than not.

When we let feelings and experience *follow* truth, they take their God-given place in our walks—blessings from God for which we should be grateful. But when we begin to define spirituality in terms of experience or states of feeling, we erect an idol of Christian thrill-seeking.[16]

Complaint 2: Reason Is Not a Cultural Bias

God is serious about truth. And the fact that truth is important means that God is also the Creator of *rationality* and *reason*. Reason isn't just the product of European culture, but a quality inherent in the Word and nature of the eternal God. God appealed to lost sinners by saying, "Come, let us reason together" (Isaiah 1:18). Long before anyone ever dreamed of the Enlightenment, Paul said the truth about God is "evident" and "clearly seen" even by people without the Bible (Romans 1:19–20). Truth is "evident from what has been created." In other words, people can use their minds to draw reasonable conclusions from nature—that God exists, and that his nature is infinite and personal. This passage flies directly in the face of postmodern contempt for reason.

Some Christian thinkers have given far too much ground in this area. Consider this assessment by Middleton and Walsh, who assert that traditional hermeneutics—the rules of scripture interpretation—are no longer workable:

> The interpreter of the Christian faith is pictured as somehow standing *outside* both the Christian faith and the contemporary context in order to magisterially correlate the two. But this is a profoundly modernist conception which naively ignores the fact that there is no neutral place to stand outside of a culturally encoded narrative. Interpretation, we have come to realize, is intrinsically tradition-dependent."[17]

Before evangelicals nod in agreement with this, we must think through the implications of their view. If interpretation is "intrinsically tradition-dependent," there is no sense in trying to "interpret" in the sense we normally use the word. We can never assess any interpretation for reasonableness, consistency, contextual flow of thought, or consistency with language and grammatical rules. To accomplish any of these, to make such judgments, we would have to stand in a position of neutrality. But we stand trapped within our culture and religious tradition, according to these postmodern-influenced evangelical professors, unable to look at it any other way.

This is a perfect example of how some Christian leaders are prepared to "sell the farm down the river." From that framework, Paul's admonishment to "handle accurately the word of truth" is nonsense, because it assumes we can determine what is accurate or inaccurate, and what is right or wrong. We have already pointed out that without reason, we cannot have truth. Perhaps we should be more explicit on this point.

Why Does Truth Require Reason?

God says in Hebrews 9:27 that "It is appointed for men to die once and after this comes judgment." But Hindus, Taoists, Buddhists, and New Agers believe people die and are reincarnated, only to die again. We as Christians say they are mistaken on this point because of Hebrews 9:27. But why? Our verse never actually says reincarnation is wrong. It teaches, though, that there is only one death for people, and we use our *reason*, including the law of noncontradiction, to conclude that if there is only one death for people, the Hindus are wrong when they say there are many deaths. Reason is essential for the application of this or any truth in the Bible. When we deny reason, we automatically deny truth.

Recent revivalists have called on Christians to forsake their fixation on "head-knowledge." Several top authors have complained that the church is "left-brained," focused too much on reason and knowledge and too little on feelings and creativity. A nationally known revivalist visiting our area pleaded to his audience that what matters is "not what's in our head, but in our hearts" and that when the Bible says "heart," it means our "feelings." He said Paul abandoned the knowledge-orientation of the Greeks in favor of the power of God.

Actually, Paul deplores the "wisdom of this world," not the *knowledge* of this world (1 Corinthians 1:20). As fallen people, we prefer to think autonomously, apart from God. When we do, our value system warps our knowledge. But this never implies that reason is wrong, carnal, or unnecessary. Again, the power of God in this passage is not some state of feeling, but "Jesus Christ and him crucified," one of the old left-brain truths we had better never forget! The same passage says of Christians that "we have the mind of Christ" (v. 16).

Enlightenment Europe made the mistake not of *using* reason but of *abusing* reason, elevating it to a place of deity, arguing that reason *alone* could tell us all things. This is what Francis Schaeffer called *autonomous* reason. Postmodernists have correctly, I believe, critiqued the value of autonomous reason. But unless we believe reason is a valid guide to reality, we can't argue for objective truth of any kind. Grenz is another example of an evangelical thinker prepared to go too far, we think, in order to modify theology to fit postmodern assumptions. He calls for a "postmodern evangelical theology" that is "post-individual," "holistic," "post-rational," and "focused on spirituality." He claims that in his new postmodern form of evangelicalism we cannot "continue to collapse truth into the categories of rational certainty that typify modernity. Rather, our theology must give place to the concept of 'mystery'—not as an irrational aspect alongside the rational, but as a reminder of the fundamentally non-rational or supra-rational reality of God."[18]

When we deny reason, we automatically deny truth.

Reason and Revelation

Reason is *reliable*, but not *sufficient*. As biblical Christians, we believe reason can tell us much about the world, but not everything. And if reason can't tell us everything about the world, it certainly can't tell us everything about the infinite personal Creator. We believe that in addition to our own reason we need revelation from

God. Revelation, whether in the Bible or even directly in our hearts, is *not* irrational, but we do not *acquire* it through reason. Instead, a personal and reasonable God speaks to us and tells us the truth about his character and actions.

Christians are utterly mistaken when they toy with the idea that reason is unreliable or unbiblical. Some Christians have claimed that the doctrine of the trinity demonstrates that God isn't subject to the law of non-contradiction. After all, doesn't 3=1? But a God who is "three in person and one in essence" (as the creed says) is hardly a contradiction. We should leave the Eastern mystical traditions to their contradictions, and affirm that our God doesn't *need* to contradict himself. Any God who "cannot lie" is definitely a God who does *not* contradict himself.

I may not be able to explain in rational terms why I like a certain painting. But this doesn't mean my feeling is irrational. Transcendent and mystical or experiential knowledge should never contradict reason. Again, I may not understand what makes my computer work, but that doesn't mean it is irrational. Just because my understanding is limited doesn't mean the universe is irrational.

The moment we agree that Christianity teaches contradictions, we lose the ability to stand for truth. Think about it: If we can contradict ourselves and still be telling the truth, then what is a lie? How can we judge right from wrong?[19] Postmodernists complain that reason implies exclusion. Yes, reason does dictate exclusion—exclusion of *falsehood*! This divisiveness isn't a bad thing; it's the will of God. Jesus declared that he came not to bring peace but a sword (Matthew 10:34). We betray him when we try to dash that sword of truth from his hand.

Paul and Reason

Paul says, "Knowing the fear of the Lord, we *persuade* men." Luke also says that "According to Paul's custom, he went to them [the Thessalonians] and for three Sabbaths *reasoned* with them from the Scriptures, *explaining* and giving *evidence* that the Christ had to suffer . . ." (Acts 17:2–3). We also notice that ". . . some of them were persuaded . . ." (v. 4). Again we read that, at Corinth, Paul was "*reasoning* in the synagogue . . . and trying to *persuade* Jews and Greeks." For Christian sympathizers of postmodernism who suggest that reason will never lead to personal faith, we have this question: If reason doesn't lead to God, why did Paul "persuade men" and "reason" with them for weeks?

According to the Bible, not only our hearts and wills but also our minds must come to agree with God (Matthew 22:37). How will we be able to call on people to surrender to the truth if we have already permitted ourselves to be unfaithful to it?

Complaint 3: Culture Does Not "Construct" Truth or Reality

The Christianity of the Bible isn't an ethnic or national religion. Christianity is truly a universal faith, directly applicable to all cultures (Matthew 28:19–20). Christianity can be expressed in different cultural forms, but its message is transcultural. The truth stands *over* culture as its judge, not *under* culture as its product.

Consider just two examples. Neither Jesus nor Paul uttered a message compatible with their own cultures. Jesus should have been, according to postmodern logic, a Pharisaic-style Jewish Rabbi reflecting the attitudes of his day—and postmodern sympathizers have indeed tried to paint him this way. But no honest reader of the Gospels can come away with the conclusion that Jesus basically reflected his cultural milieu. He *confronted* his culture and its religion on every front, as seen in his position on racism, women, the law, ritual, Rabbinic tradition, hatred of the Romans, and his view of the Old Testament.[20] According to postmodernism, people can't do this!

Paul was no different. He directly denies postmodern theories of the cultural origins of "metanarratives" when he says "For I would have you know, brethren, that the gospel which was preached by me is not according to man. For I neither received it from man, nor was I taught it, but I received it through a revelation of Jesus Christ" (Galatians 1:11–12). Paul rejected even the values held most dear by his native Hellenistic Jewish upbringing (Philippians 3:5–8).

In one striking example, Paul says, "There is neither Jew nor Greek, there is neither slave nor free man, there is neither male nor female; for you are all one in Christ Jesus" (Galatians 3:28). This was a message neither Hebraic nor Greco-Roman culture wanted to hear. Jews believed there was a huge difference between Jew and Gentile. Romans kept an iron-clad distinction between free and slave. Neither believed men and women were equal. How would a postmodernist account for this position? What cultural reality was Paul reflecting when he said this? Who conditioned him to say this? What features of the Greek, Aramaic, or Hebrew language caused Paul to believe this? Postmodern orthodoxy breaks up on the rocks of biblical revelation. If Paul, under the leadership of the Holy Spirit, could break with his so-called "cultural reality," we can too.

Christians have no debate with the observation that people usually adopt their culture's point of view. Our problem is with the postmodern position that they cannot do otherwise because they are imprisoned in the reality constructed by their language and culture. We must reject cultural determinism.

Complaint 4: Language Can and Does Communicate Objective Truth

Postmodernists can't accept the notion of objective revelation in the Bible. To them, language is never objective. Because every reading is an interpretation, it's pointless to wonder what God meant when he said something to the authors of Scripture. We will never know what these words meant to them, or what the author—in their view, not God, but culturally conditioned humans—intended. "How do we ever get from the sentences in the Bible to the proposition?" one postmodern thinker recently asked me in a personal letter. What he meant was that we have only words on a page, but we can never know what they meant to the one who spoke them (the proposition). We can only know how they *resonate* with us.

This is why postmodern theologians call for a "reader-centered" hermeneutic, or a "reader-centered" method of reading and interpreting Scripture. Reader-centered hermeneutics rehashes postmodern literary theory, applying it to the Bible. Edgar McKnight explains:

> The sort of knowledge that is provided by the Bible as literature may be seen as different from the sort of knowledge provided by the Bible as theology or history . . . the biblical text is like

> the artistic text in general, which is so filled with meaning that it transmits different information to different readers in proportion to each one's comprehension. A sensitive reader may, in fact, be "creating" a new world in the process of reading. . . . Experience with the text is an experience that alters needs and possibilities. The reader is then creating a world effectively in experience with the text.[21]

This is constructivism applied to the Bible. Readers *construct* their own meanings. The very thing traditional methods of scripture interpretation were designed to rule out—personal bias and opinion—are now the heart of what reader-centered interpreters look for! But when readers are free to generate new meaning in biblical texts, they are in the position formerly occupied by God—that of revealer and source of truth. Suddenly, God is no longer in authority, but *under* the authority of the postmodern reader!

To postmodernists, language is a prison house limiting us to the world of our own cultural reality. But God has chosen language as his primary medium of revelation, and we believe that we can accurately understand the intent of God's revelation to a *substantial degree*. The mission of hermeneutics—the science of interpretation—is to adjust our understanding based on cultural and language differences at the time of writing, so we may know the author's intended meaning. This mission has been largely successful. The Bible is fundamentally understandable in every area of significant doctrine. Postmodern critics love to camp out on the fringe of difficult passages where Christian readers cannot agree. But isolated problem texts cannot alter the picture significantly: the main doctrines of Christianity are easily understood from Scripture.

Evangelicals should be clear on this point: attacks on the usefulness and objectivity of language are automatically also attacks on biblical revelation.

Our Position

As evangelicals, we are not modernists. Modernism isn't compatible with Christianity any more than postmodernism is. What do we think about modernism? Most of its assumptions are wrong because they ignore the supernatural and deny human spirituality and dignity. At the same time, biblical Christians remain convinced that reason is useful, science can discover truth, and that universal (transcultural) truths are knowable.

Our position with postmodernism is no different. Postmodernists aren't wrong in everything they say, but their fundamental thrust is completely wrong, and incompatible with biblical Christianity. As we have seen, we can acknowledge those areas where postmodernists are closer to the truth than were modernists. Yet we must critique the many other areas where they are flat wrong. Postmodernists may share our criticisms of modernism, but they do so for completely different reasons—unacceptable reasons. Therefore, the hope of some Christian leaders that postmodernism might be an ally is forlorn and mistaken. So too is any hope for respect and acceptance from postmodern thinkers. Unless we are prepared to sell out the truth, we will be antagonists to the end.

Biblical Christianity is a distinct third way, established by God long before either modernists or postmodernists (or medieval kings and popes) roamed the earth. We have what people today need—the truth. In a time when people are coming to believe that nothing is knowable, that nothing is sure, we have something completely sure. Jesus said, "Heaven and earth will pass away, but My words shall not pass away" (Matthew 24:35). His Word is not only more timeless and certain than the culture of his day, but more timeless and certain than the heavens and the earth itself! This is the foundation, the certainty, that people increasingly long for in our postmodern world. But there is more to having the truth. We must figure out how to get it out to those who don't, which is the topic of our last chapter.

In Brief

- Liberal and neo-orthodox Christian leaders sought in vain to compromise with modernism and failed. Now, evangelicals must resist the temptation to seek compromise with postmodern culture or they too will fail. We must remain faithful to God in the area of truth, reason, and transcultural absolutes.
- Postmodernists make a number of valuable points, including the need to remain critical of our own culture and laws, and the

constant presence of human subjectivity.

- Christians must resist postmodern conclusions that people cannot be rational, that people are cultural constructs, that language is inherently unable to communicate universal truths, and indeed, that no universal truths exist.
- Standing up for truth and revelation requires that we stand up for reason and the *perspicuity*—understandability—of language in Scripture.
- We have the truth, and our world needs truth. As postmodern nihilism, anarchy, and alienation deepen, people's aching hearts will cry out more and more for the certainty and security of the truth. If we are unapologetically faithful and able to express the truth in meaningful ways, we will be able to meet that cry with the Word of Christ.

Notes

1. Thomas J. La Belle and Christopher R. Ward, *Multiculturalism and Education: Diversity and Its Impact on Schools and Society*, p.13.
2. Edgar V. McKnight, *Postmodern Use of the Bible: The Emergence of Reader-Oriented Criticism* (Nashville: Abingdon Press, 1988), p. 57.
3. We are not suggesting that the pragmatic desire for acceptance was the only motivation for adopting modernist and existential assumptions. Sadly, many pastors and professors were genuinely won over, in their own minds, to the new agendas. Also, Christian scholars wanted to retain respectability among their scholarly friends and colleagues. In a day when belief in the supernatural was *prima facie* evidence of ignorance, professors of religion, especially in Europe, where faculties from both theological and secular fields worked together at the same universities, had good reason to reinterpret Christianity in secular terms. This same motive is evident today, when Christian scholars and leaders don't want to be considered exclusive, modernistic, naive, or judging.
4. George Barna, *The Barna Report: What Americans Believe* (Ventura, Calif: Regal Books, 1991), pp. 292–294. He also shows that nearly four of five people today are relativists, and that there is surprisingly little difference between

teenagers who believe this inside versus outside the church. George Barna, comments during his conference: *What Effective Churches Have Discovered*, pp. 23–25.

5. Granted, this did include miraculous healings. But the power of God he refers to here is not an experience but "Jesus Christ and him crucified" (v. 1). He had just said that the cross of Christ was "the power of God and the wisdom of God" (1:24). This passage is not juxtaposing rational discourse over against miracles and experience as the true path of evangelism. He is contrasting "human wisdom or superiority of speech" (Greco-Roman rhetorical style) over against the offensive or foolish "message of the cross" (1:18). The worldly wisdom he refused to pander to included not only Greeks on a quest for human "wisdom" but also Jews seeking "signs" (1:22).
6. Stanley J. Grenz, "Postmodernism and the Future of Evangelical Theology," *The Challenge of Postmodernism: An Evangelical Engagement*, David Dockrey, ed. (Wheaton: Bridgepoint/Victor Books, 1995). He thinks that, "In their attempt to replace the individualistic foundational rationalism of modern Western thinking with an understanding of knowledge and belief that views them as socially and linguistically constituted, postmodern social theorists provide helpful assistance in understanding the role of propositions." We have not seen the helpful insights that sociology of knowledge contributes to evangelical theology.
7. Well critiqued in Hank Hanagraaf, *Christianity in Crisis* (Eugene, Ore.: Harvest House, 1993). I must add that as I encounter large numbers of Christian lay people, I for one have not seen any signs of the left-brain focus deplored by a number of church growth enthusiasts today. Neither have I seen the tendency to intellectualize Christianity, as deplored in several recent best-selling books. American Christianity is anything but intellectualized and left-brain. Our focus is on transcendence and experience today, as it has always been. How can we claim that American Christians are overly intellectual when George Barna shows that nearly half of our born-again Christians deny absolute truth? George Barna, *What Effective Churches Have Discovered*, p. 12.
8. Victims need to be believed as the first part of their recovery. See an example of extremist victimology in Marilyn D. McShane and Frank P. Williams, "Radical Victimology: A Critique of the Concept of Victim in Traditional Victimology," *Crime & Delinquency*, Vol. 38, No. 2 (April 1992): 258–271. Like postmodern historians, postmodern counselors argue that we can never know what happened, "only the experiences of those who suffer."
9. Paul cited Grecian poets and playwrights in Acts 17 and Titus 1.
10. I have also written a simple explanation of why rationality is incompatible with naturalistic assumptions in *Christianity: The Faith That Makes Sense* (Tyndale House, 1992), Chapter 4.
11. Charlene Spretnak is typical of what I would consider inconsistent critics. As an eco-feminist, and advocate of goddess spirituality, she depends on postmodern assumptions to build her case. Yet while deploring all "patriarchal" sources of moral knowledge—like the Bible—she vigorously though ineffectively resists the loss of all truth and morality at the hands of deconstructive postmodernists. See Charlene Spretnak, *States of Grace: The Recovery of Mean-*

ing in the Postmodern Age (San Francisco: HarperSanFrancisco, 1991), p. 233ff.

12. See K. A. Kitchen, a noted British orientalist who issues a general rebuke aimed at modernist theological scholars who are, he says, far more skeptical about the Bible than they are any comparable ancient document. *Ancient Orient and Old Testament* (Downer's Grove, Ill.: InterVarsity Press, 1966), pp. 15–34.
13. Postmodern relativism excuses a new trend in ignorance. See Allan Bloom, *The Closing of the American Mind* (New York: Simon & Schuster, 1987).
14. Andrew Altman, "Liberalism and Campus Hate Speech," in John Arthur and Amy Shapiro, eds., *Campus Wars: Multiculturalism and the Politics of Difference* (Boulder: Westview Press, 1995), p. 123. Altman points out that unlike harassment laws, these "hate-speech rules do not require a pattern of conduct: a single incident is sufficient to incur liability." Altman, as a liberal in favor of such speech codes, goes on to explain that unlike most laws in a liberal democracy which are viewpoint-neutral—they apply to all viewpoints equally—"rules against hate-speech are not viewpoint-neutral. Such rules rest on the view that racism, sexism, and homophobia are morally wrong," p. 123. Viewed objectively, such laws are a naked assertion of power by interest groups who want to be able to declare that another has impinged on their self-esteem. As we saw in the chapter on the law and postmodernism, they don't believe laws are ever neutral, and therefore this is a direct application of their views.
15. J. Richard Middleton and Brian Walsh, *Truth Is Stranger Than It Used to Be* (Downers Grove, Ill.: InterVarsity Press, 1995), p. 37.
16. I have discussed the relationship between truth and experience in more detail in Dennis McCallum, *Walking in Victory: Experiencing the Power of Our Identity in Christ* (Colorado Springs: Navpress, 1994), p. 147ff.
17. J. Richard Middleton and Brian Walsh, *Truth Is Stranger Than It Used to Be*, p. 174.
18. Some of his statements seem to be *koans* that are apparently contradictory. He affirms rationality and irrationality at the same time, as in this statement: "We must continue to acknowledge the fundamental importance of rational discourse, of course, and hence of propositions. Yet, our theology cannot remain fixated on the propositionalist approach of the older evangelical theologies, which viewed Christian truth simply as correct doctrine." Stanley J. Grenz, "Postmodernism and the Future of Evangelical Theology: 'Star Trek' and the Next Generation."
19. Listen to this postmodern description of reason and its role in society: "Western reason's fundamental attachment to the law of non-contradiction can thus be seen as based on the instrumental utility of that principle in the attempt to assert control. The repression of contradiction both within the self and within the social body favors integrity and unanimity over difference and multiplicity. The boundaries that traditional reason draws between the integral, non-contradictory thing and its others are now seen as a process of excluding contents that were included in a more complete, if also more chaotic,

whole before reason began its divisive work." John McGowan, *Postmodernism and Its Critics* (1991), p. 19.

20. On racism and women, see his willingness to converse with the Samaritan woman at the well (John 4). On sexism see his insistence that Mary was doing the right thing by learning from a Rabbi (Luke 10:38ff). On Rabbinic tradition see Mark 7:1–23. On hatred of the Romans see Matthew 22:21. On their view of the Old Testament, see the Sermon on the Mount (Matthew 5–7).
21. Edgar V. McKnight, *Postmodern Use of the Bible: The Emergence of Reader-Oriented Criticism* (Nashville: Abingdon Press, 1988), pp. 168, 176, citing Jurij Lotman, *The Structure of the Artistic Text.*

15

Practical Communication Ideas

Dennis McCallum, Contributor

A friend of mine told me that when Christian apologist and author Ravi Zaccharias visited Columbus to speak at The Ohio State University, his hosts took him to visit the Wexner Center for the Arts. The Wexner Center is a citadel of postmodern architecture. It has stairways leading nowhere, columns that come down but never touch the floor, beams and galleries going everywhere, and a crazy-looking exposed girder system over most of the outside. Like most of postmodernism, it defies every canon of common sense and every law of rationality.

Zaccharias looked at the building and cocked his head. With a grin he asked, "I wonder if they used the same techniques when they laid the foundation?"

His point is very good. It's one thing to declare independence from reality when building a monument. It's another thing when we have to come into contact with the real world. Reason and science suddenly matter again!

The Wexner Center is a memorable picture of the internal contradictions within postmodernism. For those of us who want to dialogue with postmodernists, the Wexner Center also highlights an opportunity. Many people who accept postmodern notions have never realized such contradictions exist. The contradictions, therefore, become entry-points to communication.

Postmodernism's views of so-called creativity and constructed truth provide one of the most striking contradictions.

Goose-Stepping on Campus

Those of us working with college students today are amazed at how uniform their responses are to every question about religion or values. The same relativistic formulas invariably slide out with hardly any difference—even in word order! This brings up a crucial question: If truth and reality are so up-for-grabs that anyone can create new reality at will, why is everybody saying exactly the same thing? Shouldn't we be hearing a wide variety of worldviews and ideas? Where is all the *diversity*? Where is all the anticipated *creativity*? Instead of wildly diverse approaches to thought, we see today students goose-stepping smartly to a party line that allows no variation.

The reason we see such conformity is that postmodernism is nothing less than a *totalistic metanarrative*—an all-pervasive account of reality—the very thing they dread the most. Though advanced under the slogan of tolerance, postmodernism has shown no inclination to tolerate any deviation from its narrow party line. Postmodernists have successfully demonstrated that those in earlier decades and centuries who believed in absolutes often were not tolerant. What they haven't shown is that those who *deny* absolutes *are* tolerant.

If truth and reality are so up-for-grabs that anyone can create new reality at will, why is everybody saying exactly the same thing?

The landscape today isn't becoming more tolerant. Postmodernists bequeath tolerance only on certain views and groups. Others are experiencing rejection, judgment, and even compulsion at the hands of supposedly inclusive thinkers. Some speech codes and behavior codes appearing on campuses today are even more controlling than those in extreme fundamentalist colleges.

Take, for example, these rules from the "University of Michigan Policy on Discrimination and Discriminatory Harassment." According to this policy, students are subject to discipline, including possible expulsion from the university, for:

> Any behavior, verbal or physical, that stigmatizes or victimizes an individual on the basis of race, ethnicity, religion, sex, sexual orientation, creed, national origin, ancestry, age, marital status, handicap, or Vietnam-era status and that . . . creates an intimidating, hostile, or demeaning environment for educational pursuits . . . or participation in extra-curricular activities.

The accompanying interpretive guide explains:

> You are a harasser when . . .
>
> You exclude someone from a study group because that person is of a different race, sex, or ethnic origin than you are;
>
> You tell jokes about gay men and lesbians;
>
> Your student organization sponsors entertainment that includes a comedian who slurs Hispanics;
>
> You laugh at a joke about someone in your class who stutters;
>
> You comment in a derogatory way about a particular person or group's physical appearance or sexual orientation, or their cultural origins, or religious beliefs;
>
> A male student makes remarks in class like "Women just aren't as good in this field as men," thus creating a hostile learning atmosphere for female classmates.[1]

Imagine it. Now we have groups about whom no one is allowed to make a joke! Worse still, you can be hauled in not only for telling a joke but for *laughing* at a joke! They're not kidding, either. The article that details these campus codes cites examples of students prosecuted under these rules. Postmodernists, as the guardians of the oppressed, are prepared to pursue their theories of language-constructed reality even to the radical extreme of controlling when people laugh! Orwell himself would be shocked.

One University of Michigan student filed a lawsuit to defend his right to report his laboratory findings involving differences in competencies between men and women. No, postmodernism's denial of truth has not resulted in any great upsurge of tolerance. It has ushered in a lack of concern for freedom.

The uniformity of postmodern culture leaves biblical Christians feeling left out. We find ourselves saying something widely different from other people, and we find we are the only ones saying it.

Cross-Cultural Communication

When communicating with postmodernists or those influenced by the postmodern shift, we as evangelicals have the sure answers people need. But we stand a greater distance from those with whom we communicate than we did just thirty years ago. At that time, substantial Judeo-Christian assumptions were still common in secular culture. To bridge the gap today, we need to introduce additional steps in the communications process. It's not *impossible* to communicate with postmodern culture; it's just *more difficult*.

Suppose a villager in another land engaged me in conversation about how we could fend off the forest worm-demons who are boring holes in people's teeth. Some villagers are pressing for an immediate sacrificial ceremony, but he might try to convince me that this has been tried before. He thinks that we should move the village to a new location with fewer demons. At some point I would probably interrupt him. "Excuse me," I say with my hand raised. "We have a problem here. I can't share my views about how to fend off these demons, because I don't believe they exist!"

The gap between the villager's starting point and my starting point is too great for us to communicate about demon countermeasures. This analogy falls short, however. The distance between us and postmodern thinkers is far greater than that between the villager and myself. As Christians we not only believe differently from postmodern thinkers, our perspectives are *automatically offensive* to one another.

To grasp the difficulty of our task, we need a different analogy. Suppose I live in the Pacific Northwest. I am an avid environmentalist, and I am going to my neighbor's house to ask him to sign a petition to save the trees. On the way to his house, I meet him walking on his way to my house. He works for a local logging company, and wants me to sign *his* petition to strengthen the bridge over a nearby creek so they can use larger trucks, thus increasing lumber production by felling some of the trees too fat to fit on their present trucks! How likely is it that either one of us will sign the other's petition? These positions are worse than antithetical. They are mutually offensive.

In the same way, when we argue for absolute truth and universal objective ethics—not to mention the exclusive claims of Christ—we offend our postmodern hearers profoundly. No wonder some evangelicals are tempted to soft-sell truth and look for common ground in the area of experience! No wonder others are ready to write off an entire generation and build forts to hide out from them!

Bridging the Gap

Again, the communication dilemma here isn't hopeless. It's just more demanding than anything most Western Christians have had to face. Missionaries know that success in cross-cultural communication requires patience and care in how we approach each discussion. Careless communicators are rarely successful in a cross-cultural context, and they menace all other Christians as they blithely offend people in the name of Christ.

Missions experts are well aware of the need for careful research, patient development of relationships within the community, and fluency in local language, including the ability to deliver the gospel in the local vernacular. The same principles translate to our own culture. If we expect to be successful at witnessing to postmodern people, including our own kids and their friends, we need to understand the postmodern outlook. By reading this book you have already taken a big step in the right direction.

Optimism Lives

Along with our problems in communication today, we also have good reasons for optimism. Here is only a partial list:

A house divided: Jesus warned that a house divided cannot stand. Today, Satan's house is divided. Modernists and postmodernists slug it out with one another in culture, government, and universities. The new force in society—postmodernism—is no closer to Christianity than our old foe, modernism. But perhaps their struggle with one another means opportunity for us.

Postmodernism nihilism: As Dr. Fidelibus pointed out in his chapter on psychotherapy, no worldview is more likely to produce depression and despair than postmodern nihilism ("nothing-ism," the belief that nothing matters). We may well see a rebound from postmodern extremes as society recognizes the need for norms of some kind. However, this possibility contains dangers of its own. When Germany reacted to the moral anarchy of the Weimar period, the result was Hitler. Today, we sense a cry for social order and moral norms, but often this cry is for a new secular morality based on utilitarian grounds. Christian leaders are naive when they welcome moral authoritarianism without Christ. On the positive side, may not the search for norms open doors for Christian witness in a way similar to that in the former Soviet Union?

The power of God: God declares that his invisible attributes and eternal nature are "evident within them" (Romans 1:19). He also predicted that the Holy Spirit would convict the world of their need for Christ (John 16:8–11). In other words, people know in their heart that truth exists, that they are separate from their Creator, and that they need personal conversion. Therefore, with God preparing the way, we will experience more success than we might expect. (Of course, the same passage warns that people "suppress the truth in unrighteousness.") A logger or an environmentalist would be lucky to win the other over one time in a thousand. But we will do far better if we move ahead carefully and prayerfully. Postmodernism is a fortification raised up against the knowledge of Christ (2 Corinthians 10:5). But we are fully equipped to overcome such fortifications with the truth.

Postmodern loneliness: Jesus said, "Let your light shine before men in such a way that they may see your good works, and glorify your Father who is in heaven" (Matthew 5:16). Among our most powerful "good works" in the present situation is our ability to love one another as Christ loved us. At its core, postmodern culture is profoundly lonely. When people exchange the possibility of a servant-style love for the hollow values of "respect" and "toleration," the result is interpersonal distance. They become wrapped up in avoiding "off-limits" statements, avoiding disagreement with another's views, and standing up for their own rights. Christians are free from these concerns under the security of God's authority and love. We can build real relationships and community the secular world can only envy. Many postmodernists have been won to Christ after they beheld a group of Christians sharing the love of Christ with one another.

Detailing how to witness to postmodernists is a subject too large to cover in this book, which has mainly sought to describe the challenges of postmodernity. We will, however, offer some promising strategies for Christians to explore in sharing Christ in a postmodern culture. To preview our argument, we advocate the following steps:

- Discovering and understanding people's presuppositions
- Clarifying those presuppositions in the minds of our hearers
- Carefully moving our hearers to the point of tension
- Supplying the Christian alternative when we see a new receptiveness forming.

Discovering Presuppositions

When talking to people in our postmodern culture, we find that few fully understand the basis for the views they have adopted. Therefore, the first step for effective communication often is helping people understand their own views as well as a few of the problems inherent in those views.

Some groups in our church have used a discussion format to draw out postmodern presuppositions. We share this model—what we call *Conversation and Cuisine*—not because we think it's the only way to communicate with postmodern culture, but because it illustrates the kinds of new approaches we need to develop.

In a *Conversation and Cuisine* event, a Christian group gathers in a home with their non-Christian friends for a dinner-party discussion group. Guests are reassured that all views are welcome, and that this isn't a church meeting. After dinner, the discussion topic might be "To Judge or Not to Judge." The discussion facilitator presents pairs of situations involving different types of judgments, and the group discusses whether they would feel comfortable casting judgment in that situation.

For example:

Scenario 1:

Your white workmate is helping an African-American workmate unravel a problem in the computer database. You over-

hear the white, in his frustration, call the African American a "dumb N——." She looks up with hurt on her face. You denounce the white worker for prejudice and for hurting another's feelings.

To judge your white workmate is: Okay Bad

Scenario 2:

Your other friend at work announces she is getting divorced. She has fallen in love with another man, and although she has two children she has told her husband she "cannot continue to live a lie." Her husband and children are crushed, but she feels she must be true to herself. You charge her with selfishness, lack of loyalty, and willingness to hurt others' feelings.

To judge your friend is: Okay Bad

Both judgments involve someone having feelings hurt through the actions of another. But most postmodern-influenced thinkers are more willing to approve passing judgment in scenario #1 than in scenario #2. While there are several valid points people might raise—such as the fact that we don't know what the adulterer's husband was like—the main effect of the pairing is to create confusion.

At this point, the facilitator raises an interesting question. "How would people have answered this same pair thirty years ago?" Most agree that judgment in #2 would have been made without hesitation two or three decades ago. And although people thirty years ago might have resented the racial epithet in #1, they may have concluded that "sticks and stones will break my bones, but names will never hurt me." Today, most secular people believe that the crime in #1 is morally far worse than that in #2, if indeed #2 represents anything wrong at all—just the reverse of what the same crowd would have concluded thirty years ago.

Why the difference between today and thirty years ago? Scenario #2 is definitely more socially acceptable today, even though the damage from family breakup may dwarf the actual damage from saying something wicked. Racism, of course, is by no means a minor problem whether today or thirty years ago. The purpose of the discussion isn't to promote racism but to uncover presuppositions. When postmodern guests begin to suggest that the change from thirty years ago to today is the result of morality being a product of cultural paradigms, we pose this question: "So are we suggesting that using the 'N' word was okay thirty years ago? Or was it wrong, but they just *thought* it was okay?"

This question causes postmodern thinkers to seize up in confusion. If they say it was really okay to call someone by a racial slur, they condone the racism of the past. But if they say people only thought it was okay, they suggest that a universal standard of right and wrong exists—one which people thirty years ago may have missed, but which we now know. Either position contradicts central postmodern assumptions.

By struggling with these internal contradictions in an accepting atmosphere, postmodern-influenced people realize they *are* willing to judge. Yet they are perplexed by their own unspoken rules governing judgment. Modernists have problems here as well. They have no more solid basis for moral judgments than postmodernists, and neither can they explain why they hold to moral views now or why they were held to in the past. Underlying the whole question is the obvious need for moral authority.

Guiding Others Into Discovery

Of course, we don't want to merely leave people confused. We create confusion in order to *thaw the dogmatism of postmodern thinking*. The next step is to gently push postmodern thinkers to realize the logical outcome of their presuppositions. Again, an example may help us see one way this can be done. The same group discussing judgment later introduces another scenario:

> *You visit an African tribe during their female circumcision ritual and behold a teenage girl receiving a clitorectomy. When you complain to your tour guide, he points out your Eurocentric values are interfering with your judgment.*
>
> *To judge the tribal ritual is: Okay Bad*

This scenario raises more complicated contradictions for the postmodern thinker. Female circumcision is a manifestation of misogyny and control of women. The procedure guarantees women will never experience orgasm, and therefore will take no pleasure from sex. In the words of one African apologist, the practice "frees women from their bondage to lust to find their true identity as mothers." The girls have little or no say in whether they receive the procedure. Viewed objectively, this practice is a savage and brutal violation of women, as feminists have rightly pointed out.

But there's a problem. Female circumcision is also a time-honored religious rite of passage *in another culture*—in an *oppressed, non-Western, non-white* culture at that. It is, therefore, off-limits to postmodern judgment of any kind. In culturally postmodern groups, we often find those who agree with the tour guide. They feel we cannot judge this situation because we have no context from which to view it other than our own cultural reality. Someone might suggest that we can't force our view on them, but this is a different point. The question is not *how* to change their culture—by force or by persuasion—but *whether we should even try*. Some postmodern-influenced thinkers are confused by this dilemma, while the more militant postmodernists are clear: We cannot judge their social reality. Condoning clitorectomies naturally makes the women in the group nervous.

But we don't let them off the hook so easily. Suppose we consider New Guinea, where for centuries tribes have hunted members of other tribes and taken their heads as totems, talismans, or fetishes. Today, under the influence of Western colonial culture, the government of New Guinea has outlawed head-hunting. Do those in our discussion agree with this move, or not? More confusion. The militant postmodernists stand their ground. "How can we judge a practice that has been going on for hundreds of years, and is a religious practice to boot?" "Who do we think we are to judge this culture, when we have *x*, *y*, and *z* evils in our own culture?"

Their point is good. We usually show that they are merely repeating a truth observed two decades ago by Francis Schaeffer: "If there is no absolute by which to judge the state [or here, the culture] then the state [culture] is absolute." We have to agree that for us to judge events in another culture isn't possible apart from the existence of a moral absolute that applies to all cultures, whether it is acknowledged or not. When we put such a point on it, the postmodernists' position either hardens or begins to soften.

Finally, we are ready to consider one more example: What about

Hitler's Germany? They had a rich cultural heritage of anti-Semitism, including killing Jews, that went back for centuries. Were we wrong to judge Nazi culture and intervene militarily to stop what we considered oppression?

Now we're really confused. At one discussion, a postmodernist spoke up after a short silence to say that this was different because it was our own culture—we are Europeans too.

"So if it was in India or China, we'd have no problem with it?" I wondered.

He nodded reluctantly—faithful and dogmatic to the bitter end.

Others in the room were groaning by now. We might not be able to win the most militant postmodernists, but the majority of people follow postmodern ideals like they do clothing fashions. They aren't deeply committed to the postmodern agenda, and they will reconsider their position if they find their assumptions failing the test. In this instance, my postmodern challenger came to me afterward and admitted I had disrupted his belief system to the point where he had to consider it all over again. I gave him a book on apologetics and he went home saying he would read it. I doubt he would have been willing to read it before this discussion.

Timing in Communication

Please note that we didn't share the gospel itself at the discussion I described. We left them with nothing more than the suggestion that perhaps our culture has discarded the concept of judgment too quickly and completely. We reminded them that we need to discover a universal basis for moral judgment—and other types of judgment—if we are to have anything to say about evil in other cultures or in our own. And we pointed out that as Christians we believe we have answers in this area.

If the guests from that discussion go home rethinking their positions, our pre-evangelistic task is complete, successful for the time being. If we maintain relationships with these people, we can follow up our first conversations. Once people's thinking has been thawed—or even shocked—out of their totalistic postmodern patterns, they will have a new receptiveness to the gospel and apologetic material. They will begin to take our concepts seriously, examining the rational validity of our arguments and the consistency between our "walk" and our "talk." If we have brought together the other elements of successful evangelism—including the subjective, relational parts—we will do well with many of these hearers.

We use a number of subjects as a basis for *Conversation and Cuisine* discussions in our church. Examples of relevant, interesting subjects where postmodern contradictions abound include the following:

The environment
The family in modern culture
Social ethics
The existence and nature of God
Forgiveness in relationships
Workplace ethics
Dealing with guilt feelings
Medical ethics
Education
The causes of urban crime
What is love?
Different views of the afterlife
The ethics of wealth
Animal rights and human responsibility
Current event(s) like the O.J. Simpson trial or the Rodney King trial

Again, this isn't a book on witnessing, and space prevents us from sharing fully on even this one example. But you can get more free information on how to hold *Conversation and Cuisine* events as well as other practical ideas by calling the number at the back of this book, or visiting our World Wide Web site, also listed at the back.

Legitimate Subjective Witness

In John 13:34–35 and John 17:21–23, Jesus taught that the unity and love Christians express with each other is compelling evidence of the truthfulness of Christianity. The New Testament also envisions Christians bringing their friends to Christ through what can be considered relational, or friendship evangelism (see John 1:41–51, Acts 16:30–34). Both of these areas suggest that because Christianity is relational, Christian outreach should often also contain a strong relational aspect. We believe that in a postmodern culture, friendship evangelism and the subjective evidence of a caring Christian community are going to be more important than ever.

We already noted that postmodernism breeds profound loneliness. When postmodern people insist that everyone's reality is different, they destroy any basis for closeness. Communication itself is of questionable value under postmodernism. When everyone's opinion is of equal value, no opinion is of *any* value. The result? People have nothing to talk about. Respect may be distributed more fairly, but the postmodern definition of respect virtually requires the loss of closeness. With no basis for disagreement and debate, we drift into an apathy of indifference—a devastating price for our heightened respect.

No wonder so many postmodern people are miserable, driven seekers of pleasure and meaning. Christians not only can explain why postmodernists have relational problems, but also show them a different way. We believe this is one of the most effective areas of Christian witness today. If we have even a small group of friends within a local church practicing Christian community, we have a base from which to practice evangelism. But remember: Even though the subjective witness of Christian love is important, it should *supplement* the truth of the Gospel, not *replace* it.

What Is Love Bombing?

A loving atmosphere is the ideal environment where truth can be considered with a favorable attitude. Christians will do well to form home groups where they can discuss truth rather than simply declare it, as in a sermon. However, we will never "nice" someone into the kingdom of God. Groups who use their loving demeanor to bypass truth and decision-making are guilty of *manipulating* their hearers, rather than *persuading* them.

Any time we try to win people to Christianity while bypassing their minds we are guilty of manipulation, an approach cult experts call "love-bombing." A group that "love-bombs" makes an outward show of love in order to attract and even gain control over visitors. Guests may find themselves joining the group without even knowing why.

God doesn't work this way. God may have stricken Paul down on the road to Damascus, but we aren't authorized to do likewise. Our commission is to give a defense for the hope within us (1 Peter 3:15). We are to "declare the excellencies of" God (1 Peter 2:9). We are to "speak forth the mystery of Christ" while letting our "speech always be with grace, seasoned, as it were, with salt, so that we may know how to respond to each person" (Colossians 4:3, 6).

Consider the example of Paul. He spoke to a more or less non-rationalistic world similar to ours. With isolated exceptions, mainly in large Greek cities, the first-century world had little attraction to Western-style modernistic rationalism. Yet, Paul says, "Knowing the fear of the Lord, we *persuade* men" (2 Corinthians 5:11a).

Biblical Christians should hold forth both experience *and* reason when calling others to follow Christ.

Sailing Into the Future

As evangelicals sail off into an uncertain future, we have plenty of things to fear. Our children will be subjected to a program of social indoctrination that will challenge even the most careful parents. Our churches as well are embattled, perhaps in some cases even cowering before a world that seems too hostile to Christian ideals. Social institutions will likely continue to propagate postmodern and modernist views antithetical to Christianity. Laws and court interpretations will no doubt continue to cause problems as well.

What is the church to do?

We must advance! The power of God is great. Whatever the dangers we face when we actively engage our postmodern culture, the dangers of flight are greater still. Once we adopt a posture of flight, we guarantee defeat. A church on the defensive is a church without vision. The people of our culture today need us more than ever. But remember this: Our battle isn't against flesh and blood (Ephesians 6:12). We have no war to fight with the people in our society. They are the victims of our true enemy, the Evil One. We cannot and should not construct fortress communities to protect ourselves from postmodernism. Only when we advance toward postmodernists in love do we develop the mental and spiritual fiber we need to live victoriously for God.

The Next Generation

We don't protect our children merely by hiding them from the influence of postmodern ideology. They are only safe when they are familiar with postmodern arguments and are prepared to answer them confidently.

None of us who have children want them to die from drowning. But how can we prevent it? One way is to keep them away from bodies of water deeper than two feet. It works. Kids won't drown if they don't get into water. But, of course, we can also guard them from drowning by another method: teaching them to swim. Most of us choose this method. Though it isn't foolproof, it works rather well and provides more freedom. Besides—do we really think we can keep our kids from ever in their lives falling into water too deep for wading? Even if we could, we would run the risk of turning them into social misfits.

This illustration suggests solutions for the problems we parents face in the postmodern world. God is explicit: He wants us to guard our children from drowning by teaching them to swim. For one thing, the other method—avoidance—is ineffective. Children eventually go away to college or into business and encounter all the things we guarded them from.[2] Will they be ready?

We have one final reason to teach our kids to swim. Jesus said to the Father, "I do not ask that you take them out of the world, but to keep them from the Evil One" (John 17:15). Paul said God doesn't intend that Christians distance themselves from the wicked of this world (1 Corinthians 5:9–10). Avoidance costs the lost people of the world the light they so desperately need.

In Brief

- Because of the loss of the Judeo-Christian undergirding of our society, evangelicals and culture stand at a greater distance from each other than in previous decades. The rise of postmodernism calls for cross-cultural communication, which is more demanding, more time-consuming, and more annoying to our flesh—but not impossible.
- Our reasons for optimism include the power of God, the loneliness of postmodern culture, postmodern nihilism, and a vacuum of truth.
- By discovering the presuppositions of others and gently leading them to discover the problems with their own views, we can

thaw the dogmatism of postmodern consensus and create a new openness to alternatives.

- We must be prepared to speak the truth and resist the temptation to merely try to take people to a higher pleasure state than their earlier postmodern options could.
- We can also use subjective forms of witness to good effect if they are legitimate and subordinate to the truth. Foremost among these is authentic Christian love.

Conclusion

We hope you have been challenged by our study of postmodernism. We could have said much more! If you would like to learn more about postmodernism, we have included at the back of this book our World Wide Web address as well as an 800 number where you can access detailed information on most subjects as well as a free group study guide for this book.

As we move forward to engage postmodern culture in dialogue, we know we have God's power, the truth, and our love for lost and needy people to buoy us up. May God enable us to move forward not with fear but with excitement about what we have to share.

Notes

1. All cited in "Campus Speech Codes: Doe v. University of Michigan," in John Arthur and Amy Shapiro, eds., *Campus Wars: Multiculturalism and the Politics of Difference*, pp. 116–119.
2. I don't believe this argument applies to young children. We can make a good case for protection at ages where children cannot reasonably be expected to think for themselves. If we are wise, however, we will even then work to train them for the day when we introduce them to the rest of life.

The Postmodern Analytical Framework

Discipline	Author	Text	Reader	Key Figure
Literature	*Writer, playwright, poet.* The author is viewed as irrelevant to meaning or unaware of meaning of the text. The author doesn't stand over text as an authority.	*Literary work.* Texts are to be deconstructed, freed from logocentrism.	*Audience, reader.* The reader is the center of meaning. The focus of authority over the text shifts from the author to the reader.	Terry Eagleton, Stanley Fish, Jacques Derrida, Frederick Jameson
History	*Historian, chronicler.* Authors write from a particular social perspective which serves to perpetuate their power.	*Recorded data of a culture.* Texts can be deconstructed. Critical analysis will identify aspects of authors "reification," etc.	*Student of history.* The reader stands over the text of history, identifying ways that it serves or challenges his cultural identity.	Francois Lyotard, Michel Foucault
Art	*Artists.* Artists express their socially constructed outlook.	*Painting, sculpture, theater, architecture.* Any self-expression can be art.	*Public, critic.* Viewers identify ways the material expresses social reality.	Dadaism (visual arts), post-structuralism (architecture), absurdism (theater)
Religion	*Sage, disciple, priest, mystic.* Religious figures either sanction the social elite, or rebel against it.	*Sacred texts and rituals.* These are "metanarratives" that explain reality and the human condition.	*Modern religious person.* Readers seek to actualize themselves through religious forms.	New Age Consciousness; Joseph Campbell, Feminist spirituality, etc.
Law	*Framers of the Constitution; Legislature.* These are representatives of the cultural elite.	*Constitution; laws.* These tools inflict the will of the powerful on the rest of society.	*Contemporary legislation, litigation, and constitution interpretation.* These are the means by which power can be redistributed.	Critical Legal Studies, Feminist legal studies, Race critical legal studies.

(continued)

THE POSTMODERN ANALYTICAL FRAMEWORK (continued)

Discipline	Author	Text	Reader	Key Figure
Science	*Scientist; scientific method.* These constitute a "logocentric" expression of the modernist worldview, or "paradigm."	*Experimental data.* This material is interpreted in accordance with the existing social paradigm.	*Scientists.* Interpretation and application of data to technology to serve the accepted scientific paradigm.	Feyerabend; Thomas Kuhn
Psychotherapy	*Author is client.* Patient's view of self as represented in personal narrative.	*Client's Story.* Focus of therapy.	*Psychologist and psychiatrist as interpreters.* Viewing humans as social constructs.	Kenneth Gergen, Jacques Lacan in psychoanalysis
Sociology/ Anthropology	*Human cultures and subcultures.*	*Social forms, mores and customs. Also worldviews and religions.*	*Sociologists and anthropologists.* Identify interpretative communities and "reification processes."	Karl Mantheim; Neo-Marxists; Peter Berger
Linguistics	*Communication; Language users.* Reality presents itself as linguistic symbols.	*Human symbolic communication, including written texts.*	*Linguistic analysts and anthropologists.* Analyze language games, interpretative communities, semiology (the study of signs and symbols)	Clausc Levi-Strauss; Edward Sapi; Benjamin Whorf; Alfred Korzybski

Glossary

AAL ▪ African American Language. A variant of English believed by some to have been influenced by African languages.

Absolutism ▪ The belief that truth and values are objective and universal. "Objective" means that truth exists outside of the individual, and "universal" means that truth applies to every person in every place at every time.

Agnosticism ▪ The belief that we cannot have knowledge of God and that it is impossible to prove that God does or doesn't exist.

Amoral ▪ Lacking moral distinctions or judgments. Nothing is objectively good or bad.

Annales ▪ The French school of historiography which sought underlying causes for historical developments. A forerunner of postmodern cultural and social history.

Anthropomorphism ▪ Attribution of human forms and characteristics to God, the gods, or natural forces.

Apologetics ▪ The branch of theology concerned with the defense or proof of Christianity, and refutation of opposing worldviews.

Atheism ▪ The naturalistic view of reality; the belief that no gods or God exists; the lack of belief in a particular God.

Atman ▪ A Hindu term for the human essence.

Ayurvedic Medicine ▪ A form of alternative medicine based on Hindu concepts of *Prana* energy. *Prana* is similar to one's "astral body" or "aura." The key to health is proper balance in the flow of *Prana*. See Chapter 5.

Basic Beliefs ▪ Ideas individuals accept about the nature of reality, human nature, values, and truth. Basic beliefs are the foundation of a worldview.

Behaviorism ▪ The belief that human behavior, including actions and thoughts, can be explained by biological and environmental conditioning.

Brahman ▪ The Hindu concept of God as impersonal spiritual reality.

Centering ▪ A form of meditation used by practitioners of Therapeutic Touch and some other New Age and mystical religions. Centering is supposed to allow the practitioner to become well-attuned to the human energy field. See Chapter 5.

Constructivism ▪ The postmodern belief that knowledge about the world is not discovered, but "constructed" in the minds of observers. Constructivism denies that people can ever understand an objective or fixed universal reality. Reality instead is a social construct—a creation in people's minds, colored by their social background.

Critical Legal Studies Movement ▪ A postmodern approach to law that denies laws can be fair or impartial. This movement views all law as politically motivated by those who have power in our society—mainly whites, males, and the wealthy.

Cultural Relativism ▪ A theory that truths are true only to the particular society or culture holding to them.

Deconstruction ▪ The postmodern literary discipline of uncovering the opposing ideas implied in a text and demonstrating how the author has favored one side over the other because of his or her social context. Demonstrating how texts' truth claims defeat themselves.

Dissociation ▪ In the context of psychology and religion, dissociation means a separation of attention—that is, one's attention to the real world is severed, usually resulting in a trance-like state. Profound dissociation could be sleep, hypnosis, or unconsciousness. Mild dissociation could be daydreaming or "zoning out," including through drug use.

Duality ▪ The existence of distinct physical and spiritual realms; can also refer to ultimate distinctions between true and false, good and evil.

Empiricism ▪ Basing all knowledge on sense experience alone.

Enlightenment Era ▪ The period of Western history whose motto—according to Immanuel Kant—was "Dare to know." The Enlightenment regarded optimistically the possibility of reason controlling human life. The progress and perfectibility of the human race were believed possible, and according to some intellectuals, inevitable.

Epistemology ▪ The study of how we know things, a search to answer the questions "Is our knowledge reliable?" and "How can we be sure?"

Essentialism ▪ Belief that there is a universal and objective human nature. Postmodernists deny essentialism. They say that human nature is culturally constructed, and varies from culture to culture.

Existentialism ▪ The attempt to create meaning and personal identity out of a meaningless universe by the exercise of free will.

Family Systems Therapy ▪ A school of psychotherapy originally developed by Murray Bowen at Georgetown and now in wide use, especially in the recovery movement. Family systems therapy grew out of Freudian theory but sees the family of origin—rather than the individual—as the source of neuroses. Postmodernism has seized on family systems theory because it teaches that one's culture—one's family—determines their reality.

Hermeneutics ▪ The science of literary interpretation. The rules for interpreting a text.

Hinduism ▪ A religion that originated in India during the early 2nd millennium BC and the basis of many other pantheistic religions.

Humanism ▪ A philosophy that regards the rational individual as the highest value and considers the individual to be the ultimate *source* of value. It is dedicated to fostering the individual's creative and moral development in a meaningful and rational way, usually without reference to the supernatural.

Islam ▪ Theistic religion founded by Mohammed; term means "submission to God."

Karma ▪ The structure of one's life, resulting from one's prior actions in an earlier existence. The karmic law of cause and effect keeps the unenlightened bound to the cycle of life.

Koran ▪ The sacred book of Islam; the term means "the reading" or "the lesson."

Marginalize ▪ To "marginalize" is to exclude people by pushing them to the margins of society. People who are marginalized are oppressed by the "dominant culture."

Marxism ▪ A materialistic ideology based on the teachings of Karl Marx. Marxism sees history as a sequence of class struggles ultimately leading to the formation of a classless society. Postmodernism draws on Marxism for its view of social oppression of the weaker groups in society, and for its view that different classes or social groups have different ways of understanding reality.

Materialism ▪ The belief that nothing exists other than matter, which implies that everything happening in the world can, in principle, be explained by material objects guided by natural law. See Naturalism.

Maya ▪ The Hindu term for this material world, from an ancient stem meaning "illusion." Maya represents the human dilemma of being caught up in the illusion of the material world, and failing to recognize the actual unity of *atman* (the individual) with *Brahman* (the universal ALL).

Metanarrative ▪ According to postmodernism, a religious tradition or philosophical system that commits acts of cultural tyranny by promoting the fiction that all knowledge reduces to a set of universally applicable truths.

Metaphysical dualism ▪ Reality consists of two distinct realms: spirit and matter. Theists, including Christians, are metaphysical dualists.

Modernism ▪ Another term for enlightenment thought; modernist thought centered on a belief in human progress; reason as the ultimate source of authority; human autonomy.

Monism ▪ The belief that everything is part of one essence—the essential unity of all things. Spiritual Monism is the philosophical concept underlying major schools of Hinduism, Buddhism, and Taoism, as well as much New Age Consciousness. Western naturalism is also monistic in a different sense—that all things are material.

Monotheistic ▪ Belief that there is one and only one God. He is both personal and knowable.

Multiculturalism ▪ An educational movement designed to facilitate awareness and appreciation of diverse cultures. In postmodern ideology, it teaches that all cultures should be empowered to preserve, unchanged, their unique cultural reality. Any effort to change or reform a cultural group is actually repression, domination, and colonizing of one group by another.

Muslims ▪ Those who professes the faith of Islam; followers of Mohammed and the *Koran*.

Mysticism ▪ The belief that ultimate truth about reality can be obtained neither by ordinary experience nor by the intellect but only by non-rational intuition.

Naturalism ▪ The belief that everything that exists is material and natural. Naturalists deny the supernatural. See Materialism.

New Age Mysticism ▪ A diverse assortment of modern mysticism, ranging from the occult to traditional Eastern and Native American spirituality.

Nihilism ▪ From the Latin, *nihil* nothing. Nothingism. The theory that the universe is meaningless and without purpose, human life and its activities are of no value or significance, and that nothing is worth living for.

Nirvana ▪ The final state, according to Buddhism, in which the individual is merged with the universal all, and ceases to exist as an individual. The term comes from an ancient Sanskrit word meaning to "blow out," as in the snuffing out of a candle.

Objective Truth ▪ Truth that exists independent of human thought rather than truth that depends on human thought or experience. See Subjective Truth.

Pantheism ▪ Belief that God is identical with the universe; God and nature are synonymous. (*pan* all, *theo* God)

Paradigm ▪ A model. In postmodernism, a paradigm is a way of looking at reality specific to one social group. The rules of thought and consistency apply within a given paradigm, but cannot be applied to any other.

Patriarchy ▪ "The rule of the father." In postmodern usage, patriarchy often refers to norms or authority arising from male-dominated culture.

Political Correctness ▪ The demand for conformity to attitudes, and behaviors and speech deemed important for the sake of tolerance and acceptance.

Politicization of Truth ▪ The result of truth claims being viewed as subliminal attempts to gain or maintain power.

Positivism ▪ The theory that the only legitimate basis of knowledge is empiricism, or science.

Postmodernism ▪ The movement in late twentieth-century thought that rejects enlightenment rationalism, individualism, and optimism. Postmodernism is characterized by nihilism and radical subjectivity. "Affirmative" postmodernists believe that social reality can be changed by activism.

Prana ▪ The Hindu word for people's life energy, or aura. See Chapter 5.

Quantum Physics ▪ The branch of physics that studies the movement of subatomic particles within atoms. Findings in this field have attracted popular attention because mystics claim that they prove certain monistic principles. See Chapter 11.

Rationalism ▪ The belief that reason is a faithful and—according to modernists—sufficient guide to reality and truth. An ideology that extols antonomous reason above all things, while denying the vailidty of any other source of truth.

Reader-Centered Interpretation ▪ The postmodern idea that interpretation depends not on what the text says or what the author intended but on how the reader reacts to a text. The meaning is "constructed," or created, by the reader.

Reification ▪ Confusing language about reality with reality itself. Postmodernists charge that others "reify" concepts when they forget that all their ideas and observations are merely linguistic constructs.

Reincarnation ▪ To again become flesh in some form, based on karmic law. The transmigration of the spirit.

Scientism ▪ The belief—and the worldview—that science is the only method for obtaining knowledge.

Self-evident ▪ An idea that appears to be true in such a way that no explanation or proof is necessary.

Social Constructions ▪ The theory that reality cannot be objectively known, because beliefs about reality are shaped by the culture of which the individual is a product. Social Constructions are relative to the culture.

Subjective Truth ▪ Truth that is "true to me," as opposed to truth that is true independent of our thought or experience. See Objective Truth.

Syncretism ▪ The joining together of different views, especially religious views, often blending even contradictory religions into one.

Syntax ▪ A language's rules of grammar that govern the way words are linked together in sentences.

Taoism ▪ The popular Chinese philosophy of life based on the *Tao*, or "Way." The Way is the divine principle—a balance between seeming opposites, Yin and Yang.

Theism ▪ The belief in an infinite-personal God. The religious worldview based on the Old Testament that includes Judaism, Christianity, and Islam. Also referred to as monotheism.

Therapeutic Touch ▪ A therapy based on the Hindu notion of *Prana*, or life energy. Therapeutic Touch seeks to heal by balancing people's flow of *Prana*. See Chapter 5.

Totalization ▪ The artificial gathering together of all knowledge and reality into a worldview or ideology that claims to explain the world. Postmodern thinkers deny the validity of any of these overarching concepts which see a pattern or truth in the particulars of the world, and claim to explain everything. See Metanarrative.

Transcendent ▪ God is distinct from the universe; his existence is not bound by or limited to space and time.

Transcendental Meditation ▪ A twentieth century attempt to fuse Hindu philosophy with pseudo-scientific beliefs.

Upanishads ▪ Hindu scriptures that describe the pantheistic worldview.

Worldview ▪ A philosophy of life. A worldview is a set of interrelated basic beliefs.

Zeitgeist ▪ The spirit of the time; a general trend of thought or feeling characteristic of a particular period of time.

Index

For More Information on Postmodernism:

The authors of this book are part of an apologetics ministry called *The Crossroads Project*. You can:

- contact the authors with questions or comments
- receive a *free* group study guide for *The Death of Truth*
- receive additional *free* articles and essays relating to postmodernism and other apologetics issues
- receive a free catalog of tapes
- receive a conference schedule and brochure.

You can receive a free listing of materials and a conference schedule:

- by calling 1–800–698–7884
- or visiting http://www.crossrds.org
- or E-mailing crossroads@office.xenos.org
- or write

The Crossroads Project
℅Xenos Christian Fellowship
1340 Community Park Drive
Columbus, OH 43229